ANTHROPOLOGY IN USE

A Source Book on Anthropological Practice

John van Willigen

Westview Special Studies in Applied Anthropology

ANTHROPOLOGY IN USE

ANTHROPOLOGY IN USE

A Source Book on Anthropological Practice

John van Willigen

WESTVIEW PRESS

Boulder • San Francisco • Oxford

Westview Special Studies in Applied Anthropology

This Westview softcover edition is printed on acid-free paper and bound in library-quality, coated covers that carry the highest rating of the National Association of State Textbook Administrators, in consultation with the Association of American Publishers and the Book Manufacturers' Institute.

Copyright © 1991 by Westview Press, Inc.

Published in 1991 in the United States of America by Westview Press, Inc., 5500 Central Avenue, Boulder, Colorado 80301-2847, and in the United Kingdom by Westview Press, 36 Lonsdale Road, Summertown, Oxford OX2 7EW

Library of Congress Cataloging-in-Publication Data
Van Willigen, John.
    Anthropology in use : a source book on anthropological practice /
by John van Willigen.
        p. cm.—(Westview special studies in applied anthropology)
    Includes bibliographical references and index.
    ISBN 0-8133-8250-5
    1. Applied anthropology—Bibliography. 2. Applied anthropology—
History—Chronology. I. Title. II. Series.
Z5118.A54V37 1991
[GN397.5]
016.301–dc20   90-25495
                                                                          CIP

Printed and bound in the United States of America

⊗   The paper used in this publication meets the requirements
     of the American National Standard for Permanence of Paper
     for Printed Library Materials Z39.48-1984.

10   9   8   7   6   5   4   3   2   1

To the Memory of Jeannette Van Willigen

CONTENTS

ACKNOWLEDGMENTS

This publication was accomplished with the help of many people. I am grateful to Terry Warth and Bill Marshall of the Special Collections and Archives Division of the Margaret I. King Library for help in managing the Applied Anthropology Documentation Project collection upon which this book is based; Anne Van Willigen for preparing the index; Gil Kushner for sharing project descriptions; Chris Pool for assisting with the wordprocessing software; Steve Morin, Kirin Cunningham, Russell Rhoades and Steven Maas for preparing project profiles; and LaVine Thraikill of the University of Kentucky Computing Center for scanning the original manuscript. Many people have submitted materials to the collection through the years. Although I cannot list them all I would like to acknowledge the contributions of Elizabeth Adelski, Tom Arcury, Steve Arvizu, Doraine Bailey, Martha Balshem, Elizabeth Briody, Antoinette Brown, Carol Bryant, Pam Bunte, Claire Cassidy, Michael Cernea, Jason Clay, Nancy Yaw Davis, Bill DeWalt, Kathleen DeWalt, Michael Dove, Ted Downing, Lathel Duffield, Chris Dyer, Sandy Ervin, Harvey Feit, Shirley Fiske, Sylvia Forman, George Foster, Tim Frankenberger, Robert Franklin, Art Gallaher, Irene Glasser, Walter Goldschmidt, Thomas Hakansson, Joel Halpern, Art Hansen, Joe Harding, Fred Hess, Don Hochstrasser, Mike Horowitz, Sue Ellen Jacobs, Jeff Johnson, Margaret Knight, Josea Kramer, Gil Kushner, Margaret Lantis, Constance McCorkle, Jim Merryman, Nancy Merryman, Don Messerschmidt, Michael Painter, Bill Partridge, the late John Price, Joel Savishinsky, Jay Schensul, Steve Schensul, Norm Schwartz, Rich Stoffle, Don Stull, Bob Trotter, Allan Turner, Monica Udvardy, Peter Van Arsdale, Murray Wax, Tom Weaver, Hazel Weidman, and Bob Wulff. I also wish to thank Erve Chambers, Benita Howell and Patricia Higgins for their support during their editorships of *Practicing Anthropology*. I recognize the support of Jacqueline Van Willigen in this and other projects.

John van Willigen

INTRODUCTION

This source book has two purposes. First, it is intended to help readers find information about cases in which anthropologists applied their knowledge and skills to solve practical problems. Second, it is intended to serve as a chronicle of the development of applied anthropology and anthropological practice. It is an expanded, reorganized and up-dated version of a 1981 publication entitled, *Anthropology in Use, A Bibliographic Chronology of the Development of Applied Anthropology*. That volume included about 320 entries about projects and events and was arranged chronologically. This volume contains 530 entries and is arranged topically. The new materials are derived from project profiles published in the Sources column in *Practicing Anthropology*.

I started to compile the first version of this book when I began to teach applied anthropology courses around 1975. Teaching materials were difficult to find. It was clear that documentation of anthropological practice was neither easily accessible nor complete. Since the publication of the original bibliography there are many important improvements of the documentation of applied anthropology which should be noted here. The most important are the publication of a number of useful case books. These include *Anthropological Praxis, Translating Knowledge into Action* (Wulff and Fiske 1987); *Collaborative Research and Social Change* (Stull and Schensul 1987); *Advocacy and Anthropology: First Encounters* (Paine 1985); *Anthropology and Development in North Africa and the Middle East.* (Salem-Murdock, Horowitz, Sella 1990), *Practicing Development Anthropology* (Green 1978); *Applied Anthropology in America: Past Contributions and Future Directions* (Eddy and Partridge 1987) and *Making Our Research Useful: Case Studies in the Utilization of Anthropological Knowledge* (van Willigen, Rylko-Bauer, McElroy 1989). Also contributing to improvements in documentation are the *Training Manuals in Applied Anthropology* published by the American Anthropological Association under the editorship of William L. Partridge; the *Bulletin Series* of the

National Association for the Practice of Anthropology currently edited by Ralph Bishop and Pamela Amoss and *Practicing Anthropology* edited by Erve Chambers and subsequently Benita Howell and Patricia Higgins. While the situation is now much improved the basic causes of inaccessibility remain. First, the written materials produced as a direct result of the applied process are inappropriate to most disciplinary publication outlets. Reports written by practicing anthropologists frequently have to be substantially rewritten in order to be suitable for journal publication, as a result existing anthropology journals do not publish much about practice. The articles written by practicing anthropologists are often published in journals that relate to a specific interdisciplinary problem area such as farming systems research rather than anthropology itself. This causes problems of bibliographic control, and thereby inaccessibility. Second, practicing anthropologists are not often provided with incentives to publish in the traditional disciplinary sense. That is, in contrast to academic anthropologists, their salary increments and promotions are infrequently tied to this activity.

Clearly many practicing anthropologists produce a lot of written material in the course of their work. These "naturally occurring" documents play an essential role in learning what practicing anthropologists actually do. Further, many of them serve as excellent sources about the sociocultural situation to which they are addressed. Unfortunately these documents rarely are published and frequently become "fugitive" literature. One small solution to this problem was the creation of the Applied Anthropology Documentation Project at the Margaret I. King Library of the University of Kentucky in 1978. The Project, which engaged the problem of collecting and organizing an archive of the written materials produced by practicing applied anthropologists in the course of their work, has the sponsorship of the Society for Applied Anthropology, the Washington Association of Professional Anthropologists, the Society for Applied Anthropology in Canada, the National Association for the Practice of Anthropology and the Society for Medical Anthropology. Readers who care to contribute technical reports and other materials to the Project may send them to: Applied Anthropology Documentation Project, Margaret I. King Library, Special Collections, University of Kentucky, Lexington, Kentucky 40506. The collection would benefit from the contribution of technical reports and other limited circulation documents, specifically such things as social impact assessment reports, evaluation studies, feasibility studies, technology assessments, and proposals relating to the same. Materials relating to the development of training in aspects of anthropology for various kinds of change agents, health care professionals, government officials, educators and the like would be most welcome. Documents relating to applied anthropology training programs are also sought. Materials submitted to this project are often described in Project Profiles in the "Sources" section of *Practicing Anthropology.*

Historical Overview

Applied anthropologists seem to have generally poor comprehension of the history of the field, yet one must agree with George Foster's comment that the "current forms and place [of applied anthropology] within the broad discipline can be fully appreciated only with knowledge of the several stages of its development" (1969: 181). Limited documentation leads to a poor understanding of history. Poor understanding of history limits the development of the field. To recast Santayana's aphorism as Karl Heider did in reference to ethnographic film, if we don't understand our history we will be lucky enough to repeat it.

The history of applied anthropology and anthropology proper seem to be of roughly equal lengths; that is, the applied and non-applied portions of the discipline developed in parallel. Frequently the earliest professional anthropologists were engaged in research or instruction which was motivated by policy questions. In Europe, the first Departments of Anthropology were justified as training programs for practitioners, usually in the context of colonial administration. Early faculty consisted of practitioners turned academics. In the United States, the first organizations to hire anthropologists were policy research operations. It is clear that theoretical anthropology grew out of applied anthropology. Historical accounts of the development of the discipline do not make this point (Voget 1975, Harris 1968).

Applied anthropology and anthropology proper influenced each other. This may seem like an obvious statement but in fact, commentaries on the nature of the relationship between the two categories often overlook the contribution of applied anthropology to the field in general. The most striking contribution is that anthropologists seeking data which addressed policy problems often led the way into new areas of inquiry. This pattern of adaptive-radiation continues to the present. Although it is more difficult to illustrate, various anthropologists have asserted that through use anthropological knowledge is tested and improved. This suggests that applied anthropology has improved the quality of anthropology proper.

The history of applied anthropology can be depicted in four eras. These are: the predisciplinary period, which ends in 1860 and has no specified beginning; the research-consultant period, which covers the period between 1860 and 1941, and the role-extension period, which encompasses 1941 to 1970 and the policy research period extending from 1970 to the present.

The predisciplinary period consists of a small number of documented cases in which persons use cultural knowledge to engage a practical problem and attempt to solve it. This era also is characterized by the creation of early associations of people concerned with the use of cultural knowledge and early policy research projects.

The research consultant period is named after the most prevalent activity in the period. Its beginning is marked by the identification of anthropology as a distinct discipline, and its end by the emergence of applied anthropology as a separate branch of the discipline manifested by the founding of the Society for Applied Anthropology.

During this period the first academic programs in anthropology were developed and numerous policy research organizations were created which hired anthropologists. Anthropologists were frequently hired to serve various purposes in government. Numerous cases of administrative trouble-shooting in cross-cultural settings are to be found. The most striking are James Mooney's work with the Ghost Dance among the Sioux; W. S. Rattray's work among the Ashanti; and F. E. Williams's work concerning New Guinea cargo-cults. Another frequent use of anthropologists is the training of colonial administrators. Early examples are found in the Netherlands, France, South Africa, Great Britain, Belgium, and New Guinea. Perhaps the most interesting of the activities which emerge during this period are special purpose policy research groups which were set up by various governments. Among the earliest were the Direccion de Anthropologia established by the Mexican government at the time of the Revolution and the Institute of Ethnography established by the government of the Soviet Union. Later a number of applied research groups were established in the United States. These include the Rio Grande Socioeconomic Survey of the United States Department of Agriculture, the Applied Anthropology Unit of the Bureau of Indian Affairs, the Technical Cooperation-Bureau of Indian Affairs group, the Rural Life Studies of the United States Department of Agriculture, the Committee for National Morale, and the Committee on Food Habits.

While this period saw a dramatic expansion into new topical areas, the role of the applied anthropologist remained quite limited in scope. That is, applied anthropologists limited their role activities to that of researcher and teacher. The typical applied anthropologist of this period worked as a research or training consultant in government on private sector development activities. They rarely activated a central role in decision making. It is during the next period that we see an increase in the number of action-involved roles activated by anthropologists. This shift is referred to in the name given this period; that is, the period of role extension.

Clearly World War II dramatically changed applied anthropology. In both the United States and Britain, anthropologists were involved in the war effort. The American Anthropological Association passed a resolution pledging anthropological support in the war effort. Many American anthropologists came to work for the War Relocation Authority. Others worked on research which was to identify the psychocultural nature of both enemy and allies or to prepare technical background on areas in anticipation of postwar administration. The war seemed to accelerate trends toward more intense involvement already at work which formed during "New Deal" times.

In American applied anthropology, new patterns of practice begin to emerge as early as 1941. An early example is Laura Thompson's use of action research techniques to help improve American Indian administration. Constructive attempts to improve the public health status of American Indians also occurred.

The development by anthropologists of action-involved, extended role approaches for social intervention began to occur shortly after the war. The first of these is action anthropology, developed by Sol Tax and his associates. Action anthropology had both development and research goals. Research and development anthropology was developed a few years later by Allen Holmberg. Research and development involved the use of a sophisticated conception of values coupled with economic educational and political interventions. Action anthropology was used in some other contexts, including urban Chicago, pan-Indian leadership, Chicano education, and Cheyenne religious revival. Research and development anthropology was replicated in a number of settings in Peru, as well as in Los Angeles and southern Utah.

At about the same time that both action anthropology and research and development anthropology developed, anthropologists were beginning to contribute to the so-called community development movement. This contribution included consultation on program development, evaluation, development of training materials, and administration.

Other approaches for applying anthropological knowledge were developed later. Action research was used by Stephen Schensul in the late 1960s. This approach was to be rooted in the first generation techniques, such as action anthropology, and was an adaption to big city ethnic politics. The other significant second generation approach to applying anthropological knowledge is cultural brokerage. Hazel Weidman developed this technique to improve the functioning of the health care system of Dade County, Florida. She, it should be noted, does not regard this approach as a kind of applied anthropology.

Other than the development of these approaches, the most significant events during this period are the various legislative acts which stimulated research efforts among anthropologists. Of course many of these were passed quite a while ago, but they continue to have their effects. Relevant legislation which influenced work opportunities for anthropologists includes the Antiquities Act of 1906, the Historic Sites Act of 1935, the Indian Reorganization Act of 1934, the Colonial Development and Welfare Act of 1940 (British), the Indian Claims Commission Act of 1946, the Peace Corps Act of 1961, the Economic Opportunity Act of 1964, the National Environmental Policy Act of 1969, the Foreign Assistance Act as amended in 1973, and the Community Development Act of 1974.

Note that during the period of role-extension, applied anthropologists continued to perform much the same kinds of research and consulting activities which they had carried on previously. This included research on various policy-relevant topics such as agriculture, alcoholism, bilingual education, business administration, communication, community health, drug use, employment, and ethnic relations. Also appearing are genocide, housing, land use, law, migration, nutrition, population studies, sanitation, and welfare reform.

The period of policy research sees substantial increases in the number of anthropologists working in applied roles and is characterized by what Angrosino called the "new applied anthropology" (Angrosino 1976). This consists of an increased emphasis on policy research done outside of academic employment. These developments were entailed by both push and pull factors. The push factors consist of the general decline in the academic job market. The important pull factors consist of increased allocation toward policy research by the federal government. The typical applied anthropologist was no longer academically employed but was hired directly by an agency or a consulting firm. For this and other reasons the term practicing anthropologist emerged and appeared in the names of newly developed organizations and publications. In some contexts people reserve the term applied anthropology for work of a practical nature done by anthropologists who work for universities. I interchange the terms practicing anthropology and applied anthropology.

There are a number of important changes in applied anthropology at this stage. One important factor is the radical increase in the numbers of anthropologists involved in applied work. As experience in policy research brings new methodological skills, anthropologists are increasing their involvement in impact assessment, evaluation studies and technology development research. Their research methods have become more time-effective and utilization oriented. In the 1970s there was a substantial increase in the number of graduate training programs offering specialized training in applied anthropology in its many aspects. Organizations oriented toward the needs of the practicing anthropologists emerged at both the local and national level. There are now many functioning local practitioner organizations around the country. The patterns of documentation are changing too, with new kinds of publications such as *Practicing Anthropology* and the *NAPA Bulletins*.

Ironically, as application became more common amongst anthropologists, the idea of "applied anthropology" became increasingly awkward -- indeed, some might say obsolete. More and more it seems that applied work is done in the context of specific multi-disciplinary networks of social scientists who do both applied and basic research work. They participate in specific domains of application such as the agricultural development, educational evaluation or population planning. In these contexts people seem to think of themselves more as agricultural anthropologists, etc. rather than as applied anthropologists. Educational and medical anthropologists went through this shift long ago.

The future of anthropological practice will be characterized by even greater diversity. One can only guess about the content of future versions of this source book. The shape of the field will be formed by both the challenges created by forces outside the discipline and the adaptations of individual anthropologists and their associations. The importance of external factors must be understood. Most important factors are the changing academic job market and the changing federal commitment to policy research.

A Note on Content

Each entry consists of a statement describing an activity, often a project or event. These statements are coupled with one or more bibliographic citations which may be either descriptions or products of activities noted. The dates indicate the starting point of activities. The geographic location of the event is indicated by the terminology which was relevant at the time. In other words, a term such as Tanganyika would be used in place of the current name Tanzania. Geographic terms are almost always national, although occasionally larger geographic regions are used. There is a general index, which includes persons, subjects, and a geographic descriptors. The index includes persons referred to in the annotation as well as authors cited in the bibliographic entries.

While the book contains much useful information, the coverage of the book is uneven in a number of ways. One source of bias in coverage is the extent that coverage is based upon who has chosen to send materials to the Applied Anthropology Documentation Collection. The most obvious bias is that I almost never receive either physical anthropology or archaeology. It is likely that because of the nature of my networks the sections on agricultural and forestry anthropology are well developed. I do not think that any section represents complete coverage of a topic. To a large extent this is not possible because of the limits of bibliographic control in these fields and the fugitive nature of publication.

8

I think that the book would be most useful to a person teaching a course on applied anthropology or anthropological practice. In that context it will serve as a source for case study material. Students may find it useful as a beginning point for doing analysis of cases as part of their self-study.

References Cited

Angrosino, Michael V. 1976. The Evolution of the New Applied Anthropology. In *Do Applied Anthropologists Apply Anthropology?* Michael V. Angrosino, ed., Athens, Georgia: University of Georgia Press.

Eddy, Elizabeth M. and William L. Partridge, eds., 1978. *Applied Anthropology in America: Past Contributions and Future Directions.* New York: Columbia University Press.

Foster, George M. 1969. *Applied Anthropology.* Boston: Little, Brown.

Green, Edward, ed., 1986. *Practicing Development Anthropology.* Boulder, CO: Westview.

Harris, Marvin. 1968. *The Rise of Anthropological Theory: A History of Theories of Culture.* New York: Crowell.

Paine, Robert. 1985. *Advocacy and Anthropology: First Encounters.* St. John's, Newfoundland: Institute of Social and Economic Research, Memorial University.

Salem-Murdock, Muneera, Michael M. Horowitz, and Monica Sella. eds. 1990. *Anthropology and Development in North Africa and the Middle East.* Boulder, CO: Westview Press.

Stull, Donald D. and Jean J. Schensul, eds., 1987. *Collaborative Research and Social Change.* Boulder, CO: Westview.

van Willigen, John. 1981. *Anthropology in Use: A Bibliographic Chronology of the Development of Applied Anthropology.* Pleasantville, NY: Redgrave Publishers.

van Willigen, John, Barbara Rylko-Bauer and Ann McElroy. eds. 1989. *Making Our Research Useful: Case Studies in the Utilization of Anthropological Knowledge.* Boulder, CO: Westview Press.

Voget, Fred W. 1975. *A History of Ethnology.* New York: Holt, Rinehart and Winston.

Wulff, Robert M. and Shirley J. Fiske. eds., 1987, *Anthropological Praxis: Translating Knowledge into Action.* Boulder, CO: Westview.

PREDISCIPLINARY ACTIVITIES

- **Syncretism Advocated by Holy Roman Church**
  Great Britain, 596

Pope Gregory I made recommendations to his missionaries in Britain that the pagan temples not be destroyed so as to minimize conflict with the British tribals, and thereby facilitate conversion. He suggested that the pagan animal sacrifices be converted in their meaning to feastdays honoring the saints.

Jeffereys, M.D.W. 1956. Some Rules of Directed Culture Change Under Roman Catholicism. *American Anthropologist* 58:721-731.

- **Understanding Innovation Diffusion Theory**
  Guides Mission Program
  Congo, 1682

Capuchin priest and missionary to the Congo Fr. Jerome Merolla da Sorrento developed various "policies" to increase the effectiveness of the mission program. One policy was to attempt to convert those who might be called today "opinion leaders" so as to accelerate conversion of the population.

Jeffereys, M.D.W. 1956. Some Rules of Directed Culture Change Under Roman Catholicism. *American Anthropologist* 58:721-731.

- **New World Source of Ginseng Sought**
  New France, 1718

Joseph-Francois Lafitau [1681-1746] was a French Jesuit priest who went to Canada as a missionary. Early in his stay there he carried out explorations seeking a source for ginseng to respond to the market for the plant that was generated by the China trade. Lafitau interviewed Iroquois and Hurons who were knowledgeable about ethnomedicine and ethnobotany in order to find a source of the plant that benefited those who were involved in the plant trade. This practical research project may have led to his research into social organization. This illustrates a common but little-recognized pattern that is, many theoretically significant projects are derived from practical concerns. Lafitau's later basic research is note worthy for its high standards of data collection, its disclosed research design, and its priority conception of classificatory kinship terminology, age-grading, and matriliny. Fenton called Lafitau the father of comparative ethnology.

Fenton, William N. and Elizabeth L. Moore. 1974. Introduction. In *Customs of The American Indians Compared with the Customs of Primitive Times.* Toronto: Champlain Society.

Lafitau, Joseph F. 1718. Memoire...concernant la precieuse plante du Ginseng, decouverte en Canada. Paris.

Lafitau, Joseph F. 1974 [original 1724] *Customs of The American Indians Compared with the Customs of Primitive Times.* Toronto: Champlain Society.

- **Charles III Prohibits Items of Dress**
  Spain, 1766

One of Charles III's ministers, a certain unpopular Sicilian named Marquis de Squillaci, attempted to prohibit various items of popular dress. This prohibition resulted in a crisis that included the banishment of the King. Ultimately the goal of prohibition was achieved by making the items of dress the official "uniform of the public executioner."

Foster, George. 1956. Applied Anthropology and Modern Life. In *Estudios Antropologicos, publicados en homenaje al doctor Manuel Gamio.* Mexico, D. F.

- **Judge's Language Studies Form Basis for Historic Linguistics**
  India, 1783

Sir William Jones was appointed to a judgeship of the Supreme Court at Calcutta. This led him to study Sanskrit to understand Hindu legal texts in the original language. He had previously studied Hebrew, Arabic, Persian and Turkish. From these scholarly efforts emerged the foundations of comparative Indo-European linguistics specifically and historic linguistics generally. In this case research done for practical reasons resulted in significant advancement in basic research.

Voget, Fred W. 1975. *A History of Ethnology.* New York: Holt, Rinehart and Winston.

- **John Company Hires Cultural Researcher**
  India, 1807

Francis Buchanan was appointed by Governor-General of the East India
Company to study life and culture in Bengal in response to a need
expressed by the Court of Directors of the Company. At this time the
Company was the de facto civil government of much of India.

Buchanan, Francis. 1820. *History, Antiquity, Topography and Statistics of Eastern
India.* London.
Sachchidananda. 1972. Planning, Development and Applied Anthropology in
India. *Journal of the Indian Anthropological Society* 7:11-28.

- **Early Professional Societies Established**
  United Kingdom, 1838

The Aborigines Protection Society, established in London, was concerned
with both research and social service for the native population of Great
Britain's vast empire. A more academically oriented faction of the society
became formalized as the Ethnological Society of London in 1843. These
organizations were strongly reformist.

Keith, Arthur. 1917. How Can the Institute Best Serve the Needs of
Anthropology? *Journal of the Royal Anthropological Society* 47:12-30.
Reining, Conrad C. 1962. A Lost Period of Applied Anthropology. *American
Anthropologist* 64:593-600.

- **Early Change Agent at Work**
  United States, 1860

William Duncan, a missionary, made efforts at social reform among
Northwest Coast Indian groups. This is an early example of a culturally
aware change agent.

Barnett, H. G. 1942. Applied Anthropology in 1860. *Applied Anthropology*
1:19-32.

- **Self-determination Programs Developed for Greenland Natives**
  Denmark, 1862

Hinrich Rink was trained as a natural historian and served as an
administrator. He contributed to the early development of
self-determination among Greenland natives.

12

Nellemann, George. 1969. Hinrich Rink and Applied Anthropology in Greenland in the 1860s. *Human Organization* 28:166-174.

EARLY DISCIPLINARY EVENTS

▪ Early Policy Study Funded by Congress
United States, 1852

Henry R. Schoolcraft, one of the founders of the American Ethnological Society, was retained by the United States Congress to compile *Information Respecting the History, Condition and Projects of the Indian Tribes of the United States.* He was motivated by the idea that the information would lead to a more objective policy toward the native American.

Partridge, William L. and Elizabeth M. Eddy. 1978. The Development of Applied Anthropology in America. In *Applied Anthropology in America.* Elizabeth M. Eddy and William L. Partridge, eds. New York: Columbia University Press.
Schoolcraft, Henry R. 1852-57. *Information Respecting the History, Condition, and Prospects of the Indian Tribes of the United States.* 6 vols. Philadelphia, PA: Lippincott.

▪ Bureau of American Ethnology Founded to do Applied Work
United States, 1879

The Bureau of American Ethnology was founded "to produce results that would be of practical value in the administration of Indian affairs." Thus the first organization to hire anthropologists in the United States was an applied research organization, not an academic program. Later annual reports of the Bureau spoke of "applied ethnology." Their contribution to theory was significant. The term acculturation was first used in a BAE document.

Powell, John Wesley. 1881. *First Annual Report of the Bureau of American Ethnology (1879-80).* Washington, DC: Government Printing Office.

▪ Tylor Gets First Academic Job
United Kingdom, 1883

E. B. Tylor received the first academic appointment in anthropology. Tylor was appointed Reader in Anthropology at Oxford. Justification of this position included the training needs of the colonial regime. That is, the first anthropology department was an applied anthropology training program. What may be the first use of the term applied anthropology appears in an article that describes the Oxford program. C. H. Read wrote, "The great importance to an imperial nation of what may be called 'Applied Anthropology' has been pointed out so often that it is unnecessary to insist upon it further here" (1906:56).

Foster, George. 1969. *Applied Anthropology*. Boston: Little, Brown and Company.
Read, C. H. 1906. Anthropology at the Universities. *Man* 38:56-59.

- **Applied Ethnology Proposed for BAE Work**
  United States, 1902

W. J. McGee, Director of the Bureau of American Ethnology, proposed that the Bureau focus on what he called applied ethnology. This reemphasized the policy research mission of the Bureau at a time when it was involved in a crisis brought about by J. W. Powell's death and a financial scandal. McGee's prospectus for applied ethnology proposed various kinds of policy studies focused on the United States and its colonial possessions. McGee was actually a geologist like Powell but assumed the title Ethnologist-in-Charge in 1893.

Hinsley, Curtis M., Jr. 1976. Amateurs and Professionals in Washington Anthropology, 1879 to 1903. In *American Anthropology, the Early Years*. John V. Murra, ed. New York: West Publishing Co.

- **Early Cambridge Faculty Were Ex-Practitioners**
  United Kingdom, 1904

Early development of academic anthropology in Great Britain was based upon the justification of potential application. Many early faculty were in fact ex-colonial administrators. At Cambridge, what Fortes calls the "first inaugural lecture" on anthropology was given by Sir Richard Temple who was ex-Indian Civil Service. Other early faculty were T. C. Hodson and J. H. Hutton, both ex-civil servants.

Fortes, Meyer. 1953. *Social Anthropology at Cambridge Since 1900*. Cambridge: Cambridge University Press.

- **The Golden Stool Incident**
  Gold Coast, 1921

Capt. W. S. Rattray, government anthropologist, investigated the cultural meaning of the Golden Stool which had been the focus of conflict between the British and the Ashanti of West Africa. The Ashanti saw the stool as a repository of the nation's soul, while the British assumed the Stool was a symbol of royal authority. In response to their assumptions the British attempted to obtain the Stool to solidify their leadership. This led to armed and bloody conflict with the Ashanti. Rattray suggested that the British view was wrong and that they desist from attempting to obtain the Stool. This advice was followed and had the proper ameliorative effect.

Rattray, R. S. 1923. *Ashanti.* Oxford: Clarendon Press.

- **Early Use of Term "Applied Anthropology" Cited**
  United Kingdom, 1930

The phrase, "Applied Anthropology," according to H. Ian Hogbin, was first used by Radcliffe-Brown in a 1930 article. It does appear as early as 1906, however.

Hogbin, H. Ian. 1957. Anthropology as Public Service and Malinowski's Contribution to It. In *Men and Culture, an Evaluation of the Work of Bronislaw Malinowski.* R. Raymond Firth, ed. London: Routledge and Kegan Paul.
Radcliffe-Brown, A. R. 1930. Applied Anthropology. *Proceedings of the Australian and New Zealand Association for the Advancement of Science.* Pp. 267-80.

ETHICS

- **SFAA Issues Code of Ethics**
  United States, 1949

The Society for Applied Anthropology published their first Code of Ethics based on a process begun in 1946. After much discussion, the committee's report was published in the Society's newly renamed journal, *Human Organization.* The ethics code has been subsequently changed periodically. This appears to be the first ethics code published by a professional association in anthropology.

Mead, Margaret, Eliot D. Chapple and G. Gordon Brown. 1949. Report of the Committee on Ethics. *Human Organization* 8(2):20-21.

- **Project Camelot Rolled Out**
  United States, 1964

Project Camelot was a multidisciplinary project designed to produce improved understanding of the causes of civil war in Latin America. Sponsored by the United States Department of Defense, the project led to a significant ethical debate in anthropology in spite of the fact that the amount of participation by anthropologists was limited.

Horowitz, Irving Louis, ed. 1974. *The Rise and Fall of Project Camelot: Studies in the Relationship Between Social Science and Practical Politics.* Cambridge: M.I.T. Press.
Nisbet, Robert A. 1974. Project Camelot and the Science of Man. In *The Rise and Fall of Project Camelot.* I. L. Horowitz, ed. Cambridge: M.I.T. Press.

- **Vietnam War Brings Ethical Crisis**
  Thailand, 1970

Representatives of the Student Mobilization Committee to End the War in Vietnam stole papers from an UCLA anthropologist that were used to mount an attack on the involvement of anthropologists and other social scientists in Thailand research during the Vietnam War. The documents were perceived as indicating that anthropologists were involved in secret research funded by the U.S. Government that focused upon "accelerating rural development" and village security. These perceptions resulted in an extensive investigation and debate within the American Anthropological Association.

Belshaw, Cyril S. 1976. *The Sorcerer's Apprentice: An Anthropology of Public Policy.* New York: Pergamon Press.
Wolf, Eric and Joseph Jorgensen. 1970. Anthropology on the Warpath in Thailand. *New York Review of Books* 15(9): November 19.

PUBLICATIONS

- **Early Publication of Applied Anthropology**
  United Kingdom, 1866

The Anthropological Society of London began to publish the *Popular Magazine of Anthropology.* This periodical contained articles on applied topics. Many articles promoted the use of anthropology to mitigate the abuses of the colonial systems.

Reining, Conrad C. 1962. A Lost Period of Applied Anthropology. *American Anthropologist* 64:593-600.

■ Policy Needs Produce Classic Works
Sudan, 1908

C. G. Seligman was hired to do an ethnographic survey of the Sudan to help inform colonial administration. The applied research report is now seen as a classic product of basic research. Many important early studies by British anthropologists were funded for policy reasons. Their original purpose as policy studies was reconstructed, in reflecting on this we can see that the effects of "applied work" on the discipline are under estimated.

Seligman, C. G. 1932. *Pagan Tribes of the Nilotic Sudan.* London.

■ Administrator-Anthropologist Publishes Guide to Tribes and Castes of India
India, 1908

H.H. Risley prepared *The People of India*, which extensively covered the diversity of the Indian population. Risley and his work are respected by the Indian anthropological community, yet they realize that this study and others like it served to further institutionalize ethnic and communal differences the British Raj used to maintain control of their Indian empire. In addition to its ostensible purpose as a basic reference work, it served British political goals. The cultural "sensitivity" that anthropologists produce can be a mechanism for establishing hegemony over the powerless.

A.K. Kalla. 1987. Physical Anthropology: Its Relevance in National Building. In *Anthropology, Development and Nation Building.* A.K. Kalla and K.S. Singh, eds. New Delhi: Concept Publishing.
H.H. Risley. 1908. *The People of India.* Calcutta: Thackerspink.

■ Nadel Does Classic Ethnography for Government
Sudan, 1938

S. F. Nadel was appointed Government Anthropologist in the Sudan. There he carried out work among the Nuba tribes which resulted in the publication of *The Nuba*, showing the value of practitioners publishing.

Nadel, S. F. 1947. *The Nuba.* London: Oxford University Press.

- **USDA Rural Life Studies Started**
United States, 1939

U.S. Department of Agriculture commissioned the Rural Life Studies, a series of six community studies in selected parts of the United States. They focused on community responses and potentials for change and were done with a holistic perspective. The team included anthropologists. Additional studies were planned but Congressional opposition developed for ideological reasons.

Bell, Earl H. 1942. *Culture of a Contemporary Rural Community: Sublette, Kansas.* U.S. Department of Agriculture, Rural Life Studies, No. 2.
Kollmorgen, W. H. 1942. *Culture of a Contemporary Rural Community: The Old Order Amish of Lancaster County, Pennsylvania.* U.S. Department of Agriculture, Rural Life Studies, No. 4.
Leonard, Olen and Charles P. Loomis. 1941. *Culture of a Contemporary Rural Community: El Cerrito, New Mexico.* U.S. Department of Agriculture, Rural Life Studies, No. 1.
MacLiesh, Kenneth and Kimball Young. 1942. *Culture of a Contemporary Rural Community: Landoff, New Hampshire.* U.S. Department of Agriculture, Rural Life Studies, No. 3.
Moe, E. O. and Carl C. Taylor. 1942. *Culture of a Contemporary Rural Community: Irwin, Iowa.* U.S. Department of Agriculture, Rural Life Studies, No. 5.
Olson, Philip. 1964. Rural American Community Studies: The Survival of Public Ideology. *Human Organization* 23(4):342-350.
Wynne, Waller. 1943. *Culture of a Contemporary Rural Community, Harmony, Georgia.* U.S. Department of Agriculture, Rural Life Studies, No. 6.

- **Applied Anthropology Journal Published**
United States, 1941

Initial issue of the journal *Applied Anthropology*, later to be called *Human Organization*, was published.

Society for Applied Anthropology. 1941. Editorial Statement. *Applied Anthropology* 1(1):1-2
Srb, Jozetta H. 1966. Human Organization: The Growth and Development of a Professional Journal. *Human Organization* 25(3):187-197.

- **Anthropologist Writes Industrial Relations Textbook**
United States, 1945

Human Relations in Industry, by Burleigh Gardner, was published. The textbook remained widely used in the industrial relations field for a decade.

Gardner, who was trained in anthropology, had been associated with the personnel department of Western Electric.

Gardner, Burleigh B. and David G. Moore. 1945. *Human Relations in Industry*. Chicago: Richard D. Irwin.

- **Area Studies Handbook Published**
  United States, 1946

The first volume of *The Handbook of South American Indians* was published. This encyclopedic work was "initiated as a wartime activity under a State Department program for promoting cultural relations with Latin America" (Beals 1969:55) and thus was a policy relevant publication.

Beals, Ralph L. 1969. *Politics of Social Research: An Inquiry into the Ethics and Responsibilities of Social Scientists*. Chicago: Aldine Publishing Company.
Steward, Julian H. 1946-59. *Handbook of South American Indians*, Vols. I-VII. Washington, DC: U.S. Government Printing Office.

- **AAA Development Anthropology Publishing Venture**
  United States, 1951

The American Anthropological Association sponsored the preparation of "Intercultural Transfer of Techniques, A Manual of Applied Social Science for Point IV Technicians and Administrators Overseas." This was later published for the general public under the title *Introducing Social Change*.

Arensberg, Conrad M. and Arthur N. Niehoff. 1964. *Introducing Social Change: A Manual for Americans Overseas*. Chicago: Aldine Publishing.

- **Important Case Book Published**
  United States, 1952

Human Problems in Technological Change was published by the Russell Sage Foundation. Based on a conception of Alexander H. Leighton, the book grew out of Cornell University seminars in applied anthropology and consisted of various case studies.

Spicer, Edward H., ed. 1952. *Human Problems in Technological Change*. New York: Russell Sage Foundation.

- **Technical Change Manual Published**
  United States, 1953

Cultural Patterns and Technical Change was published by the United Nations Educational, Scientific and Cultural Organization. Edited by Margaret Mead, it was intended for use by persons engaged as change agents cross-culturally and focused on the question, "How can technical change be introduced with such regard for culture pattern that human values are preserved?"

Mead, Margaret, ed. 1953. *Cultural Patterns and Technical Change*. Paris: UNESCO.

- **Change Text Published**
  United States, 1963

Cooperation in Change concerns the application of cultural theory to problems of development and technical assistance. It was one of three manuals for administrators stimulated by the Cornell Summer Field School in Applied Anthropology in the early 1950's.

Goodenough, Ward H. 1963. *Cooperation in Change: Anthropological Approaches to Community Development*. New York: Russell Sage Foundation.

- **McGimsey's Public Archaeology Text Published**
  United States, 1972

Charles R. McGimsey's *Public Archaeology* was the result of his work organizing the Arkansas Archaeological Survey and his assistance in writing and promoting the Moss-Bennett Bill, later to become the Archaeological and Historical Preservation Act of 1974. This book was compiled in order to (1) remind American archaeologists of the rapid destruction of their data base, (2) inform them of the current Federal and state legislation related to cultural resources, (3) suggest ways to pass protective legislation, and (4) explain the 1969 National Environmental Policy Act (NEPA). This book became the standard textbook for training in cultural resource management.

McGimsey, Charles R., III. 1972. *Public Archaeology*. New York: Seminar Press.
King, Thomas F., P. P. Hickman, and G. Berg. 1979. *Anthropology in Historic Preservation: Caring for Culture's Clutter*. New York: Academic Press.

Schiffer, Michael and George J. Gumerman, eds. 1977. *Conservation Archaeology*. New York: Academic Press.

- **Academic Job Crunch Paper Published**
  United States, 1975

In the 1970's there emerged a general downturn in the amount of academic employment opportunity for anthropologists. This was clearly demonstrated by research published by R. G. D'Andrade, E. A. Hammel, D. L. Adkins and C. K. McDaniel on the demographics of Ph.D. supply and demand. They state, "our most optimistic assessment of the future of academic employment in anthropology indicates that after 1982 over two-thirds of all anthropology Ph.D.'s will have to find employment outside academia" (772). This influenced non-academic hiring.

D'Andrade, R. G., E. A. Hammel, D. L. Adkins, and C. K. McDaniel. 1975. Academic Opportunity in Anthropology 1974-90. *American Anthropologist* 77(4):753-773.

- **Technical Manual for Social Soundness Analysis Published**
  United States, 1979

The Cultural Appraisal of Development Projects by anthropologist Glynn Cochrane was published. This technical guide to development research was derived from a technical manual used by the U.S. Agency for International Development in the project planning process. The book describes the social soundness analysis process put in place in 1974. Cochrane was largely responsible for the original manuals.

Cochrane, Glynn. 1979. *The Cultural Appraisal of Development Projects*. New York: Praeger.

RESEARCH AND PROFESSIONAL ORGANIZATIONS

- **Ethnographic Survey of United Kingdom Formed**
  United Kingdom, 1892

The Ethnographic Survey of the United Kingdom, sponsored by a number of learned societies, was initiated. The early surveys were established for policy research purposes.

Myres, J. L. 1928. The Science of Man in the Service of the State. *Journal of the Royal Anthropological Institute of Great Britain and Ireland* LIX: 19-52.

- **Ethnographic Survey of Ireland Formed**
Ireland, 1893

The Ethnographic Survey of Ireland was formed and sponsored by the Royal Irish Academy.

Haddon, A. C. 1897. *The Study of Man.* London: J. Murray.

- **Survey of India Organized**
India, 1905

Ethnographic Survey of India was initiated with H. H. Risley as its first director. The survey resulted in a series of basic ethnographies. After 1945 the Survey becomes known as the Anthropological Survey of India.

Majumdar, D. N. 1953. India, Pakistan, and Ceylon. In *International Directory of Anthropological Institutions.* William L. Thomas, Jr., and Anna M. Pikelis, eds. New York: Wenner-Gren.

- **Philippines Ethnological Survey Organized**
Philippines, 1906

The Philippine Ethnological Survey, patterned after the Bureau of American Ethnology, was active for four years. The project was directed by American anthropologist Albert E. Jenks. Jenks later developed applied anthropology programs at the University of Minnesota.

Kennard, Edward A. and Gordon MacGregor. 1953. Applied Anthropology in Government: United States. In *Anthropology Today.* A. L. Kroeber, ed. Chicago: University of Chicago Press.

- **Revolutionary Mexico Creates Anthropology Organization**
Mexico, 1917

The revolutionary government of Mexico created the Direccion de Anthropologia within the Department of Agriculture and Development. Headed by Manuel Gamio, this organization is presented by Edward H. Spicer as the first manifestation of applied anthropology in Mexico.

22

Although this organization lasted only until 1924 it "was a powerful influence for the application of anthropology in Mexico" (Spicer 1977:117). Gamio's ideas came to be expressed in the book *Forjando Patria,* which focused upon the process by which the various cultures of Mexico could be integrated.

Comas, Juan. 1975. *Manuel Gamio, Antologia.* Mexico: Universidad Nacional Autonoma de Mexico.
Gamio, Manuel. 1916. *Forjando Patria.* Mexico: Pronacionalismo Porrua Hermanos.
Spicer, Edward H. 1977. Early Applications of Anthropology in North America. In *Perspectives on Anthropology, 1976.* Anthony F. C. Wallace, et al., eds. Washington, DC: American Anthropological Association.

- **October Revolution Changes the Rules in Anthropology**
  Union of Soviet Socialist Republics, 1917

The October Revolution radically changed the nature of the development of ethnography in the Soviet Union. Following the Revolution state sponsorship increased resulting in the creation of the Institute of Ethnography of the USSR Academy of Sciences. Soviet ethnography was very closely tied to the goals of the Revolution. As Bromley notes, "the tasks of Lenin's national policy and the need for radical changes in the life and culture of the formerly backward peoples called for a thorough research into the ethnic composition of the population and the national peculiarities of its culture" (1976:99). Thus virtually the entire Soviet ethnography apparatus was a kind of applied anthropology enterprise.

Bromley, Yu. V. 1976. Ethnographical Studies in the USSR 1965-1975. In *Soviet Ethnography: Main Trends.* Moscow: USSR Academy of Sciences.

- **African Studies Institute Organized**
  Africa, 1926

The establishment of the International Institute of African Languages and Cultures was based on the need for scientific data relevant to problems of administrating colonial Africa. The institute was supported by the governments of Germany, France, United Kingdom, Belgium, Italy, and South Africa. The Institute emphasized research in problem areas and published the journal *Africa.*

International Institute of African Languages and Cultures. 1937. Annual Report: The Work of the Institute in 1936. *Africa* 10:108-9.

Lugard, F. D. 1928. The International Institute of African Languages and Cultures. *Africa* 1:1-14.

Malinowski, Bronislaw. 1929. Practical Anthropology. *Africa* 2:23-38.

Richards, A. I. 1944. Practical Anthropology in the Lifetime of the International African Institute. *Africa* 14:289-301.

▪ Applied Anthropology Unit Established in BIA
United States, 1936

The Applied Anthropology Unit was created to review prospects of certain American Indian tribes to develop self-governance organizations in response to the Indian Reorganization Act of 1934. Research topics included settlement patterns, education policy, and prospects for economic development. The group's research had very little impact on the direction of political development. Critics suggest that the research took too long. Scudder Mekeel was hired by John Collier as the first director. Participants included Julian Steward, Morris Opler, Claude Schaeffer, Abraham Halpern, Charles Wisdom, Margaret Welpley Fisher, David Rodnick and Gordon MacGregor.

Collier, John. 1936. *Instruction to Field Workers, Applied Anthropology Unit.* Office of Indian Affairs, Applied Anthropology Unit.

_____. 1944. Collier Replies to Mekeel. *American Anthropologist* 46:(3):424-25.

MacGregor, Gordon. 1936. *Washo Indians of the Sacramento Jurisdiction.* Office of Indian Affairs, Applied Anthropology Unit.

_____. n.d. *Report on the Pit River Indians of California.* Office of Indian Affairs, Applied Anthropology Unit.

McNickle, D'Arcy. 1979. Anthropology and the Indian Reorganization Act. In *The Uses of Anthropology.* Walter Goldschmidt, ed. Washington, DC: American Anthropological Association.

Mekeel, H. Scudder. 1936. Social Science and Reservation Programs. *Indians at Work* IV:7.

_____. 1944. An Appraisal of the Indian Reorganization Act. *American Anthropologist* 46:2.

Opler, Morris E. 1936. *Report on Observations at Mescalero Reservation.* Office of Indian Affairs, Applied Anthropology Unit.

Rodnick, David. 1936. *Report on the Indians of Kansas.* Applied Anthropology Unit Report Series. Washington, DC: Office of Indian Affairs, Department of the Interior.

Schaeffer, C. E. 1936. *Future Possibilities of Self-Government Among the Flathead.* Office of Indian Affairs, Applied Anthropology Unit.

Thompson, Laura. 1956. U.S. Indian Reorganization Viewed as an Experiment in Social Action Research. *Estudios Antropologicos Publicado en Homenaje a Doctor Manuel Gamio.* Mexico: Direccion General da Publicaciones.

Wisdom, Charles. 1936. *Report on the Great Lake Chippewa.* Office of Indian Affairs, Applied Anthropology Unit.

_____. n.d. *Origin of Keetoowah Society.* Office of Indian Affairs, Applied Anthropology Unit.

_____. n.d. *Memorandum on the Present Condition of the Oklahoma Choctaw.* Office of Indian Affairs, Applied Anthropology Unit.

- ## Rhodes-Livingstone Institute Founded
Rhodesia, 1937

The Rhodes-Livingstone Institute, established by the governor of Northern Rhodesia, focused on central African studies. The Institute was to improve "native" and "non-native" relations and to determine the effect of culture contact on native African society. The Institute was established independently of the government and directed by a board of trustees to investigate policy relevant issues. Early directors of the operation included Godfrey Wilson and Max Gluckman. About one-half of the Institute's budget was government supplied. The Institute was "intended as a contribution to the scientific efforts now being made in various quarters to examine the effects upon native African society of the impact of European civilization, by the formation in Africa itself of a center where the problem of establishing permanent and satisfactory relations between natives and non-natives. . . may form the subject of special study."

International Institute on African Languages and Cultures. 1946. Notes and News. *Africa* 16(2).

Mair, Lucy. 1960. The Social Sciences in Africa, South of the Sahara: The British Contribution. *Human Organization* 19:(3):98-107.

Wilson, Godfrey 1940. Anthropology as a Public Service. *Africa* 13:43-60.

- ## USDA Applied Research Unit Established
United States, 1937

The U.S. Department of Agriculture established the Technical Cooperation-Bureau of Indian Affairs Unit. TC-BIA was supported by the Soil Conservation Service but assisted the Bureau of Indian Affairs as a research unit. Various researches were carried out that focused on improving natural resource use.

Kennard, Edward A. and Gordon MacGregor. 1953. Applied Anthropology in Government: United States. In *Anthropology Today*. A. L. Kroeber, ed. Chicago: University of Chicago Press.

- **Inter-American Indian Institute Established**
  The Americas, 1938

The Inter-American Indian Institute was established in Mexico with Manuel Gamio as its first director. The organization has encouraged direct action as well as more traditional anthropological activities.

Gamio, Manuel. 1945. Some Considerations of Indianist Policy. In *The Science of Man in the World Crisis*. R. Linton, ed. New York: Columbia University Press.
Instituto Indigenista Interamericano. 1941. Instituto Indigenista Interamericano. *America Indigena* 1(1):1.

- **Society for Applied Anthropology Founded**
  United States, 1941

The Society for Applied Anthropology was established. The Society has provided for an expressive outlet for the work of applied anthropologists in its journal and annual meetings. In its early days the Society served as an intermediary between its members and potential clients. The Society has also served to define ethical standards.

Foster, George M. 1969. *Applied Anthropology*. Little, Brown and Company, Boston.

- **Instituto Nacional Indigenista Founded**
  Mexico, 1948

The Instituto Nacional Indigenista was founded. Staffed largely by anthropologists, INI came to bear a major responsibility in the education and development of the native population of Mexico through its coordinating centers. The role of anthropologists was sharply reduced in the 1970s.

Caso, Alfonso. 1958. Ideals of an Action Program. *Human Organization* 17(1):27-29.
de la Fuente, Julio. 1958. National Indigenous Institute of Mexico: A Report - Results of an Action Program. *Human Organization* 17(1):30-33.

Huizer, Gerrit. 1968. Community Development and Conflicting Rural Interests: Some Observations on the Programme of the National Indian Institute in Mexico. *American Indigena* 28(3):619-629.

Instituto Indigenista Interamericano. 1948. Creation of the National Indian Institute. *Boletin Indigenista* 8(3-4):259-63.

- ### Anthropological Survey of India Established
India, 1945

The Anthropological Survey of India was established to document the biological and ethnic diversity of the Indian nation following Independence. Published sources state that currently the ASI is the largest employer of anthropologists in the world with a staff of over 400 professionals located in regional institutes in Calcutta, Nagpur, Mysore, Shillong, Dehra Dun, Port Blair, Udaipur and Jagdalpur. Under its first Director, B.S. Guha, the Survey was established as a basic research organization that was intended to provide information that would be of use to planners, administrators and other researchers. This has been expressed in large numbers of publications with an emphasis on tribal research. Recently the Survey has become somewhat more involved in policy issues. The current Director-General of the Survey, K. S. Singh, serves as advisor to the Government of India on Tribal Affairs. With the promulgation of the current Seventh Five Year Plan, the Survey has become increasingly involved in providing anthropological input on plan programs relating to environment, alleviation of poverty and malnutrition, women's welfare and the development of depressed sectors of the population.

Director-General Anthropological Survey of India. 1987. *Anthropological Survey of India, 1945-1987.* Calcutta: Government of India, Ministry of Human Resources Development.

K.S. Singh. 1987. Anthropology, Development and Culture. In *Anthropology, Development and National Building.* A.K. Kalla and K.S. Singh, eds. New Delhi: Concept Publishing.

- ### Clearing House for Research in Human Organization Established
United States, 1950

The Society for Applied Anthropology established the Clearinghouse for Research in Human Organization "as a center for coordinating research in social science disciplines dealing with relations of human beings to one another." It had as its purpose the dissemination of social science data to people who might apply the data. The Clearinghouse published the *Human Organization Clearinghouse Bulletin* in the early 1950's.

Society for Applied Anthropology. 1955. *Clearinghouse Bulletin of Research in Human Organization.* Society for Applied Anthropology.

- **International Potato Center Started**
  Peru, 1971

The International Potato Center (CIP) was established as an International Agricultural Research Center (IARC) to increase the yield of potatoes in the developing countries. Located in Lima, CIP maintains research and training programs in the agronomic and social sciences. Anthropologists have been more extensively employed at CIP than other IARCs. Research efforts focus on the entire potato using process from growing to storage and processing.

Rhoades, Robert E. 1984. *Breaking New Ground: Agricultural Anthropology.* Lima: International Potato Center.
Werge, Robert W. 1977. *Anthropology and Agricultural Research: The Case of Potato Anthropology.* CIP Socioeconomic Unit. Lima: Centro Internacional de la Papa.

- **First Local Professional Organization Formed**
  United States, 1974

The Society of Professional Anthropologists was formed in Tucson, Arizona, to provide support to practicing anthropologists in southern Arizona. Services provided include information on job seeking, theoretical up-dating, and national political developments. Following SOPA's lead, similar organizations developed elsewhere. Linda A. Bennett reports seventeen local practitioner organizations functioning in her recently published study of these groups (1988). SOPA, which in a sense started it all, ceased to meet in 1983.

Bainton, R. Barry. 1975. Society of Professional Anthropologists Formed in Tucson. *Anthropology Newsletter* 16(8):4-6.
Bennett, Linda A. 1988. Bridges for Changing Times: Local Practitioner Organizations in American Anthropology. *NAPA Bulletin 6.* Washington, DC: American Anthropological Association.

- **Early Public Interest Anthropology Group Established**
  United States, 1975

The Anthropology Resource Center was established as one of the first public-interest anthropology organizations in the United States. This type of anthropology "differs from traditional applied anthropology in what is considered the object of study, whose interests the researcher represents, and what the researcher does with the results of his or her work. Public-interest anthropology grows out of the democratic traditions of citizen activism rather than the bureaucratic needs of management and control. It is based on the premise that social problems--war, poverty, racism, sexism, environmental degradation, misuse of technology--are deeply rooted in social structure, and the role of the intellectual is to work with citizens in promoting fundamental social change" (1979:5).

Davis, Shelton H. and Robert O. Mathews. 1979. Anthropological Resource Center: Public Interest Anthropology -- Beyond the Bureaucratic Ethos. *Practicing Anthropology* 1(3):5,25-26.
Nader, Ralph. 1975. Anthropology in Law and Civic Action. In *Anthropology and Society*. Bela C. Maday, ed. Washington, DC: Anthropological Society of Washington.

- **Society of Applied Anthropology in Canada Formed**
  Canada, 1981

The Society of Applied Anthropology in Canada (SAAC) has developed an active program for its national constituency including annual meetings, a highly informative newsletter and an ethics statement. It is also working on the certification issue. While it is a national organization, SAAC does have local chapters in Quebec, Manitoba and Saskatchewan. According to John A. Price, SAAC developed in response to efforts of the Society for Applied Anthropology to increase its membership (1987:28). Price played a very important role in developing the organization. John Matthiason of the University of Manitoba was the first president.

Ervin, A. M. 1989. On the Current Viability and Future of SAAC. *Newsletter, Society of Applied Anthropology in Canada/Societe D'Anthropologies Appliquee du Canada*. 8:1.
Price, John A. 1987. *Applied Anthropology: Canadian Perspectives*. Downsview, Ontario: SAAC/York University.

- **National Practitioners Organization Formed**
  United States, 1983

The National Association for the Practice of Anthropology (NAPA) was established as a unit of the American Anthropological Association. NAPA defines "practicing anthropologists" as "professionally trained anthropologists who are regularly employed or retained by nonacademic clients, such as social service organizations, government agencies, business and industrial firms, and public educators, and who apply their specialized knowledge to problem solving." NAPA organizes sessions at the American Anthropological Association's meetings, publishes a Bulletin series, and has recently established a mentor program.

Bennett, Linda A. 1988. Bridges for Changing Times: Local Practitioner Organizations in American Anthropology. *NAPA Bulletin 6.* Washington, DC: American Anthropological Association.

- **British Association for Social Anthropology in**
  Policy and Practice Formed
  United Kingdom, 1988

BASAPP is an umbrella organization for a number of small associations of anthropologists who do applied work in health, education, community work, industry and international development. Currently there are three groups associated with BASAPP; ATE [Anthropology, Training and Education], GAPP [Group for Anthropology in Policy and Practice], SASCW [Social Anthropology and Community Work]. The organization publishes a newsletter and has an annual meeting.

Lloyd, Peter. 1989. Editorial. *BASAPP Newsletter* No. 2.

CASES OF APPLICATION AND PRACTICE

AGRICULTURE

- **Zande Scheme Evaluated**
  Sudan, 1952

The Zande Scheme was part of a program for the development of agriculture in British Africa. The ultimate goal was the creation of, "happy, prosperous, literate communities, based on agriculture and participating in the benefits of civilization." The region within which the Azande lived was selected as a pilot project area. Conrad C. Reining carried out research to determine the effects of the project with the financial support of the government of Anglo-Egyptian Sudan.

Reining, Conrad C. 1966. *The Zande Scheme: An Anthropological Case Study of Economic Development in Africa.* Evanston: Northwestern University Press.

- **Early FAO Study in Agricultural Anthropology**
Philippines, 1957

Harold C. Conklin began his Philippine research program following the Second World War. This included work with the Hanunoo, a group on the island of Mindoro. While his research was basic in nature, it did attract the attention of the Food and Agriculture Organization of the United Nations, which published Conklin's monograph on swidden or shifting agriculture of the Hanunoo. This was presented as a kind of policy-relevant monograph. The FAO-provided foreword notes, "It will perhaps come as a surprise to some readers that Dr. Conklin has not concluded his work by suggesting possible ways of improving the standards of living of the group he has studied. It is felt, however, that in this particular case there was no urgent need for such suggestions. It is a case of almost perfect equilibrium between man and his environment, and if there is any deterioration on either side it is an extremely slow process" (1957:v). The actual support for the research project came from the Social Science Research Council and the Ford Foundation.

Conklin, Harold C. 1957. *Hanunoo Agriculture: A Report on an Integral System of Shifting Cultivation in the Philippines.* FAO Forestry Development Paper No. II.

- **Maasai Livestock and Range Development Project Organized**
Tanzania, 1964

The Government of Tanzania developed the policy goal of increasing livestock production in order to improve balance of payments and transform the traditional economy of the Maasai and other pastoral people. This, as well as other issues, led to the organization of the Maasai Livestock and Range Development Project. Shortfalls in the initial stages of the project lead to its reorganization including a social science component. The project made use of anthropologists in a variety of roles over its long history. In the initial stages of the project it was their role to explain and overcome Maasai resistance to the proffered livestock and range management innovations and to disseminate innovations developed by the technical staff. Later there was more direct participation on the part of anthropologists in the development of the technology.

Moris, Jon R. and Colby R. Hatfield. 1982. A New Reality: Western Technology faces Pastoralism in the Maasai Project. In *The Role of Anthropologists and Other Social Scientists in Interdisciplinary Teams Developing Improved Food Production Technology.* Los Banos, Philippines: International Rice Research Institute.

■ **North Shaba Agricultural Development Project Planned**
Zaire, 1975

U.S. Agency for International Development initiated the design process for the North Shaba Project. This small farmer development project used a flexible and incremental approach to planning and development which stressed small farmer participation in decision making. Anthropologists A.H. Barclay, Jr., Thomas Blakely and Pamela Blakely provided research services to this effort.

Barclay, Jr., A. H. 1979. *Anthropological Contributions to the North Shaba Rural Development Project.* Occasional Staff Papers, No. 9 Washington, DC: Development Alternatives, Inc.

■ **Potato Center Researches Farmer Practices**
Peru, 1976

The International Potato Center, using direct hire social scientists including anthropologists, began research on farming practices in the Mantaro Valley. The valley is the largest agricultural area of Central Andes region of Peru. According to Werge, "the primary purpose was to provide baseline data on technical and socioeconomic constraints to potato production which might help to orient the agricultural investigation at [the center] toward appropriate technologies." Research projects on indigenous storage and processing technology have been carried out.

Werge, Robert W. 1977. *Potato Storage Systems in the Mantaro Valley of Peru.* Lima: Centro Internacional de la Papa.
Werge, Robert W. and G. Frerks. 1978. *Evaluation of Solar Dehydration Techniques.* Lima: Centro International de la Papa.

- **ICRISAT Hires Anthropologist for Watershed Development Project**
India, 1976

Preliminary economic analysis suggested that small watershed development (8-16 ha.) would be a productive development alternative. Because this scale required farmer to farmer cooperation, the International Crops Research Center for the Semi-Arid Tropics (ICRISAT), Economic Program added anthropologist Victor S. Doherty to their staff. Doherty worked on a number of aspects of the program including investigations into cooperative action. As the project developed he participated in the on-farm research team that analyzed farmer's assessments of the new watershed technology.

Doherty, Victor S., Senen M. Miranda and Jacob Kampen. 1982. Social Organization and Small Watershed Development. In *The Role of Anthropologists and Other Social Scientists in Interdisciplinary Research Teams Developing Improved Food Production Technology.* Los Banos, Philippines: International Rice Research Institute.

- **Social Stratification in ICRISATs Study Villages Examined**
India, 1982

Victor S. Doherty developed an approach for the study of caste in the sample of ten villages within which ICRISAT's agricultural scientists develop and test new technology. The Village Level Studies (VLS) villages have been selected from 5 different districts representative of soil and agroclimatic regions of the Indian dry semi-arid tropics. For a period of time data on this panel of villages was collected monthly. Doherty developed an approach for comparing caste rank differences between the geographically dispersed villages.

Doherty, Victor S. 1982. *A Guide to the Study of Social and Economic Groups and Stratification in ICRISAT's Indian Village Level Studies.* Patancheru, Andhra Pradesh: ICRISAT.

- **Integrated Pest Management Project Makes Use of Anthropologist**
Philippines, 1978

The International Rice Research Institute (IRRI) developed a program to improve integrated pest management (IPM) technology for small-scale irrigated agriculture in Southeast Asia. The team working on the project included anthropologist Grace Goddell. IPM has the general purpose of reducing pesticide use and thereby input cost and pesticide dependence.

Pesticide use is reduced through a complex of behaviors requiring farmer to farmer cooperation and more complex management. In the case of IRRI the package included synchronous planting over a large area, group pest monitoring, group fallowing and group pesticide purchase. The IRRI technology development process made use of a quasi-experimental research design. A group of 15 villages were studied by using a "top-down" approach in five, a "bottom-up" approach in another, while five villages served as a control. In the course of the study, anthropologist Goodell lived in villages of each type.

Goodell, G. E., P. E. Kenmore, J. A. Litsinger, J. P. Bandong, C. G. de la Cruz and M. D. Lumaban. 1982. Rice Insect Pest Management Technology and Its Transfer to Small-scale Farmers in the Philippines. In *The Role of Anthropologists and Other Social Scientists in Interdisciplinary Teams Developing Improved Food Production Technology.* Los Banos, Philippines: International Rice Research Institute.

■ **Subsistence Farmers Write Agricultural Technology Textbook**
Bolivia, 1979

The Traditional Practices Project produced textbooks on traditional agricultural techniques in three geographic regions of Bolivia, including highland plateau, temperate valleys, and the tropical lowlands. The project, done by Rural Development Services, was sponsored by the Bolivian Ministry of Agriculture and the U.S. Agency for International Development. The texts were produced to a large extent by the farmers themselves. The core data were diaries kept by the hundreds of male and female household heads that participated. Interestingly many of the diarists were illiterate, they succeeded by using school children or project staff as translators and scribes. The records documented their daily subsistence activities, such as crop tasks, herding livestock, gathering water and fuel, preparing meals, washing and mending clothes, making craft products, providing health care, as well as family celebrations. The diary materials were supplemented with transcripts of interviews between Bolivian project staff and the participating agriculturalists. It was thought that subsistence farmers could learn from each other through the medium of these texts and that outsiders might gain appreciation for what these farmers know.

Hatch, John K. 1983. *Our Knowledge, Traditional Farming Practices in Rural Bolivia. Volume I: Altiplano Region.* (AID Contract No. GOB-AID-511-113) New York: Rural Development Services.

- **Potential for Development Among Pastoralists Assessed**
  Kenya, 1980

James L. Merryman and Nancy H. Merryman carried out a study to inform the design of a plan for the rehabilitation of some irrigation schemes in the Garissa area of northeastern Kenya. Garissa is one of the least developed areas of Kenya. It is arid and in the 1970's was part of the eastern extension of the disastrous Sahelian drought. The drought resulted in the loss of over half of the area's livestock herds and the consequent impoverishment of its primarily pastoral population. The irrigation schemes and the settled agriculture which they permitted were established to relieve the tremendous economic hardship caused by the drought. There was, of course, almost no precedent for agriculture. The study revealed that many of the irrigation schemes had failed and that technical reliability was the most frequent problem. In addition, the workability of the schemes was limited because of problems associated with marketing and cash flow. The research demonstrated that the nomads preferred stable residence if it was economically feasible. The research was conducted for the Kenyan Ministry of Cooperative Development and the Danida Mission of the Danish Embassy.

Merryman, James L. and Nancy H. Merryman. 1980. *The Potential for Agricultural Development in a Pastoral Society: A Sociological Study of the People's of Garissa District.* Report No. 6. Nairobi: Research and Evaluation Unit, Development Planning Division, Ministry of Cooperative Development.

- **CIMMYT Anthropologist Contributes to
  Development of On-farm Research Techniques**
  Ecuador, 1980

The International Center for Improvement of Corn and Wheat (CIMMYT) working in association with Ecuador's national agricultural research institute initiated a series of on-farm research projects. On-farm research involves the carrying out of agronomic research on a farm rather than in the more controlled environment of an experiment station. Part of the conceptual framework of this research approach is the recommendation domain, which is "a set of farmers who work land with similar features and who have access to similar resources." This concept guides site selection. A major motivation for doing agronomic research on-farm is that it improves the probability of effective technology transfer in later stages because it tends to take into account a wider array of production problems which impinge on small-farmer decision-making. The anthropologist, Robert Tripp developed relations with participants, data recording forms and strategies for site selection.

Tripp, Robert. 1982. *Data Collection, Site Selection and Farmer Participation in On-Farm Experimentation.* Mexico: Centro Internacional de Mejoramiento de Maiz y Trigo.

- **Farming Systems of Alachua County, Florida Examined**
  United States, 1980

Although farming systems research (FSR) has been widely used in international development situations, it has been rarely used in domestic settings. An apparently early attempt to use FSR domestically was carried out by University of Florida anthropologists, Art Hansen, David Griffith, John Butler, and Sandra Powers along with others. The research started with the collection of secondary data, visits to the research, area and interviews with University technical staff. This was coupled with a "rapid, unstructured survey" in two areas of the county. Various formal surveys emerged out of this work, including general and commodity-focused work. These surveys resulted in the identification of three "distinct production strategies," that is crop production, animal production and mixed strategies. Focusing primarily on "low resource" farmers the researchers reported a number of conclusions and recommendations.

Hansen, Art, David Griffith, John Butler, Sandra Powers, Elon Gilbert, Robin Lauriault, and Masuma Downie. 1981. *Farming Systems of Alachua County, Florida: An Overview with Special Attention to Low Resource Farmers.* Gainesville, FL: Center for Community and Rural Development, Institute of Food and Agricultural Sciences, University of Florida.

- **Common Pasture Use by Andean Pastoralists Researched**
  Peru, 1981

One of the most significant problems faced in the development of traditional livestock production is overgrazing of commonly held pastures due to the inability to control stocking rates. The problem, often attributed to Hardin's idea of the "tragedy of the commons" is widespread and to a large extent intractable. Working with the support of the Small Ruminant Collaborative Research Support Program, Keith A. Jamtgaard carried out a research program in a community in highland Peru to better understand community and farmer factors that control access to communal pasture resources. The community within which the research was done was well documented through earlier CRSP-supported research. Data were collected from household production units using participant-observation, key - informant interviews, and survey census techniques. The research indicated that decision-making relating to the use of pasture resources was strongly influenced by the interaction between livestock and crop production. Further the distance to pastures was related to variation in use levels. The primary remedies for reducing overgrazing involve strengthening community organizations.

Jamtgaard, Keith A. 1984. *Limits on Common Pasture Use in an Agro-pastoral Community: The Case of Toqra, Peru.* Technical Report Series Number 42. Columbia, MO: Small Ruminant Collaborative Research Support Program, University of Missouri.

- **Andean Pastoralism Examined for Small Ruminant CRSP**
  Peru, 1981

Constance McCorkle researched the technological and ecological organization of herding among Quechua-speaking peasants resident in the village of Usi in the Department of Cuzco, Peru for the Small Ruminant Coordinated Research Support Program. The research made use of a variety of data collection techniques including a set of questionnaires administered to a stratified sample of stock-owning families; topically focused, in-depth, open-ended interviewing with key informants; as well as participant observation. These data were presented as a series of descriptive ethnographies stressing the interaction of various components of the livestock production system.

McCorkle, Constance M. 1982. *Organizational Dialectics of Animal Management.* Technical Report Series Number 6. Columbia, MO: Department of Rural Sociology, University of Missouri.
_____. 1983. *The Technoenvironmental Dialectics of Herding in Andean Agropastoralism.* Technical Report Series Number 30. Columbia, MO: Department of Rural Sociology, University of Missouri.

- **Kordofan Farming Systems Examined**
  Sudan, 1981

Anthropologists Edward B. Reeves and Timothy Frankenberger conducted a farming system and marketing analysis in North Kordofan, Sudan. This was carried out as a component of INTSORMIL, the International Sorghum/Millet Collaborative Research Support Program (CRSP) funded by the Agency for International Development. INTSORMIL sponsors collaboration in research and development at a number of U.S. land grant institutions, international research centers and various in-country research programs. The research was directed at identifying constraints for improving sorghum and millet production and marketing.

Reeves, Edward B. and Timothy Frankenberger. 1981. *Socio-economic Constraints to the Production, Distribution, and Consumption of Millet, Sorghum, and Cash Crops in North Kordofan, Sudan.* Report No. 1, Lexington, KY: University of Kentucky, College of Agriculture, Department of Sociology.
_____. 1982. *Farming Systems Research in North Kordofan, Sudan.* Report No. 2., Lexington, KY: University of Kentucky, College of Agriculture, Department of Sociology.

- **Asian Vegetable Gardens Studied**
  Taiwan, 1981

Asian Vegetable Research and Development Center instituted the AVRDC Garden Program to demonstrate feasibility for this type of development for various Southeast Asian sites. Anthropologist Jack Gershon participated in research which identified some nutritional problems which could be alleviated through the inclusion of specific vegetables in garden developments. The goal was the growing of "gardens that contain a culturally acceptable intercrop of vegetables which contain significant amounts of the nutrients that will alleviate the Vitamin A, Iron and calcium deficiencies."

Gershon, Jack. 1982. *Progress Report, AVRDC Garden Programs.* Tainan, Taiwan: Asian Vegetable Research and Development Center.

- **Sorghum Development Effort Informed**
  by Anthropological Research
  Honduras, 1981

A site in rural Honduras was selected for study as part of the social science component of the International Sorghum/Millet Program. The research, directed by Billie R. DeWalt and Kathleen M. DeWalt, was intended to improve the production, marketing, and use of sorghum and millet world-wide. The research is being used to inform sorghum and millet development efforts carried out at a number of American universities with the cooperation of host countries.

DeWalt, Billie R. and Kathleen M. DeWalt. 1982. *Farming Systems Research in Southern Honduras.* Report No. 1, Department of Sociology, Department of Anthropology, Agricultural Experiment Station College of Agriculture, University of Kentucky, Lexington.

- **Ministry of Agriculture Research Efforts Supported**
  Malawi, 1981

USAID provided a technical assistance team to the Ministry of Agriculture of Malawi. The team consisted of a number of agricultural scientists and one anthropologist, Art Hansen. Hansen's responsibility consisted of initiating a national FSR program and developing capabilities within a unit of the Ministry of Agriculture to administer it. In addition he participated in the developing research program. This started with literature review and rapid diagnostic survey work.

Hansen, Art. 1985. Farming Systems Research in Phalombe, Malawi: The Limited Utility of High Yielding Varieties. In *Social Sciences and Farming Systems Research: Methodological Perspectives on Agriculture and Development.* Jeffrey R. Jones and Ben J. Wallace, eds. Boulder, CO: Westview Press.
Hansen, Art, Emmanuel N. Mwango and Benson S. C. Phiri. 1982. *Farming Systems in Phalombe Project, Malawi: Another Approach to Smallholder Research and Development.* Gainesville, FL: Center for Tropical Agriculture, University of Florida.

- **Zambia Agriculture Project Led by Anthropologist**
  Zambia, 1982

The Zambia Agricultural Training, Planning and Institutional Development Project was based on a cooperative agreement between USAID, Iowa State University, and the Government of Zambia. Anthropologist D. M. Warren was leader of the team that saw to the implementation of the project that was to improve various Zambian government agencies' ability to plan and make policy in relation to small-scale agricultural producers.

Warren, Dennis M. 1985. Anthropology and Agricultural Planning in Zambia. Unpublished paper presented at American Anthropological Association.

- **Ethnosemantic Elicitation Used to Understand
  Potential Domesticate**
  Botswana, 1982

The morama bean is a wild plant that grows in the Kalahari and is gathered and consumed by the Basarwa who live there. The bean known to be nutritious, delicious, drought resistant, and high in protein and oil was targeted by the National Academy of Sciences of the United States as a promising legume for domestication. A research group including Megan Biesele and Robert E. Murry, Jr. proposed doing an ethnography of the bean to the National Science Foundation. The goal of this research was to serve the information needs of various agricultural scientists who were working on the potentials of the bean at various universities and research institutes in the American southwest. The field research on the bean done in Botswana included three components; ethnological observation of practices relating to the bean; ethnosemantic elicitation of knowledge of the collectors and users; and collection of germ plasm and ecological information. Knowledge of the bean was limited. As the report noted, "Nearly everything that agronomists needed to know in order to disseminate this plant had yet to be discovered." Data about natural growing conditions was especially important to collect.

Biesele, Megan and Robert E. Murry, Jr. 1982. *Morama and Other Plant Foods of Kalahari Foragers: An Applied Ethnobotanical Study.* Report to the Applied Ethnobotanical Study.

- ## Small Ruminant CRSP Does Goat Production Diagnostic
  Brazil, 1982

An early research project of the Small Ruminant CRSP was a basic diagnostic study of goat production of smallholders in selected municipios of North Bahia, Brazil. This area was selected because of its high concentration of goat production. The research determined some of the variation in the production system. Using an interview guide the researchers interviewed about fifty farmers. The data collected addressed many aspects of the goat production system as well as data about other commodities.

Primov, George with Paulo Luiz Santos de Almeida. 1984. *Goat Production within the Farming System of Smallholders of Northern Bahia, Brazil.* Research Report No. 35. Title XII. Small Ruminant CRSP. Department of Rural Sociology, University of Missouri, Columbia.

- ## Supply of Rural Credit to Haitian Farmers Studied
  Haiti, 1982

Glenn R. Smucker studied the availability of credit for Haitian farmers under an USAID contract. There is high demand for credit in rural Haiti and many of the available sources are usurious. The study was coupled with research on the demand for low interest loans from the Bureau de Credit Agricole of the Haitian Ministry of Agriculture. The study relied on key informant interviews with Bureau de Credit Agricole staff and clients, peasant farmers, market ladies, provincial merchants, pawnbrokers, money lenders and others. Representatives of various other credit supplying agencies were also interviewed. Smucker's report describes the "salient aspects of peasant economy, traditional strategies for access to credit, the range and variation of non-formal lending sources," while it compared formal and informal credit suppliers.

Smucker, Glenn R. 1983. *Supplies of Credit Among Haitian Peasants.* Washington, DC: Development Alternatives, Inc.

- **Sorghum Production Constraints Studied in Mexico**
  Mexico, 1983

As part of the social science program of INTSORMIL, Elizabeth Adelski researched aspects of sorghum production in Sinaloa, Mexico. Her research documented the agricultural system with special attention to the role of sorghum and identified the incentives and constraints to sorghum production in this important agricultural state. Sinaloa is an important agricultural producer and contributes substantially to Mexican agricultural production. Her research focused on a newly irrigated area in the northern part of the state. Production on these irrigated lands is constrained by shortage of tractors, insect infestation and delays in getting credit approval. In response to these problems farmers have largely switched to a soybeans and wheat rotation.

Adelski, Elizabeth. 1987. *Sorghum Production in the Small-Farmer Sector of Sinaloa, Mexico.* Lexington, KY: College of Agriculture, University of Kentucky.

- **Potato Production and Variety Selection Studied for the International Potato Center (CIP)**
  Nepal, 1982

Agricultural anthropologist Robert E. Rhoades researched potato production and post-harvest practices of traditional Eastern Nepal farmers. Data were collected through open-ended, ethnographic interviews in both lowland and highland ecological zones. This research complemented the substantial research of Rhoades on Andean potato production done with CIP and was done as part of an evaluation of Nepal's National Potato Development Programme. Rhoades was able to characterize the potato production system of two regions in terms of cultivation practices, exchange and marketing, storage and processing, seed sources and flows, selection and use of germplasm and variety descriptions used by farmers.

Rhoades, Robert E. 1985. *Traditional Potato Production and Farmers' Selection of Varieties in Eastern Nepal.* Potatoes in Food Systems, Research Series, Report No. 2. Lima: International Potato Center (CIP)

- **Fresh Produce Market Potential Assessed for the Bluegrass**
  United States, 1983

At the instigation of the Kentucky Department of Agriculture and the Lexington-Fayette Urban County Government, anthropologist Grace M. Zilverberg and nutritionist Anita Courtney undertook a study of the feasibility of the expansion of a fresh fruit and vegetable market for the Bluegrass region. The research project had a number of goals. These were (1) the determination of the current status of the fruit and vegetable market in the Bluegrass region; (2) grower and buyer interest in expanding the market; and (3) identification of constraints for the development of the market. Data were collected from buyers and growers through face-to-face interviews and by telephone. Inquiry was made concerning interest in the establishment of a packing-marketing facility, expansion of the local farmer's market and contract arrangements with food processors. The research revealed strong interest in such developments by growers and buyers. A number of constraints to market development were identified.

Zilverberg, Grace M. and Anita Courtney. 1984. *The Status and Potential of the Fruit and Vegetable Market in the Kentucky Bluegrass Region.* Frankfort, KY: Kentucky Department of Agriculture.

- **Barter and Other Exchange Studied by Small Ruminant CRSP**
  Peru, 1984

As part of the Small Ruminant Collaborative Research Program, a series of related research projects have been carried out in highland Peru. One project, carried out by Paula Bilinsky focused on the role barter and labor exchange in agricultural production systems of the central Andes. This project was carried out in Aramchay, an agricultural community in the Mantaro Valley. Bilinsky found that barter and labor exchange was extensively used to obtain various production inputs in this region. One interesting means of exchange was the *sunay* in which a planting season

42

laborer is given the produce from a certain number of rows of crop at harvest. Labor exchange was found to be very common. Barter for goods often occurred between the local and regional economies.

Bilinsky, Paula. 1986. *Barter and Non-monetary Exchanges of Labor in a Highland Peruvian Community.* Small Ruminant CRSP, Technical Report Series Number 74. Columbia, Missouri: Department of Rural Sociology.

- **Literature on Household Gardens Reviewed for CIP**
  Peru, 1984

As part of their social science research program, the International Potato Center (CIP) sponsored research into the household garden. The project, carried out by anthropologist Vera K. Ninez, was based on literature review. The research considered a number of aspects of the topic, these included evidence from prehistoric and early historic times, role of gardens in the diffusion of plant material, and the nutritional significance of gardens. Perhaps the most interesting aspect of the project was the development of a definition and typology for the household garden. The analysis was supplemented with ethnographic case examples from around the world.

Ninez, Vera K. 1984. *Household Gardens: Theoretical Considerations on an Old Survival Strategy.* Potatoes in Food Systems Research series, Report No. 1. Lima, Peru: International Potato Center.

- **Fallow and Cropping Practices Examined for ICARDA**
  Syria, 1984

The International Center for Agricultural Research in the Dry Area (ICARDA) supports an in-house farming systems research program as part of its agronomic research efforts. Dennis Tully, an anthropologist employed by ICARDA, carried out research that was designed to determine the feasibility of substituting legume production for fallow in the cereal crop cycle among smallholder farmers in Syria. Feasibility was tested through a survey of farmers sampled from three different areas defined in terms of rainfall. The sampling and data collection units were villages. In each survey village the researchers attempted to contact the headman or other knowledgeable person. Information about the farming system was obtained from the key informant, with others sitting in on the interview so as to improve the quality and completeness of the information. Data were collected on a number of topics. these included land use, cultivation practices, hiring of labor, costs and benefits of legumes and cereals and livestock feeding practices. The research indicated that feasibility for the substitution of legumes for fallow was low. The major problem were low yields and profitability and high start-up costs and harvest-labor requirements.

Tully, Dennis. 1984. *Land Use and Farmer's Strategies in Al Bab: The Feasibility of Forage Legumes in the Place of Fallow.* Research Report No. 12. Aleppo, Syria: International Center for Agricultural Research in the Dry Areas.

- **Applications of Agricultural Technology Studied for FAO**
  World, 1985

Deborah Merrill Sands, a consultant to the Food and Agriculture Organization of the United Nations, reviewed literature that addressed what was referred to as the "technology applications gap." This refers to frequently observed limitations in the adoption by farmers with small-scale farms of newly developed agricultural technology that is thought to be effective by agricultural scientists. Merrill Sands dealt with this complex and important issue by focusing on how and with what criteria these farmers evaluate technology and how technology can be developed that is attractive to them. The product of the review was a report intended to increase awareness of these issues amongst researchers, policy makers and development planners. The review resulted in the development of a strategy for bridging the "applications gap" which is described in the report. She advocated increasing the complexity of the base of knowledge of cultural and social factors and to increase the involvement of the technology user in the technology development process. She proposed a four step process to help agricultural scientists and development planners close the "technology applications gap." Also included was an extensive annotated bibliography of the case literature.

Sands, Deborah Merrill. 1986. *The Technology Applications Gap: Overcoming Constraints to Small-farm Development.* FAO Research and Technology Paper 1. Rome: Food and Agriculture Organization.

- **On Farm Research Studied for ISNAR**
  Netherlands, 1986

The International Service for National Agricultural Research [ISNAR] located in the Netherlands organized a five year study of the organization and management of on-farm client-oriented research led by anthropologist Deborah Merrill-Sands. Also involved in the project was anthropologist

Susan V. Poats. The study drew upon the experience of scientists and research managers in Bangladesh, Ecuador, Guatemala, Indonesia, Nepal, Panama, Senegal, Zambia and Zimbabwe. The researchers produced a series of case studies of the use this approach and organized a workshop in 1989.

Bingen, R. James and Susan V. Poats. n.d. *Staff Management Issues in On-farm Client-Oriented Research: Lessons for Managers.* OFCOR Comparative Study Papers. No. 5.

Merrill-Sands, Deborah and David Kaimowitz. 1990. *The Technology Triangle, Linking Farmers, Technology Transfer Agents, and Agricultural Researchers.* The Hague: International Service for National Agricultural Research.

Merrill-Sands, Deborah, David Kaimowitz *and Jean McAllister. n.d. Strengthening the Integration of On-farm Client-Oriented Research and Experiment Station Research in National Agricultural Research (NARS): Management Lessons from Nine Country Case Studies.* OFCOR Comparative Study Papers. No. 1.

- **Sondeo Research Techniques Used to Guide Agricultural Extension and Research in Kentucky**
  United States, 1986

A research team including agricultural and social scientists carried out a sondeo or rural reconnaissance in two Kentucky counties to improve the circumstances of farm families and to evaluate this techniques' utility for guiding development projects and research programs for Kentucky. The sondeo technique is characterized by informal interviews conducted by research teams with farmers over a limited period of time. The data collected through the interviews is analyzed through group discussion and then written up. While it can have much of the validity of a sample based survey it is much cheaper and quicker. It also has advantages over an ethnographic study done by a single researcher because it incorporates the technical knowledge of a variety of individuals. The Kentucky Sondeo included agronomists, soil scientists, economists, animal scientists, and extension agents as well as social scientists. Sondeos are often done early in a farming system research/extension project to quickly scope out a region. The counties in which these sondeos were done faced a number of special problems. In both counties tobacco was grown and therefore farmers were concerned about alternative commodities to replace this valuable crop because of uncertainties about the tobacco price support program. In one of the counties farmers were uncertain about production decisions because of the federal dairy herd buyout program. In the other county, where off-farm employment in coal mining is important, farmer/miners were having difficulty because of the depressed coal market.

This was addressed in the sondeo by considering the needs of part-time farmers. The sondeo was carried out by C. Milton Coughenour, John van Willigen and Grant Thomas.

van Willigen, John et al. 1986. *The Farming Systems of Russell County.* Lexington, KY: Department of Sociology, College of Agriculture, University of Kentucky.

- **Diffusion of Agricultural Innovations Studied**
  Niger, 1988

The Communication for Technology Transfer in Agriculture project researched "farmer-to-farmer communication networks in relation to the transfer of farmer innovations" in Niger as part of their multi-nation research program. In contrast to many studies in the rich innovation diffusion literature the researchers emphasized the flow of information between farmers rather than between extensionists and farmers [See Rogers 1983]. Research was carried out in seven villages representing a mix of attributes such as presence of extension agents, access to roads, presence of development projects, and distance from town. The data were collected through individual and group interviews. Group interviews ranged from 6 to 60 in size, usually all men. The questions used to guide discussions dealt with the village, communication channels, farming activities, and innovations. The data were used to construct case studies of technology transfer. The researchers reached the following conclusions among others; (1) technology offered by extension programs is seen as inappropriate by farmers, (2) farmers tend to "reinvent" technology but do not communicate back to the technology developers, and (3) farmers seek out new workable ideas.

McCorkle, Constance M., Robert H. Branstetter, Gail D. McClure. 1988. *A Case Study on Farmer Innovations and Communication in Niger: Communication for Technology Transfer in Agriculture.* Washington, DC: Academy for Educational Development.

Rogers, Everett M. 1983. *Diffusion of Innovations.* New York: The Free Press.

- **Indonesian Farming Systems Efforts Evaluated**
  Indonesia, 1988

Anthropologist Harold J. McArthur and Kanok Rerkasem reviewed the results of farming systems research and extension activities carried out in Indonesia as part of a multi-nation study sponsored by USAID. The study had the objectives of identifying "the degree to which externally funded projects have assisted in institutionalizing the FSR/E approach into the national agricultural research and extension system and the extent to which national budgets are now supporting FSR/E activities." McArthur, who has been involved in FSR/E activities in Indonesia, collected data through key informant interviews at various project sites and institutes in Java. These data were supplemented with secondary data on the transmigration projects in Sumatra and Sulawesi. McArthur found substantial use of the FSR/E approach in Indonesia. There is a small and well-prepared cadre of senior researchers who are committed to this approach and are in a position to influence further development of the approach. A constraint has been the highly centralized nature of Indonesian research organizations which makes local-level impacts difficult.

McArthur, Harold J. and Kanok Rerkasem. 1988. *Identification of Results of Farming Systems Research and Extension Activities in Indonesia.* Prepared for the U.S. Agency for International Development, Science and Technology Bureau.

- **Inland Valley Swamp Development Project Assessed**
  Sierra Leone, 1989

In Sierra Leone there is a push to develop swamps to supplement upland rice production. One project actively involved in this is the Inland Valley Swamp Development Project sponsored by the United Nations Development Programme, the Food and Agriculture Organization, and the Ministry of Agriculture, Natural Resources and Forestry. The locus of their efforts is Moyamba District in southern Sierra Leone. The Project's objectives are to (a) increase the production of rice, Sierra Leone's staple food, and (b) to relieve pressure on the uplands, the traditional site of rice farming using swidden agriculture. They have seventy-seven farmers associations that they work with, providing low-cost resources, food aid, as well as technical advice and guidance in conjunction with government extension workers. Central to the Project are five demonstration sites, which serve as showcases of the Project's activities and successes. To enhance the Project's understanding of the local-level dynamics of swamp development, two anthropologists conducted an in-depth case study of one of the demonstration sites over a ten month period. The research focused on how farmers integrate swamp development into their farming practices, how development influences division of labor and gender relations, the dynamics of forming cooperative farmers' associations, and how local land tenure affects Project outcomes. The research used questionnaires, and informal and key-informant interviews conducted with several Project participants and non-participants, both male and female. In addition, a great deal of information was obtained through participant observation, both in the village and at Project headquarters.

Cunningham, M. Kiran and Russell D. Rhoads. 1990. *The Dynamics of Swamp Development: A Case Study of a Demonstration Site in the UNDP/FAO/MANR&F Inland Valley Swamp Development Project SIL/86/001.* An evaluation prepared for UNDP/FAO/MANR&F Project SIL/86/001.

(M. Kiran Cunningham & Russell D. Rhoads)

ALCOHOL AND DRUG ABUSE

- **Drinking Problems Project**
  United States, 1964

The McKinley County, New Mexico, Community Treatment Plan for Navaho Problem drinkers was established. The project made use of anthropologists and illustrated the increasing use of anthropologically trained persons in clinical settings.

Ferguson, Frances Northend. 1968. Navaho Drinking: Some Tentative Hypotheses. *Human Organization*   27(2):139-167.

- **Anthropology of Drugs**
  United States, 1968

Various anthropologists developed serious interest in research into the cultural dimensions of drug use. In some cases this interest developed into anthropologists acting as therapists. These therapies were based on strategies of reenculturation.

Rosenstiel, C. R. and J. B. Freeland. 1973. Anthropological Perspectives on the Rehabilitation of Institutionalized Narcotic Addicts. In *Anthropology Beyond the University.* Proceedings of the Southern Anthropological Society, No. 7, Alden Redfield, ed. Athens: University of Georgia Press.

Weppner, Robert S. 1973. An Anthropological View of the Street Addict's World. *Human Organization*   32(2):111-112.

48

- **Rural Alcohol Initiative Project Researched in Kentucky**
  United States, 1978

Anthropologist Patricia Marshall directed the research component of the Kentucky activities of the federally funded Rural Alcohol Initiative. The general thrust of the research component was to identify constraints and problems associated with "the delivery of alcohol treatment programs" in a largely rural area of Eastern Kentucky. Early research included a telephone needs assessment survey and extensive key informant interviews with representatives of health care and social service agencies, the courts, schools, alcoholics, program employees and community residents. These efforts were supplemented by a community survey carried out in all project sites. Analysis revealed the importance of religious belief in defining drinking as a problem.

Marshall, Patricia. 1979. *Executive Summary Interim Report: Rural Alcohol Initiative*. Ashland, KY: Lansdowne Mental Health Center.

- **PNG Alcohol Use and Abuse Assessed**
  Papua New Guinea, 1980

Papua New Guinea Institute of Applied Social and Economic Research researched alcohol use and abuse throughout Papua New Guinea. The project, funded by a government agency, was to make policy recommendations about beverage alcohol to national and provincial governments. The research team, consisting of Andonia Piau-Lynch, Francis H. Sumanop and Mac Marshall, used a variety of data sources. Archival research focused upon newspapers, missionary reports, government records, ethnographic data on alcohol use and the alcohol literature. Extensive field research was carried out. This included interviews with licensing officials, industry officials, bar owners, licensees, etc. Surveys and other research activities were carried out in various urban and rural settings. Assistance of researchers doing ethnographic work in New Guinea during the time of the project was obtained. Policy recommendations dealt with licensing, non-beverage alcohol imports, advertising of beverage alcohol, drinking premises construction standards, and drunk-driving.

Marshall, Mac. 1980. *A History of Prohibition and Liquor Legislation in Papua New Guinea*. IASER Discussion Paper, #33.
_____. 1981. *A Summary of the IASER Conference on Alcohol Use and Abuse in Papua New Guinea, 23-27 March 1981*. Waigani.

Piau-Lynch, Andonia, F. H. Survanna. 1981. *Policy Recommendation from the IASER Alcohol Research Project to the National and Provincial Governments of Papua New Guinea.*

- **Substance Abuse Program Implemented**
  United States, 1989

The Teen Action Project, funded by the Robert Wood Johnson Foundation, was organized through the Institute for Community Research and the Hispanic Health Council of Hartford, CT. The project focused on gaps in programing for prevention and early intervention of substance abuse among youth. Of special concern was the participation of youth as drug sellers, the lack of constructive alternative economic opportunity for youth, and insufficient knowledge of youth drug culture. The goals of the project were to be achieved through the formation of a Teen Team trained in action research and supported by staff and community mentors. The team worked on plans for improving leisure time activity and economic opportunities. The principal investigator of the project was Jean J. Schensul.

Cooper, Sandra, et al. n.d. *Teen Action Research Project.* Hartford, CT: Institute for Community Research.

COMMUNITY ACTION

- **Anthropologist Serves Early Community**
  Development Efforts
  India, 1945

W. H. Wiser, a frequent contributor to the social anthropological literature on rural India, started organizational work leading to the creation of India Village Service. I.V.S. was a privately funded experimental program which was to devise techniques for rural development in Uttar Pradesh. It was funded by various missionary groups and committed to community development ideology.

Wiser, W. H. 1958. *India Village Service, Retrospect and Prospect.* Marehra, District Etah, Uttar Pradesh: India Village Service.

- **Early Development Anthropology Project**
  Haiti, 1947

Marbial Valley Project was started to begin the process by which illiteracy, poverty and ill health in a rural Haiti region could be conquered. The project started with survey research done by anthropologist Alfred Metraux. Based on these research activities, change programs were mounted. Later, other projects were carried out by other anthropologists. The project, a cooperative effort of UNESCO and the government of Haiti, was a very early example of the use of research working in conjunction with development activities.

Metraux, Alfred. 1949. Anthropology and the UNESCO Pilot-Project of Marbial (Haiti). *America Indigena* 9:183-194.
Sylvain, Jeanne G. 1949. La Infancia Campesina en el Valle del Marbial, Haiti. *America Indigena* 9:299-332.
UNESCO. 1951. *The Haiti Pilot Project, Phase One.* Monograph on Fundamental Education No. 4. UNESCO Publication No. 796.

- **Anthropologists Advise Pilot Community Development Program**
  India, 1948

The community development approach to rural development was applied on a pilot basis to a region of the north Indian state of Uttar Pradesh. The group which designed the original program was led by town planner Albert Mayer. The team was assisted by various social scientists including anthropologists McKim Marriott and Rudra Dutt Singh. This project became the model for the national program of community development.

Mayer, Albert with M. Marriott and R. L. Park. 1958. *Pilot Project, India: The Story of Rural Development at Etawah, Uttar Pradesh.* Berkeley: University of California Press.

- **Cornell Fruitland Project**
  United States, 1948

One of the many significant applied anthropology projects in which Cornell University anthropologists came to be involved was the Southwestern Field Station Project at Fruitland, New Mexico. The activities of the project were predominantly research, focused primarily on an evaluation of the Fruitland irrigation project. The Fruitland Project was initiated some eight years earlier by the Bureau of Indian Affairs to provide irrigated farm land to Navajo Indians. The working agreement between the BIA and the Cornell group called for the determination of the social effects of the various development efforts and making of recommendations for subsequent efforts. The anthropologists involved included Tom T. Sasaki, John Adair, Alexander Leighton, Clifford Barnett, and Milton Barnett.

Sasaki, Tom T. 1960. *Fruitland, New Mexico: A Navaho Community in Transition.* Ithaca, New York: Cornell University Press.
Sasaki, Tom T. and John Adair. 1952. New Land to Farm: Agricultural Practices Among the Navaho Indians of New Mexico. In *Human Problems in Technological Change.* Edward H. Spicer, ed. New York: Russell Sage.

- ## Fox Project Starts
United States, 1948

The Fox Project, under the leadership of Sol Tax, resulted in the development of the "action anthropology" method. This is one of the first value-explicit approaches. Its goal was to bring about changes in an American Indian community in Iowa and its relationships with nearby white communities. This is one of the earliest intervention techniques developed in anthropology.

Diesing, Paul. 1960. A Method of Problem Solving. In *Documentary History of the Fox Project.* Department of Anthropology, University of Chicago.
Gearing, Frederick. 1960. The Strategy of the Fox Project. In *Documentary History of the Fox Project.* Department of Anthropology, University of Chicago.
Gearing, Frederick, Robert Mc. Netting and Lisa R. Peattie. 1960. *Documentary History of the Fox Project.* Department of Anthropology, University of Chicago.
Peattie, Lisa R. 1960. The Failure of the Means-Ends Scheme in Action Anthropology. In *Documentary History of the Fox Project.* Department of Anthropology, University of Chicago.
Piddington, Ralph. 1960. Action Anthropology. *Journal of the Polynesian Society* 69:199-213.
Tax, Sol. 1958. The Fox Project. *Human Organization* 17:17-19.
_____. 1960. Action Anthropology. In *Documentary History of the Fox Project.* Department of Anthropology, University of Chicago.

- ## Community Development Programme Initiated
India, 1952

The Government of India adopted the community development approach as official rural development policy. This was based on experiments carried out earlier at various sites including the Etowah and Nilokheri Projects. As long as the approach was used, anthropologists participated as researchers and to an extent as practitioners. Certainly the best known publication to come out of this episode in the history of applied anthropology in India is S. C. Dubey's *India's Changing Villages* (1955). Based on a study of two different types of villages in North Central India, he concluded that most positive impacts of development occurred among the elite agriculturalists of the community and left poorer agricultural and artisans largely untouched. This effect plagued various development efforts through the Green Revolution. The anthropologists that contributed to aspects of the community development programme included S. K. Dey, Oscar Lewis, Henry Orenstein, M. N. Srinivas and D. P. Sinha, among many others. Work done by Lewis with the assistance of H. S. Dhillon and I. P. Singh resulted in the publication of *Village Life in Northern India*.

Dubey, S. C. 1955. *India's Changing Villages*. Allied Publishers, Bombay.

Dey, S. K. *Community Development: A Bird's Eye View.* Bombay: Asia Publishing House.

Orenstein, Henry. 1963. Village, Caste and the Welfare State. *Human Organization* 22(1).

Lewis, Oscar. 1965. *Group Dynamics in a North India Village*. Delhi: Planning Commission.

Srinivas, M. N. 1950. The Dominant Caste in Rampur. *American Anthropologist* 61(1).

- **Research and Development Anthropology Developed**
  Peru, 1952

Under the leadership of Allan R. Holmberg, the Cornell-Peru project attempted to bring about political and economic change in a community in highland Peru. The approach used is termed "research and development" anthropology. It is one of the first systematic value-explicit approaches. The approach developed at Vicos was applied in a number of other contexts. The project had a significant research output and is very well documented.

Alers, J. Oscar. 1965. The Question of Well-being. *American Behavioral Scientist* 8(7):18-22.

Alers, J. Oscar, Mario C. Vasquez, Allan R. Holmberg, and Henry F. Dobyns. 1965. Human Freedom and Geographic Mobility. *Current Anthropology* 6(3):336.

Collier, John and Mary Collier. 1957. An Experiment in Applied Anthropology. *Scientific American* 196(1):37-45.

Dobyns, Henry F. 1965. The Strategic Importance of Enlightenment and Skill for Power. *American Behavioral Scientist* 8(7):23.

Dobyns, Henry F., Paul L. Doughty and Harold O. Lasswell. 1971. *Peasants, Power, and Applied Social Change, Vicos as a Model*. Beverly Hills: Sage.

53

Dobyns, Henry F., Carlos Monge M. and Mario C. Vasquez. 1962. A Contagious Experiment: The Vicos Idea Has Spread Through-out Peru. *Saturday Review* (November 3, 1962), pp. 59-62.

Doughty, Paul L. 1965. The Interrelationship of Power, Respect, Affection and Rectitude in Vicos. *American Behavioral Scientist* 8(7):13-17.

Freid, Jacob. 1962. Social Organization and Personal Security in a Peruvian Hacienda Indian Community: Vicos. *American Anthropologist* 64(4):771.

Holmberg, Allan R. 1954. Participant Intervention in the Field. *Human Organization* 14(1):23-26.

_____. 1956. From Paternalism to Democracy: Cornell Peru Project. *Human Organization* 15(3):15-18.

_____. 1958. The Research and Development Approach to the Study of Culture Change. *Human Organization* 17(1):12-16.

_____. 1959. Land Tenure and Planned Social Change: A Case from Vicos, Peru. *Human Organization* 18(1):7-10.

_____. 1965. The Changing Values and Institutions of Vicos in the Context of National Development. *American Behavioral Scientist* 8(7):3-8.

_____. 1966. *Vicos: Metodo y Practica de Antropologia Aplicada.* (Investigaciones Sociales, Serie: Monografias Andinas, No. 5). Lima: Editorial Estudios Andinos, S. A.

Holmberg, Allan R. and Henry F. Dobyns. 1962. The Process of Accelerating Community Change. *Human Organization* 21(2):107-109.

Holmberg, Allan R., Henry F. Dobyns and Mario C. Vasquez. 1961. Methods for the Analysis of Culture Change. *Anthropological Quarterly* 34(2):37-46.

Huizer, Gerritt. 1972. Overcoming Resistance to Change: The Vicos Experiment. In *The Revolutionary Potential of Peasants in Latin America.* Lexington, MA: D. C. Heath.

Lasswell, Harold D. 1962. Integrating Communities into More Inclusive Systems. *Human Organization* 21(2):116-121.

Lear, John. 1962. Reaching the Heart of South America. *Saturday Review* (November 3rd. 1962), pp. 55-58.

Newman, Marshall T., Carlos Collazos Chiriboga and Carmen da Fuentes. 1963. Growth differences between Indians and Mestizos in the Callejon de Huaylas, Peru. *American Journal of Physical Anthropology* 21:407-408.

Vazquez, Mario C. 1952. La Antropologia Cultural y Nuestro Problems del Indio: Vicos, un Caso da Antropologia Aplicada. *Peru Indigena* 2:5-157.

_____. 1965. The Interplay between Power and Wealth. *American Behavioral Scientist* 8:9-12.

Vazquez, Mario C. and Allan R. Holmberg. 1966. *The Castas: Unilineal Kin Groups in Vicos, Peru.* Cornell University, Department of Anthropology.

- **Community Center Proposed to the South Pacific Commission**
Palau, 1953

Anthropologist Homer G. Barnett recommended that the South Pacific Commission provide support for the construction of a community center at Koror, Palau. Koror was a rapidly growing town without much community focus. Local people and the expanding number of in-migrants were often in conflict. This proposal was made to fulfill a recommendation made by Barnett in the previous year when he was requested to investigate "Palauan unrest in Koror." The purpose of the community center was to improve "native morale" by providing a means for recreation and education. The building was constructed.

Barnett, Homer G. 1953. *An Experiment in Community Consolidation: Proposal for the Establishment of South Pacific Commission Project S. 12 (Welfare Center) in Koror, Palau Islands, Trust Territory of the Pacific Islands.*

- **Research and Development Approach Applied**
  Peru, 1959

The Kuyo Chico project was initiated as part of the National Program for the Integration of the Aboriginal population of Peru. The project, which lasted until 1960, made use of the research and development technique and is an excellent example of a diverse anthropological role set. It was developed to bring about various economic, social, and political changes in an Indian community. The project was influenced by the Vicos project.

Nunez Del Prado, Oscar with William Foote Whyte. 1973. *Kuyo Chico: Applied Anthropology in an Indian Community.* Chicago: University of Chicago Press.

- **Action Anthropology Applied in Chicago Conference**
  United States, 1961

The American Indian Chicago Conference was organized "as a test of action anthropology in response to Indian dissatisfaction with federal policy of the 1950's" (Lurie, 1976). The conference, which was coordinated by Sol Tax, stimulated the development of the National Indian Youth Council, the Great Lakes Inter-Tribal Council and the political organization of the Winnebago of Wisconsin under the provisions of the Indian Reorganization Act.

American Indian Chicago Conference. 1961. *Declaration of Indian Purpose: The Voice of the American Indian.* Chicago: American Indian Chicago Conference.
Lurie, Nancy O. 1976. Comment. *Human Organization* 35(3):320-321.

- **Yaqui Community Development Activities**
  United States, 1966

Edward H. Spicer and William Willard were employed in community development administration in a Southwestern Indian community.

> Spicer, Edward H. 1970. Patrons of the Poor. *Human Organization* 20(1) 12-19.
> Willard, William. 1977. The Agency Camp Project. *Human Organization* 36(4):352-362.

- **Papagos Use Community Development Techniques**
  United States, 1968

The Papago Tribe of Arizona hired anthropologists in various administrative positions in their community development program. These people included John van Willigen who was the Director of Community Development for the Tribe and Barry R. Bainton who was Legal Education Officer.

> van Willigen, John. 1971. The Papago Community Development Worker. *Community Development Journal* 6(2).
> _____. 1973. Abstract Goals and Concrete Means: Papago Experiences in the Application of Development Resources. *Human Organization* 32(1).
> _____. 1976 Applied Anthropology and Community Development: a Critical Assessment. In *Do Applied Anthropologists Apply Anthropology?*. Proceedings of the Southern Anthropological Society, M. Angrosino, ed. Athens: University of Georgia Press.
> _____. 1977. Administrative Problems in an Arizona Community Development Programme. *Community Development Journal* 12(1).

- **Action Research Techniques in Chicago**
  United States, 1968

"Action Research," or "Community Advocacy" anthropology approaches were developed on the Southside of Chicago. An anthropologist served as a researcher in association with the indigenous leadership of the community to assist achieving community goals. The approach is conceptually related to both research and development and action anthropology.

> Schensul, Stephen L. 1973. Action Research: The Applied Anthropologist in a Community Mental Health Program. In *Anthropology Beyond the University.* A.

Redfield, ed. Southern Anthropological Society Proceedings No. 7. Athens: University of Georgia Press.

_____. 1974. Skills Needed in Action Anthropology: Lessons from El Centro de la Causa. *Human Organization* 33:203-209.

- **Academics in Action for Native Americans**
  United States, 1971

University Year for Action, as it was implemented at the University of Wisconsin-Green Bay, used applied anthropology techniques and concepts. The program, which was both service providing and instructional, dealt with nine Native American communities in Northern Wisconsin. The project included grant-seeking and lobbying activities.

Hunter, David F. and Phillip Whitten. 1971. Fieldwork II: Applied Anthropology Among Wisconsin's Native Americans. In *The Study of Anthropology*. New York: Harper and Row.

- **Southern Cheyenne Action Project**
  United States, 1971

Karl Schlesier, an anthropologist and ethnohistorian, contacted representatives of the Southern Cheyenne in 1968 to carry out basic historical research. From this emerged a working relationship defined by Schlesier as action anthropology. Working closely with the Arrowkeeper, a traditional and sacred Southern Cheyenne leadership role, Schlesier attempted to foster and encourage the reemergence of significant traditional leadership. This was expressed both through traditional roles and a group named the Southern Cheyenne Research and Human Development Association.

Schlesier, Karl H. 1974. Action Anthropology and the Southern Cheyenne. *Current Anthropology* 15(3):277-283.

- **Vicos Model Used in Los Angeles Park Planning**
  United States, 1973

Using the rehabilitation of a community center and the creation of a new park/playground as a catalyst for group organization, the transferability of the Vicos Community development strategy was tested in the Watts section of Los Angeles. Anthropologist Robert M. Wulff was a member of the U.S. Army Reserve which carried out the project as a Domestic Action

57

Program. Wulff served as a community development specialist supervising a team of reservists. He also acted as a community liaison with the Army. The strategy of slowly sharing power and expertise was evaluated as successful.

Wulff, Robert M. 1977. *Vicos in Watts: Testing Anthropological Change Strategies in Urban America.* ERIC Microfiche (abstracted in *Resources in Education*) Princeton, NJ: Educational Testing Service.

- **Research and Development Approach Used Among Southern Paiute**
  United States, 1974

Allen C. Turner developed a program based upon principles derived from the Research and Development approach, which was to lead to development among the Southern Paiute at near Kaibab, Utah. Turner worked with Band leadership on various policy research activities.

Turner, Allen C. 1974. *Southern Paiute Research and Development Program: A Pre-Proposal.* Cedar City, Utah: Southern Utah State College.
_____. 1987. Activating Community Participation in a Southern Paiute Reservation Development Program. In *Anthropological Praxis, Translating Knowledge into Action.* Robert M. Wulff and Shirley J. Fiske, eds., Boulder, CO: Westview.

- **Project Vicos Assessed**
  Peru, 1981

Under contract to U.S. Agency for International Development, Barbara D. Lynch reported research which evaluated the long term effects of the Cornell-Peru project on the highland community of Vicos. The Vicos Project was initiated in 1952 as a product of an agreement between Cornell University and the Instituto Indigenista Peruviano. Lynch's evaluation was based on review of literature at the Cornell University Library Department of Manuscripts and Archives. The evaluator found that improved potato cultivation techniques did take hold and had beneficial effects on income. This was coupled with increases in social inequality within the community relating to unequal access to productive land. Credit and loan provisions associated with the introduction of agricultural innovations stimulated a "push toward commercialization." Attempts to broaden Vicosino participation in national life led to the establishment of military service veterans as a new power elite. This caused some displacement among the traditional elites, thus the authority

58

of older people declined. Improved education assisted Vicosinos in dealing with the outside world. Higher educational attainment often made migration necessary to obtain appropriate jobs. All things considered, evaluator found that "the impacts of the project seem to have been more positive than negative."

Lynch, Barbara D. 1981. *The Vicos Experiment, a Study of the Impacts of the Cornell-Peru Project in a Highland Community.* Submitted to the Agency for International Development.

- **Kansas Kickapoo Action Project Established**
  United States, 1982

University of Kansas anthropologists Donald D. Stull and Steven V. Lutes participated in the development of a technical assistance relationship between the Center for Public Affairs, University of Kansas and the Kickapoo Tribe in Kansas. This relationship provided the Tribal Government with proposal development services while it afforded the University internship experiences for anthropology students. Proposals were developed in a large number of areas, including water resources, elderly services, pre-school education, health services, security services, home energy use, vocational education and other areas. Interesting products of the relationship included a videotape entitled "Return to Sovereignty: Self Determination and in the Kansas Kickapoo" and a text on Kickapoo tribal studies.

Lutes, Steven V. and Donald D. Stull. 1982. *The Kansas Kickapoo Technical Assistance Project: An Experiment in Applied Anthropology.* Lawrence, Kansas, Center for Public Affairs, University of Kansas.
Stull, Donald D. 1981. Ethnohistory for the People: Methodologies, Mediums, and Professional Responsibility, Presented at SFAA meetings, Edinburgh, Scotland, United Kingdom.
Stull, Donald D. and Steven V. Lutes. 1982. In the People's Service: Two Action Anthropology Projects among the Kansas Kickapoo. In *Anthropologists in Communities.* Stull and Yamamoto, eds. Lawrence: University of Kansas Press.

CRIMINAL JUSTICE AND LAW ENFORCEMENT

- **Attica Prison Course**
  United States, 1972

In the aftermath of the Attica prison riots anthropologist Frank J. Salamone was hired to develop a course for Attica prison guards in

"Conflict Resolution." Under substantial administrative controls the course of study had limited success.

Salamone, Frank J. 1977. The Attica Human Relations Course: An Example of Leaping before Looking. *Anthropology and Education Quarterly* 8(4):227-229.

- **Correctional Institution Policy Based on Anthropological Research**
United States, 1980

Jack Alexander prepared a "Proposed Guideline for Initial Security Classification of Adult Males" for the Department of Correctional Services, State of New York. This document was adopted as policy for state prisons. The guideline was used to classify incoming inmates in terms of security. This was done to make the placement decisions more consistent. The Guideline is based on data derived from field interviews with classification analysts, inmates, and prison staff. This was supplemented with a comparison of 500 "commitment" cases, a simulation of the Guideline's operation, and a trial implementation at one prison.

Alexander, Jack. 1979. *Summary of Field Interviews, Security Classification Guideline Research Project.* Working Paper V. State of New York. Department of Correctional Services.
Alexander, Jack with Kenneth J. Martin. 1979. *Preliminary Review of Literature Relevant to Security Classification Guidelines.* Security Classification Guideline Research Project, Working Paper #4, State of New York, Department of Correction Services.
Alexander, Jack with Ken Martin and Michael Weintaub. 1980. *A Proposed Guideline for Initial Security Classification of Adult Males.* Security Classification Guideline Project, Working Paper VIII., State of New York, Department of Correction Services.
Alexander, Jack with William Chapman. 1982. *Initial Security Classification Guideline for Young Males Classification Improvement Project.* Working Paper XI, State of New York, Department of Correctional Services.

CULTURAL RESOURCES MANAGEMENT

- **Antiquities Act Passed**
United States, 1906

The Antiquities Act of 1906 (Public Law 59-209) was passed, providing for the protection of historic and prehistoric ruins or monuments on federal lands. It prohibited the excavation or destruction without permission from the Secretaries of Interior, Agriculture, and Defense and limited permission to reputable institutions and museums seeking to preserve or increase knowledge of the remains. This Act further authorized the President to declare areas of public lands as national monuments and to reserve land for that purpose. This represented the first large scale involvement of the U.S. Government in cultural resource management.

McGimsey, Charles R., III. 1973. *Archaeology and Archaeological Resources.* Washington, DC: Society for American Archaeology.

- **New Deal Has Impact on Archaeology**
  United States, 1933

The Civil Works Administration was inaugurated as a federal relief program to reduce unemployment. Money was allocated for hiring over fifteen hundred archaeological field laborers under the direction of the Smithsonian Institution. Extensive excavations were conducted, particularly in the Southeastern United States. A lull in activity followed the demise of the C.W.A. in 1934, but the creation of the Works Progress Administration in 1936 brought a resurgence of large-scale fieldwork which was to continue until World War II. This first period of massive government funding for archaeology not only resulted in an extensive amount of fieldwork, but also served as a training device and professionalization experience for the next generation of American archaeologists.

Fitting, James E. 1973. *The Development of North American Archaeology.* Garden City, NJ: Anchor Books.

- **Historic Sites Act Passed**
  United States, 1935

The Historic Sites Act of 1935 (P.L. 74-292) was passed, declaring as national policy the preservation for public use of historic sites, buildings and objects. It led to the establishment of the Historic Sites Survey, the Historic American Building Survey, and the Historic American Engineering Record. The National Historic Landmarks program and its advisory board were established under the act to designate properties of historic value. The National Historic Landmarks program was the beginning of the National Register of Historic Places which would later be expanded and strengthened by the National Historic Preservation Act of 1966 (P.L.

89-665) and by Executive Order 11593. These programs demonstrate increasing government interest in cultural resource management and the cataloging and assessment of historically significant properties.

Boisvert, Richard and Alvin Luckenbach, eds. 1976. *Kentucky's Heritage: A Public Concern.* Lexington, KY: University of Kentucky, Department of Anthropology.

- **Reservoir Salvage Research Supported Through Legislation**
  United States, 1960

The Reservoir Salvage Act of 1960 (P.L. 86-523) was enacted. This law broadened the jurisdiction and reinforced the national policy to preserve for public use, historic sites, buildings and objects of national significance for the benefit of the people of the United States established by the Historic Sites Act of 1935 (P.L. 74-292). Specifically, this act protected all historic and archaeological data threatened with destruction by the results of inundation and any other terrain alterations caused by the construction of a dam by an agency. These agencies found it necessary to contract with archaeologists to do the required survey and salvage work. The Reservoir Salvage Act of 1960 was itself broadened and strengthened by the Archaeological and Historical Preservation Act of 1974 (P.L. 93-291), better known as the Moss-Bennett Bill.

McGimsey, Charles R., III. 1972. *Public Archaeology.* New York: Seminar Press.

(J. H. Sorensen)

- **SAA Organizes Committee on Public Archaeology**
  United States, 1967

The Society for American Archaeology created the Committee on the Public Understanding of Archaeology which was later renamed Committee on Public Archaeology (COPA). COPA functions as a communication network on archaeologically-relevant political issues, such as federal agency review deadlines.

Committee on Public Archaeology, Society for American Archaeology. 1979. What Is COPA? *COPA Communication* (January) p.1.

62

- **Black Mesa Cultural Resource Management Project Started**
  United States, 1967

The Black Mesa Archaeological Project (BMAP) was one of the largest and the longest lasting cultural resources management projects. The BMAP was contracted by the Peabody Coal Company to insure that their mining operations on 160km² leased from Hopi and Navajo Tribal lands in northeastern Arizona comply with Federal, state, and tribal regulations that concern the preservation of cultural resources. From its beginning in 1967 the BMAP tried to balance its contractual obligations with academic research goals. The over 2500 archaeological sites identified on these 160km² have contributed to questions of regional culture history, cultural ecology, and the dynamics of culture change. The BMAP was by necessity a multidisciplinary operation, enhancing its understanding of archaeological resources by collecting ethnological and ethnoarchaeological data.

Andres, Peters P., Robert Layhe, Deborah L. Nichols, and Shirley Powell, eds. 1982. *Excavations on Black Mesa, 1980: A Descriptive Report.* Center for Archaeological Investigations Research Paper 24. Carbondale: Southern Illinois University, Carbondale.

Gummerman, George J. 1970. *Black Mesa, Survey and Excavation in Northeastern Arizona, 1968.* Prescott College Studies in Anthropology 2.

Holt, Barry H. 1982. Navajo Sacred Areas: A Guide for Management. *Contract Abstracts and CRM Archaeology* 2(2):45-53.

Klesert, Anthony L., ed. 1978. Excavation on Black Mesa, 1977: A Preliminary Report. *Center for Archaeological Investigations Research Paper 1.* Carbondale: Southern Illinois University.

Klesert, Anthony L. and Shirley Powell, eds. 1979. Excavation on Black Mesa, 1978: A Descriptive Report. *Center for Archaeological Investigations Research Paper 8.* Carbondale: Southern Illinois University.

Layhe, Robert, Steven Sessions, Charles Miksicek, and Stephen Plog. 1976. The Black Mesa Archaeological Project: A Preliminary Report for the 1975 Season. *University Museum Archaeological Service Report 48.* Carbondale: Southern Illinois University.

Plog, Stephen and Shirley Power, eds. 1982. *Studies in Black Mesa Archaeology.* Carbondale: Southern Illinois University Press.

- **Presidential Executive Order Issued**
  Protecting Cultural Resources
  United States, 1971

President of the United States, Richard M. Nixon, issued Executive Order 11593. This order expanded the responsibility of Federal agencies in regards to the protection of cultural properties under their control. The

63

most important feature of this order is that the heads of Federal agencies were ordered to "locate, inventory and nominate to the Secretary of Interior all sites, buildings, districts and objects under their jurisdiction or control that appeared to qualify for listing on the National Register of Historic Places." By requiring these inventories and nominations and giving the Secretary of Interior the responsibility of advising, overseeing, reviewing, and developing procedures and criteria for identification, evaluation and protection of these resources many job opportunities were created for archaeologists in various Federal agencies.

King, Thomas F., Patricia Parker Hickman and Gary Berg. 1977. *Anthropology in Historic Preservation: Caring for Culture's Clutter.* New York: Academic Press.

- **Pomo Basketry Program Designed by Corps of Engineers**
  United States, 1973

A Dam to be constructed by the U.S. Army Corps of Engineers' San Francisco District (SFD) was to flood the Pomo economic, ritual, and medicinal plant harvesting area. The Dam caused concern about the availability of plants used in basket weaving; a major cultural tradition and income source. Richard Lerner, a Corps anthropologist, was given responsibility for the loss mitigation program including plant usage determination, assessment of plant-associated values and requirements, alternative plant source identification, and economic data analysis of alternative mitigations. He served as intermediary between Pomo and the Corps. Lerner developed and managed cultural studies and horticultural research and surveyed government-owned stream banks outside the project area for transplant suitability. The Corps and a plant user's council agreed to transplanting. Experimental transplanting and testing of maintenance techniques preceded major transplanting by the Corps, Pomos, and contract specialists. Transplanted sedge (an important grass for basketry), of major concern, did well. A visitor center describing the program and basketry came to be popular with both Pomos and visitors. The transplant area, dedicated as a preserve, included a trail allowing visitor vegetation and wildlife enjoyment.

Lerner, Richard N. 1987. Preserving Plants for Pomos. In *Anthropological Praxis: Translating Knowledge Into Action.* R. Wulff and S. Fiske, eds. Boulder: Westview.

64

- **CRM Archaeologists Establish National Organization**
  United States, 1976

The Society of Professional Archaeologists (SOPA) was incorporated as a not-for-profit corporation in Cahokia, Illinois. The formation of this society was the result of a coordinated study by members of the American Society for Conservation Archaeology, the Archaeological Institute of America, the Association for Field Archaeology, the Society of Historical Archaeology and the Society for American Archaeology. SOPA has a number of purposes including the development of a comprehensive set of ethical and professional standards for archaeology and to identify individuals who meet those standards in a published directory.

Society of Professional Archaeologists. 1976. *The Directory of Professional Archaeologists.* First Edition. Washington, DC: The Society of Professional Archaeologists.
Jelks, Edward B. 1980. News from SOPA. *Journal of Field Archaeology* 7(4):495-496.

- **Karok World Renewal Sites Evaluated for Listing on**
  National Register of Historic Places
  United States, 1979

Anthropologist Gary B. Palmer was retained by the U.S. Forest Service to investigate various Karok Indian sites in the Klamath National Forest in Northern California for the purpose of nominating these sites for the National Register of Historic Places. The proposed District included 117 villages.

Palmer, Gary B. 1980. *Karok World Renewal and Village Sites: A Cultural and Historical District.* Las Vegas, Nevada: University of Nevada, Department of Anthropology.

- **CRM in Living Communities Done**
  United States, 1979

Although there has been a great deal of archaeological research done in response to the Antiquities Act of 1906, the Historic Sites Act of 1935 and the Historic Preservation Act of 1966, there has been little ethnographic work done in response to this legislation. One major example is the work done by Benita J. Howell in response to the establishment of the Big South Fork National River and Recreation Area in the Big South Fork drainage of Kentucky and Tennessee. Working in conjunction with Billie R. DeWalt, Susan Duda and Robert Tincher, Howell's work identified "folk life" resources as they related to potential inclusion in the National Register of Historic Places, potential negative effects of the new Recreation Area status as well as potential needs for mitigation. The documentation produced by the Folk Life Study was intended as a resource for future interpretation of the "local history" of the way of life of this region. The data were derived from statistical and documentary sources, and household surveys, key informant interviews including extensive oral histories, architectural evaluations, and a cemetery survey.

Howell, Benita J. with Susan S. Duda and Robert B. Tincher. 1981. *A Survey of Folklife along the Big South Fork of the Cumberland River.* Report of Investigations No. 30. Knoxville, TN: Department of Anthropology, University of Tennessee.

- **Micronesian Museums Studied Under
National Endowment for the Humanities Grant**
Micronesia, 1979

Anthropologist Harley C. Schreck Jr. served as project director for the Planning for Museum and Historic Site Development in the Islands of Micronesia project. Funded by the National Endowment for the Humanities, the project drew up development plans for museums and historic sites throughout the Trust Territory of the Pacific Islands.

Schreck, Harley C. 1982. Museums in Micronesia: Their Development and Operations in a Situation of Dependence. Presented at SfAA meetings 1982.

- **Lands Unsuitable for Mining Petition Filed to
Protect Cultural Resources**
United States, 1983

Charles M. Niquette filed a Lands Unsuitable for Mining petition with the Department for Surface Mining Reclamation and Enforcement of the Commonwealth of Kentucky to stop strip mining in a 50,000 acre area in the Green River drainage of western Kentucky. The petition was filed under the provisions of a Kentucky statute that was modeled after a section of the Surface Mining Control and Reclamation Act of 1977. The petition was upheld by Kentucky State Government, with the result that granting of mining permits is conditional on archaeological survey. This was the first use of this legislation solely on the grounds of the potential adverse effects of mining on archaeological resources.

Niquette, Charles M. 1983. Mining versus Archaeology: Time for a Compromise. *Kentucky Archaeology Newsletter* 3(2):1-2.

■ **Native American Sacred Sites Assessed for Department of Defense**
United States, 1984

A team led by Richard W. Stoffle researched the impact of Department of Defense activities on Native American sacred sites located in a section of the Fort Carson Military Reservation in southern Colorado. Their primary goal was to make mitigation recommendations concerning sacred sites on lands to be used for military maneuvers. Data were collected in the field and extended to libraries in the region as well as the Newberry Library. The field ethnography component involved public meetings, interviews with Native Americans who visited the areas and interviews with religious specialists. The field ethnography and documentary research was supplemented with oral history interviews carried out with persons familiar with the area. The report included suggested mitigations. In addition to Stoffle, the anthropologists on the research team included Henry F. Dobyns, Omer C. Stewart, Michael J. Evans and Pamela A. Bunte.

Stoffle, Richard W., Henry F. Dobyns, Michael J. Evans and Omer C. Stewart. 1984. *Toyavita Piavuhuru Koroin, "Canyon of Mother Earth" Ethnohistory and Native American Religious Concerns in the Fort Carson/Pinon Canyon Maneuver Area.* Final Report. Kenosha, WI: University of Wisconsin-Parkside.

■ **Vicksburg Cultural Heritage Project Initiated**
United States, 1986

Supported by the National Endowment for the Humanities, the Vicksburg Cultural Heritage Project was organized to examine the contributions to the social life and culture of Vicksburg of the numerous ethnic groups which settled in the area. These included the Irish, German Jewish, German Catholic, Italian, Syrian-Lebanese, and Chinese. Anthropologist Ralph Bishop conducted the project on behalf of the citizen's group that proposed the project. The project was carried out in conjunction with All Saints' Episcopal School of Vicksburg.

Bishop, Ralph. 1986. Photographic History Depicts Vicksburg Life. *Vicksburg Evening Post. March 20, 1986.*

67

- **Louisiana Crafts Program Started**
United States, 1986

The Louisiana Crafts Program of the State of Louisiana, Department of Culture, Recreation and Tourism was created to provide marketing assistance to folk artists. The manager of the program was anthropologist Maida Bergeron. An important mechanism for assisting the craftsmen is the identification by jury of the most creative craftsmen in the state. Only jury approved craftsmen are eligible to use a "Handmade by Louisiana Craftsmen" logo which is a major mechanism for promotional assistance. Jury approved craftsmen are included in *Fait a la Main: A Source Book of Louisiana Crafts* edited by Bergeron, this illustrated volume serves as a directory for buyers of hand made crafts. Since 1979 Louisiana has had an active folklife program which documented traditional cultures of Louisiana. Much of this documentation was done by anthropologists and provided a base of information about craft production in the state and used by Bergeron when the Crafts Program was designed and implemented.

Bergeron, Maida, ed. 1988. *Fait A La Main: A Source Book of Louisiana Crafts.* Baton Rouge, LA: Louisiana Crafts Program.

DESIGN AND ARCHITECTURE

- **Anthropology in the Design Process**
United States, 1973

Anthropological research techniques are used to provide data concerning Navajo desires in public school architecture and design. Working with the sanction of the local Navajo school board and through a California architectural firm, the research helped achieve a school design which was enthusiastically accepted by community members.

Clement, Dorothy C. 1976. Cognitive Anthropology and Applied Problems In Education. In *Do Applied Anthropologists Apply Anthropology?* M. Angrosino, ed. Athens: University of Georgia Press.
Harding, Joe R. 1973. *An Architectural Planning Study: Prospective User Perceptions (Form and Functions) of the Proposed Ramah Navajo Learning Center.* Berkeley: Policy Research and Planning Group.

- **NASA Design of Space Communities**
United States, 1975

Anthropologist Magoroh Maruyama was engaged by the National Aeronautics and Space Administration to research optimum extraterrestrial community design. Much of this was carried out at the NASA/Stanford Summer Study of Space Colonization.

Maruyama, Magoroh. 1976. Extraterrestrial Community Design: Psychological and Cultural Consideration. *Cybernetica* 19:45-62.

- **Anthropologist Assists in Park Design Process**
United States, 1975

Under the auspices of the Tampa Metropolitan Development Agency and Department of Recreation, Robert M. Wulff evaluated two recreation facilities: a new playground and the city's system of 18 community recreation centers. Both studies took a user-oriented approach to recreation service delivery identifying user/emic view contrasted to planner/etic view of the services.

Wulff, Robert M. 1976. *Tampa's Community Centers: An Analysis of Recreation Programming and Policy.* Tampa, Florida: Human Resources Institute and Center of Applied Anthropology, University of South Florida.

- **Anthropologist Assists Apache Community Design**
United States, 1980

George Esber worked as advisor with an architectural design team on a project to redevelop an Apache settlement outside of Payson, Arizona. The Payson Project, was a development effort to improve life conditions of Tonto Apache then living as squatters, leading to full tribal recognition and a new culturally appropriate settlement. Esber realized architects' paucity of cross-cultural knowledge made it difficult for them to address housing needs dictated by Apache behavior patterns, and insisted that extensive data collection precede planning. Esber mapped all squatter structures, identified all residents of each, conducted interviews to explore interpersonal relationships, identified space use through interior maps, supplied and analyzed interior plan model kits, and identified continuing and changing patterns.

Esber, George S., Jr. 1987. Designing Apache Homes With Apaches. In *Anthropological Praxis: Translating Knowledge Into Action.* R. Wulff and S. Fiske, eds. Boulder: Westview.

(Steven E. Maas)

- **Anthropologist Involved in Philadelphia Park Design**
  United States, 1981

Anthropologist Setha M. Low, part of the landscape architecture faculty at the University of Pennsylvania, participated in directing students in the design of the rehabilitation of Farnham Park, Camden, New Jersey. The design which was produced was based upon data derived from four research teams which focused on different types of data, including ethnographic.

Low, Setha M. 1981. Anthropology as a New Technology in Landscape Planning, Presented at meetings of the American Society of Landscape Architects.

- **Anthropological Research Informs Corporate Center Landscape Plan**
  United States, 1984

A team led by Setha Low conducted a study of recreational activities at three corporate centers in support of the development of the social component of the landscape plan for the partially completed Carnegie Corporate Center, near Princeton, New Jersey. The research design, directed at the identification of recreational elements, included behavioral observation of outdoor activities and interviews. The identified recreational elements are presented in the report as sets consisting of activities, landscape requirements and design specifications.

Low, Setha M. and Elaine L. Simon. 1984. *Working Landscapes: A Report on the Social Uses of Outside Space in Corporate Centers and Program Recommendations for Carnegie Center.*
Low, Setha M. 1984. *User Survey of Carnegie Center: A Report on the Recreational Activities of Employees Based on the Analysis of the Carnegie Center Questionnaire.*

- **Ethnosemantic Techniques in Historic Design Guidelines Development**
  United States, 1985

Anthropologist Setha M. Low in collaboration with William Ryan used "mental mapping" techniques to synthesize local views of historic architecture with those of professionals in a project in Oley, Pennsylvania. The research technique involved a task that required local residents to examine a series of drawings indicating architecture details and to rank them. These results were used to guide architects and planners in the development of guidelines for design for a program of restoration work.

Low, Setha M. 1987. A Cultural Landscapes Mandate for Action. *CRM Bulletin* 10(1):22-23, 30.
Low, Setha M. and William Ryan. 1985. Noticing Without Looking: A Methodology for the Integration of Architectural and Local Perceptions in Oley, Pennsylvania. *Journal of Architecture and Planning Research* 2:3-22.

DEVELOPMENT POLICIES AND PRACTICES

- **Anthropologists Hired by the International Cooperation Administration**
United States, 1951

Anthropologists and other behavioral scientists were hired to assist I.C.A. programs overseas. I.C.A., or the International Cooperation Administration, became known as the Agency for International Development in 1961. Anthropologists served both as administrators and "community analysts."

Boggs, Stephen T. 1960. The Organization of Anthropology in Action. *Human Organization* 23(3):193-195.
Galdwin, Thomas. 1960. Technical Assistance Programs: A Challenge for Anthropology. *Fellow Newsletter, American Anthropological Association* 1(10):6-7.
Hamilton, James W. 1973. Problems in Government Anthropology. In *Anthropology Beyond the University.* Proceedings of the Southern Anthropological Society, N 7, A. Redfield, ed. Athens: University of Georgia Press.
Mini Louis. 1964. The Use of Anthropologists in the Foreign Aid Program. *Human Organization* 23(3):187-189.
Schaeder, Richard P. 1964. Anthropology in AID Overseas Missions: Its Practical and Theoretical Potential. *Human Organization* 23(3):100-192.

- **Cornell-Peru Project Studies Community Services in the Mantaro Valley**
Peru, 1964

The project focused on the acquisition of community services as an aspect of the community development process. The research attempted to determine if there was a patterned acquisition of community services or if the process was haphazard. Identification of pattern was thought to be of interest for both theoretical and practical reasons. Aspects of pattern considered included the relationship between population size and services and the order of introduction. The data upon which the analysis was based were obtained through the use of an interview schedule that had been pretested in a preliminary survey of six communities. This was then revised and used to collect data from 27 communities in the Mantaro Valley. Funding for the project came from a contract between Cornell University and the Peace Corps.

Maynard, Eileen A. 1964. *Patterns of Community Service Development in Selected Communities of the Mantaro Valley Peru.* Socio-economic Development of Andean Communities, Report No. 3. Ithaca: Cornell Peru Project, Department of Anthropology, Cornell University.

- **Peace Corps Established**
  United States, 1961

The establishment of the Peace Corps resulted in the placement of anthropologists as administrators, policy-makers, evaluators, trainers, and volunteers.

Comitas, Lambros. 1966. Lessons from Jamaica. In *Cultural Frontiers of the Peace Corps.* Robert B. Textor, ed. Cambridge: M.I.T. Press.

Dorjahn, Vernon R. 1966. Transcultural Perceptions and Misperceptions in Sierra Leone. In *Cultural Frontiers of the Peace Corps.* Robert Textor, ed. Cambridge: M.I.T. Press.

Doughty, Paul. 1966. Pitfalls and Progress in the Peruvian Sierra. In *Cultural Frontiers of the Peace Corps.* Robert B. Textor, ed. Cambridge: M.I.T. Press.

Dupree, Louis. 1966. Moving Mountains in Afghanistan. In *Cultural Frontiers of the Peace Corps.* Robert B. Textor, ed. Cambridge: M.I.T. Press.

Heath. Dwight B. 1966. The Emerging Volunteer Subculture Bolivia. In *Cultural Frontiers of the Peace Corps.* Robert R. Textor, ed. Cambridge: M.I.T. Press.

Mahony, Frank J. 1961. Evaluation of a Pilot Project in Range Management near Afmadu. *Community Development Review* 6(1).

_____. 1966. Success in Somalia. In *Cultural Frontiers of the Peace Corps.* Robert B. Textor. ed. Cambridge: M.I.T. Press.

Maretzki, Thomas. 1965. Transition Training: A Theoretical Approach. *Human Organization* 24(2):128-134.

Szanton, David L. 1966. Cultural Confrontation in the Philippines. In *Cultural Frontiers of the Peace Corps.* Robert B. Textor, ed. Cambridge: M.I.T. Press.

72

Textor, Robert B., ed. 1966. *Cultural Frontiers of the Peace Corps.* Cambridge: M.I.T. Press.

- **Potential of Anthropology at the World Bank Examined**
  United States, 1970

Glyn Cochrane initiated a working relationship with the World Bank so as to demonstrate the utility of anthropology in international development. Cochrane did a study of World Bank operations to determine where anthropology might be useful.

Cochrane, Glyn. 1976. The Perils of Unconventional Anthropology. In *Development from Below, Anthropologists and Development Situations.* David C. Pitt, ed. The Hague: Mouton Publishers.

- **Swedish Development Cooperation Incorporates Anthropologists**
  Sweden, 1975

Although anthropologists have worked for the Swedish Development Cooperation [SIDA] for some time such involvement became more organized with the establishment of an agreement between SIDA and the Department of Social Anthropology, University of Stockholm. The relationship came to be expressed through the Development Studies Unit, a non-profit, consultancy organization that provides SIDA with consultant services, recruitment, professional resource and capacity development. As of 1989 SIDA funds seven anthropologists and one sociologist as professional staff. Although the Development Studies Unit is at University of Stockholm it serves as a means for the collaboration of Departments at Gothenburg, Uppsala and Lund. In the earliest stages of its existence it served largely as a source of information about short term consultants. This was expanded to include actually doing projects. A major portion of the Unit's work deals with rural development in Sub Saharan Africa, with emphasis on East Africa. Work of various types has been done in South Asia and Central America. The unit does not participate in training students to any extent but does have a arrangement by which they place anthropology graduates in practica to increase preparedness for development work.

Einarsdottir, Jonina. 1989. Documentation. *Development Anthropologist* 13-14: 38-39.

Freudenthall, Solveig, Anders Rudqvist, Eva Tobisson. 1989. Anthropological Participation in the SIDA Special Programmes. *Development Anthropologist* 13-14:30-37.

Krantz, Lasse and Eva Tobison. 1989. Anthropologists in Swedish Development Cooperation: An Overview. *Development Anthropologist* 13-14: 6-14.

Krantz, Lasse and Eva Tobison. 1989. Consultancy Work. *Development Anthropologist* 13-14: 16-18.

Woodford-Berger, Prudence. 1989. Recruitment and Professional Capacity Development. *Development Anthropologist* 13-14:20-23.

▪ Sahel Development Strategy
United States, 1976

As part of an attempt to develop a strategy for dealing with the development problems of the Sahel, the Agency for International Development contracted with David W. Brokensha, Michael M. Horowitz and Thayer Scudder to develop a research prospectus for the region. They proposed a long-term, multicomponent study lasting over 15 to 25 years. Some of the areas of research stressed were farming systems, social soundness analysis of dams, marketing systems, and various topics relating to health.

Brokensha, David W., Michael M. Horowitz and Thayer Scudder. 1977. *The Anthropology of Rural Development in the Sahel.* Binghamton, NY: Institute for Development Anthropology.

▪ Decentralization in Development Studied
United States, 1979

The U.S. Agency for International Development's Office of Rural Development and Development Administration commissioned a research project on the management of decentralization in development. The research, which consisted of extensive literature review, attempted to identify how people in the rural Third World might benefit from "present international interest in providing development assistance through programs that more closely match the scale and interests of rural organizations." The final report emphasized the study of rural organizations as cooperating groups for a decentralized development approach.

74

Ralston, Lenore, James Anderson and Elizabeth Colson. 1981. *Voluntary Efforts in Decentralized Management, Final Report, Project on Managing Decentralization.* Institute of International Studies Berkeley, University of California.

- **Grand Tower, Illinois Develops Community Development Plan**
  United States, 1979

The Town Council of Grand Tower, Illinois requested that Terry Alliband develop a Community Development Plan for the community. Working with students in the Community Development Program at Southern Illinois University, Alliband recommended plans for economic development, tourism, recreation, housing and government services. The process made use of surveys and community meetings to gather data which informed the plan.

Alliband, Terry et al. 1979. *A Community Development Plan for Grand Tower, Illinois.* Carbondale, IL: Southern Illinois University, Division of Social and Community Services.

- **Contribution of Community-level Social Organization Researched**
  United States, 1980

Barbara D. Miller, of the Local Revenue Administration Project at Syracuse University, investigated the role which indigenous voluntary associations can play in contributing to "project capacity in rural areas." This research was done under the sponsorship of the U.S. Agency for International Development. The research was based on literature review.

Miller, Barbara D. 1980. *Local Social Organizations and Local Project Capacity.* Syracuse, NY: Local Revenue Administration Project, Maxwell School, Syracuse University.

- **AID Planning Process Evaluated**
  United States, 1980

The U.S. Agency for International Development produces a variety of documents in the project development process. One document type are the Program Evaluation Summaries (PES). In AID's system of project implementation and longer term planning, PES's appear in the planning sequence after the development of the Project Paper (PP). The PES component of the AID planning process was evaluated by Gerald M.

Britan based on an analysis of a small judgmental sample of PES's. The ultimate goal of the evaluation was to "develop a set of criteria that good evaluations could fulfill." Evaluation found that the quality of the PES's was quite variable. One of the problems was that the PES process often ignored the special expertise of project managers.

Britan, Gerald M. 1980. *An Assessment of AID's Project Evaluation System.* Office of Evaluation Working Paper No. 34, Evanston: Northwestern University.

- ### Literature on Settlement and Deforestation in Central America Reviewed for AID
  Central America, 1986

Supported by the Fragile Lands Advisory Group of the Agency for International Development, Collins and Painter analyzed recent documents related to settlement and deforestation. The analysis addressed settlement processes, land tenure, road development, land use, and labor availability. They found that few publications were based on trustworthy data obtained from field studies. An important content area in the literature was the process by which forests are converted to pastures. A number of factors were identified as responsible for this conversion. Important among these factors was the need to increase export income to satisfy foreign debt. Small producers were found to be attracted to the cattle business because of reduced labor requirements. These small producers often had to sell their land to meet living expenses resulting in the concentration of land in the hands of the wealthy. The research literature did not seem to offer many alternatives for development.

Collins, Jane L. and Michael Painter. 1986. *Settlement and Deforestation in Central America: A Discussion of Development Issues.* Binghamton, NY: Institute for Development Anthropology. Cooperative Agreement on Human Settlements and Natural Resource Systems Analysis.

DISASTER RESEARCH

- ### Firth and Spillius Involved in Disaster Research
  British Solomons (Tikopia), 1952

In response to conditions of famine caused by a hurricane, anthropologists James Spillius and Raymond Firth developed an applied approach in the field to better assist the Tikopia. The approach was value-explicit and suggests elements of both cultural brokerage and participant intervention. This represents one of few examples of involvement in the action by "British" social anthropologists. The dimensions of role are dealt with explicitly.

Spillius, James. 1957. Natural Disaster and Political Crisis in a Polynesian Society: An Exploration of Operational Research II. *Human Relations* X(2):113-125.

- **Social Impacts of Exxon Valdez Oil Spill Assessed**
  United States, 1989

A research team from the University of South Alabama investigated social impacts of the oil spill on a community of Native Alaskans. The data were collected at four and a half months and again at eighteen months through personal interviews using a pre-tested interview schedule. The data collection was guided by a disaster impact assessment research design that apparently had been used in other projects. The persons interviewed were identified through a snowball technique and reinterviewed in a second wave. The research found that the persistent negative impacts on the community were associated with perceptions of the loss of natural resources. The team also found that family relations were initially disrupted but stabilized later.

Dyer, Christopher L., J. Steven Picou, Duane A. Gill and Evans W. Curry. 1990. *Technological Disaster and the Natural Resource Community: Social Impacts of the Exxon Valdez Oil Spill on Native Alaskans.* Revision of Paper Presented at the SFAA York meetings.

ECONOMIC DEVELOPMENT

- **Comprehensive Survey Carried Out**
  Micronesia, 1946

The Micronesian comprehensive survey was carried out. The survey, sponsored by the United States Commercial Company, dealt with economics, anthropology, and administrative management. The social scientists focused on regional variations in the population's relationship with the sea and land.

Bascom, William R. 1947. *Economic and Human Resources--Ponape.* Eastern Carolinas, U.S. Commercial Company.

Mason, Leonard E. 1947. *Economic and Human Resources--Marshal Islands.* U.S. Commercial Company.

Oliver, Douglas L., ed. 1951. *Planning Micronesia's Future: A Summary of the United States Commercial Company's Economic Survey of Micronesia, 1946.* Cambridge: Harvard University Press.

Pelzer, Karl and Edward T. Hall. 1947. *Economic and Human Resources--Truk Islands, Central Carolinas.* U.S. Commercial Company.

Useem, John. 1947. *Economic and Human Resources--Yap and Palau, Western Carolinas.* U.S. Commercial Company.

- **Applied Project for Apaches**
  United States, 1960

A research project in applied anthropology for the Jicarilla Apache Tribe dealt with political and economic development on the Jicarilla reservation. It was supported by the Tribal Government and was not an action program.

Basehart, Harry W. and Tom T. Sasaki. 1964. Changing Political Organization in the Jicarilla Apache Reservation Community. *Human Organization* 23(4):283-89.

Wolfe, Leo J. 1961. The Relationship Between Unearned Income and Individual Productive Effort on the Jicarilla Apache Reservation. *Economic Development and Cultural Change* 9(4):589-597.

- **Anthropologist Becomes Tribal Planner**
  United States, 1967

In a relationship which evolved out of a dissertation project, John H. Peterson, Jr. became chief planner for the Mississippi Band of Choctaws. In this role he participated in an array of development projects as a researcher. This included employment and housing development.

Peterson, John H., Jr. 1970. *Socio-Economic Characteristics of the Mississippi Choctaw Indians.* Social Science Research Center Report No. 34. State College: Mississippi State University.

_____. 1972. Assimilation, Separation and Out-Migration in an American Indian Community. *American Anthropologist* 74:1286-1295.

_____. 1974. The Anthropologist as Advocate. *Human Organization* 33:311-318.

_____. 1978. The Changing Role of an Applied Anthropologist. In *Applied Anthropology in America.* Elizabeth M. Eddy and William L. Partridge, eds. New York: Columbia University Press.

78

- **Alternatives to Hudson's Bay Company Developed**
  Canada, 1967

Assisted by anthropologist Walter Hlady, Cree and Meti fur trappers in the Saskatchewan River Delta area attempted to develop an alternative to the Hudson's Bay Company. Hlady was employed by the Citizenship Branch of the Canadian Department of State and given free rein to assist the community. Hudson's Bay Company held the fur trading lease in the area, but wanted to be relieved of the responsibility and thereby requested that the Province reassign the lease prior to its expiration and buy out the company's equity. Hlady's role was to provide the community with information on the various alternatives and support the community in its dealings with the Provincial government.

Lurie, Nancy O. 1973. Action Anthropology and the American Indian. *Anthropology and the American Indian, Report of a Symposium.* San Francisco: Indian Historian Press.
Hlady, Walter H. 1969. The Cumberland House Fur Project: The First Two Years. *Western Canadian Journal of Anthropology* 1(1).

- **Efforts at Developing Local Revenue Policies Aided by USAID**
  Ghana, 1977

An agreement was reached between the Government of Ghana and U.S. Agency for International Development which resulted in the implementation of a national program for the improvement of management and development planning training for district and regional officials. The Economic and Rural Development Management (ERDM) program provided technical assistance in training expressed through annual cycles of seminars that attempted to transform groups of local officials into development teams. Emphasis was placed on local participation, collaboration across government agencies, integrated development and unitary budgeting. Dennis M. Warren was associated with the project.

Warren, Dennis M. and Joe D. Issachar. 1982. The Role of Anthropology in Understanding and Changing Local Revenue Policies and Practices in Ghana's Decentralization Program. Unpublished Paper.

- **Local Taxation in Bangladesh Examined**
  Bangladesh, 1982

Using survey data on land-ownership patterns collected in 1978, anthropologist Barbara Miller and economist James A. Wozny investigated distributive effects and revenue potential of a tax levied against total land ownership in rural Bangladesh. The research was done as part of a U.S. Agency for International Development project intended to increase Bangladeshi capacity to raise and administer financial resources. Miller and Wozny estimated tax liability under two different tax rates using the available land data. The study identified certain taxation inequities.

Miller, Barbara D. and James A. Wozny. 1983. *The Land Development Tax in Bangladesh: Insights from the 1978 Land Occupancy Survey.* Occasional Paper No. 69, Local Revenue, Administration Project, Syracuse University.

- **Tax System Examined for the Government of Jamaica**
  Jamaica, 1986

Funded by the Government of Jamaica and USAID, the Metropolitan Studies Program at the University of Syracuse has been examining taxation policy alternatives for Jamaica. As part of this effort anthropologist Barbara D. Miller, working with economist Richard M. Bird, researched the incidence of various kinds of taxes in a sample of low-income Jamaican households. The data were derived from a survey of a range of different types of low-income households that formed a base-line.

Richard M. Bird and Barbara D. Miller. 1986. *The Incidence of Indirect Taxes on Low-Income Households in Jamaica.* Jamaica Tax Structure Examination Project. Staff Paper No. 26. Syracuse, NY: Metropolitan Studies Program.

- **Fish Marketing Scheme Explored in Florida**
  United States, 1987

A research team examined the feasibility of integrating fish, seafood and aquaculture into a state-supported system of 13 farmer's markets for the Florida Department of Agriculture and Consumer Services. These markets "provide sites for packing, grading, sorting, and shipping crops grown by large and small fruit and vegetable farmers and for brokers who facilitate the buying and selling of Florida produced crops." The research task was to identify the potentials and constraints for marketing various fish products. The research team visited the markets to inventory usable space, equipment, and the activities at each market. Primary data were collected through 50 key informant interviews with persons from the industries and the markets. Secondary data were also used. The researchers suggested that the inclusion of fish in the commodity mix of the state farmers' markets was feasible.

Lampl, Linda L. and Thomas A. Herbert. 1988. *The Integration of Fish, Seafood, and Aquaculture Products into the Florida Farmers' Market System.* Tallahassee, FL: T. A. Herbert & Associates

EDUCATION AND SCHOOLS

- **Anthropologist Appointed Education Official**
Philippines, 1903

William Howard Taft, then Governor-General of the Philippines, appointed David P. Barrows as General Superintendent of Education for the Philippines.

Eggan, Fred. 1974. Applied Anthropology in the Mountain Province, Philippines. In *Social Organization and the Applications of Anthropology, Essays in Honor of Lauriston Sharp.* Robert J. Smith, ed. Ithaca: Cornell University Press.

- **Anthropologist Starts School**
Italy, 1906

Maria Montessori, trained as a physician and physical anthropologist, initiated a school for young children of low-income Roman families. The school made use of what was ultimately called the Montessori Method. The diffusion of the Montessori innovation in the United States is closely related to the foundation of the American Montessori Society in the early 1960s. A primary influence of anthropology on Montessori education can be seen in the role of the teacher, who is responsible for observing and recording much like an ethnographer. The view that each child has unique growth potential is consistent with the concept of cultural relativity.

Kramer, Rita. 1976. *Maria Montessori: A Biography.* New York: G. P. Putnam.
Montessori, Maria. 1955. *Childhood Education.* New York: Meridian.
_____. 1964. *The Montessori Method.* New York: Schocken Books.
_____. 1967. *The Absorbent Mind.* New York: Dell.
_____. 1973. *From Childhood to Adolescence.* New York: Schocken Books.

- **Radcliffe-Brown Becomes a Practitioner**
Tonga, 1916

A. R. Radcliffe-Brown was appointed Director of Education of the Kingdom of Tonga. He served in this position until 1919.

Fortes, Meyer. 1949. Preface. In *Social Structure; Studies Presented to A. R. Radcliffe-Brown.* M. Fortes, ed. London: Oxford University Press.

- **Educational Survey Completed**
  Netherlands Indies, 1933

A survey of educational systems of Netherlands Indies assessed conditions and indicated aims of the native education program.

Embree, Edwin R., Margaret Sargent Simon and W. Bryant Mumford. 1934. *Island India Goes to School.* Chicago: University of Chicago Press.

- **Indian School Surveyed**
  United States, 1938

The Sherman and Phoenix School Surveys in Indian education attempted to learn whether vocational training helped in post-school attendance adjustment.

MacGregor, Gordon and Armin Sterner. 1939. The Pine Ridge Vocational Survey. *Indian Education* 31, (November 1, 1939).
_____. 1940. The Sherman-California Survey. *Indian Education* 41 (April 13, 1940).

- **Read Appointed Head of Colonial Training Department**
  United Kingdom, 1940

Margaret Read was appointed head of the Colonial Department of the University of London, Institute of Education. The department offered training, which included anthropology, to colonial administrators.

Read, Margaret. 1943. Notes on the Work of the Colonial Department, University of London Institute of Education. *Applied Anthropology* 3(1) 8-9.
_____. 1950. Educational Problems in Non-Autonomous Territories. In *Principles and Methods of Colonial Administration.* C. N. MacInnes, ed. London: Butterworths Scientific Publications.

- **Culturally Appropriate Texts Prepared**
  India, 1946

The Government of India, Department of Anthropology was established to do basic and applied research which included the development of culturally appropriate texts for village schools and a comprehensive study of the Andaman Islanders.

Majumdar, D. N. 1948. Department of Anthropology, Government of India. *American Anthropologist* 50(3):578-81.

- ### Education Project Assessed
  India, 1948

An assessment of the Madras state education program was carried out by anthropologist A. Aiyappan who submitted a report with recommendations to the Government of Madras.

Aiyappan, A. 1948. *Report on the Socio-Economic Condition of Aboriginal Tribes of Madras.* Madras.

- ### Techniques for Increasing Cultural Scope Explored
  United States, 1952

George Spindler developed an approach referred to as "cultural therapy." Used with a school principal Spindler successfully increased the principal's capacity for dealing with persons with different cultural identities. This process involved presenting the principal with data concerning his own cultural background and the nature of his selective response to students over a period of time.

Prieto, A. G. 1957. American Education--The Image in the Mirror. *Reviews in Anthropology* 2(2):286-290.

Spindler, G. D. 1959. *The Transmission of American Culture.* Cambridge: Harvard University Press.

_____. 1974. Cultural Sensitization. In *Education and Cultural Process: Toward an Anthropology of Education.* G. Spindler, ed. New York: Holt, Rinehart and Winston.

- ### Interethnic Curriculum Developed
  United States, 1953

Elmer R. Smith was invited to join the Utah State Department of Education, Committee for the Revision of the State School Course of Study in Human Relations. As an anthropologist Smith was expected to contribute to a better curriculum in the area of interethnic relations.

Hoebel, E. Adamson. 1955. Anthropology in Education. In *Yearbook of Anthropology, 1955*. New York: Wenner-Gren Foundation.

- ## School Administration Problems Examined in Dutch Colony
  Netherlands New Guinea, 1955

H.G. Barnett carried out an investigation of Dutch colonial administration problems with special reference to education to inform "administrative planning and execution." The project which apparently involved two months of field work attempted to identify native attitudes and aspirations. Barnett visited six localities where he interviewed officials and community members. The report of the research which was delivered to "His Excellency the Governor" treated a number of topics. These included the lack of connection between traditional and modern economic patterns, the relationship between land use and economic development, and the collective responsibility of kinsmen. The research focused heavily on education. Barnett noted that the teachers had little respect for the students, texts in use were not appropriate to the New Guinea situation and generally the education provided was not practical. Barnett made a number of recommendations. These included the idea that entire families participate in the education process so as to decrease the opportunity for ideological cleavages between young and old.

Barnett, Homer G. 1955. *Observations on Selected Administrative Problems, June 24 - August 26, 1955*. Dittographed Report.

- ## AAA Starts Teaching Anthropology Project
  United States, 1960

The Educational Resources in Anthropology (ERA) project, of the Department of Anthropology, University of California, Berkeley is significant for two reasons. First, it is an example of a general curriculum development project focused upon anthropology of various types and additionally it represents an early attempt to make recommendations on training in applied anthropology. Besides the various symposia which were held the project resulted in two rather substantial publications, *The Teaching of Anthropology* and *Resources for the Teaching of Anthropology*, published by the American Anthropological Association. The recommendations on applied anthropology education are encompassed in articles by Robert N. Rapoport, Laura Thompson, Kenneth Little, Homer G. Barnett and Richard N. Adams.

84

Adams, Richard N. 1963. General Use of Studies in Applied Anthropology. In *The Teaching of Anthropology.* D. G. Mandelbaum, et al. eds. Memoir 94. Washington, DC: American Anthropological Association.

Barnett, Homer G. 1963. Materials for Course Design. In *The Teaching of Anthropology.* D. G. Mandelbaum, et al. eds. Memoir 94. Washington, DC: American Anthropological Association.

Hoebel, E. Adamson. 1963. Anthropological Studies for Students of Law and Government. In *The Teaching of Anthropology.* D. G. Mandelbaum, et al. eds. Memoir 94. Washington, DC: American Anthropological Association.

Kimball, Solon T. 1963. Teaching Anthropology in Professional Education. In *The Teaching of Anthropology.* D. G. Mandelbaum, et al. eds. Memoir 94. Washington, DC: American Anthropological Association.

Paul, Benjamin D. 1963. Teaching Cultural Anthropology in Schools of Public Health. In *The Teaching of Anthropology.* D. G. Mandelbaum, et al. eds. Memoir 94. Washington, DC: American Anthropological Association.

Rapoport, Robert N. 1963. Aims and Methods. In *The Teaching of Anthropology.* D. G. Mandelbaum, et al. eds. Memoir 94. Washington, DC: American Anthropological Association.

Thompson, Laura. 1963. Concepts and Contributions. In *The Teaching of Anthropology.* D. G. Mandelbaum, et al. eds. Memoir 94. Washington, DC: American Anthropological Association.

- **Study of American Indian Education**
  United States, 1962

Studies of American Indian educational systems (particularly among the Sioux) by Murray L. Wax and Rosalie Wax encouraged the development of more encompassing American Indian educational studies by causing uneasiness in relevant educational circles. The Wax's work gave impetus to the idea of Indian control of schools.

Wax, Murray L., Rosalie H. Wax and R. V. Dumont, Jr. 1964. *Formal Education in an Indian Community.* Monograph No. 1, Society for the Study of Social Problems.

- **Elementary School Anthropology Curriculum Developed**
  United States, 1964

The U.S. Office of Education funded a project entitled "Development of a Sequential Curriculum in Anthropology for Grades 1-7," which was carried out at the University of Georgia. The project involved Wilfrid C. Bailey and Francis J. Clune, Jr., as well as various consultants.

Bailey, Wilfrid C. 1966. Anthropology Curriculum Project, University of Georgia. *Fellow Newsletter* 7(7) 9-10.

- **Drop Outs Studied**
  United States, 1964

Murray L. Wax and Rosalie H. Wax studied "dropouts" among American Indian students for the United States Office of Education. Materials derived from the research were presented before the Special Subcommittee on Indian Education of the Committee on Labor and Public Welfare.

Wax, Murray L. and Rosalie H. Wax. 1969. Dropout of American Indians at the Secondary Level. *Hearings before the Special Subcommittee on Indian Education of the Committee on Labor and Public Welfare. U.S. Senate 90th Congress.* Part 4, pp. 1457-1523, Washington, DC: Government Printing Office.

- **Headstart Makes Use of Anthropologists**
  United States, 1967

Project Headstart, which became a very important component of the "War on Poverty," made use of anthropologists in limited numbers as evaluators. One example of these activities was the work of the Bank Street College of Education, Research Division, in a number of New Jersey schools between 1967 and 1973.

Jacobsen, Claire 1973. *The Organization of Work in a Pre-school Setting: Work Relations Between Professionals and Paraprofessionals in Four Head Start Centers.* New York: Bank Street College of Education (available through ERIC).

- **Governor of Assam Requests Reconnaissance Survey on Education**
  India, 1967

N.K. Bose was recruited to do an analysis of the educational programs of the North East Frontier Agency (now the state of Arunchal Pradesh). For the most part the data were collected through group discussions with teachers, students and officials of the educational system. The experience of this work formed Bose's view of the tribal population of the Northeast which was expressed as Commissioner of Scheduled Castes and Scheduled Tribes and as advisor to Prime Minister Indira Gandhi. Sinha summarized Bose's recommendations concerning these peoples as follows: "(a) The main emphasis should be on building up an economy of unexploitative

86

interdependence between the hills and the plains; (b) The cultural policy should be extremely permissive and tolerant, providing facilities for autonomous development from the home base of specific tribes or related cluster of tribes; (c) Demand for political cessation should not be negotiable. This should be firmly and unequivocally communicated to those tribals who may be involved in such anti-national demands" (Sinha 1986:79).

Bose, Nirmal K. 1968. *Report of the Commissioner for Scheduled Castes and Scheduled Tribes, (1967-1968).* New Delhi.
Sinha, Surajit. 1986. *Nirmal Kumar Bose, Scholar Wanderer.* National Book Trust, India: New Delhi.

- **Chicano Education Project Started**
United States, 1968

The Mexican American Education Project is a research and development project initiated at California State University, Sacramento. Its initial funding came from the U.S. Office of Education. The general mission of the project was the improvement of educational opportunities for Mexican-Americans. Early leadership for the project came from Warren Snyder and Steven F. Arvizu. Programs were developed in the following areas: fellowship program for experienced teachers, curriculum development, fellowships for "high risk, high gain" individuals, prospective teachers, and an early childhood component.

Arvizu, Steven F. 1973. *The Mexican American Education Project Final Report.* California State University, Sacramento.

- **Community-School Links Explored at Sacramento**
United States, 1968

Using an approach which is termed by Rios as action anthropology, Senon Valadez developed a program of community oriented courses for Chicanos in Sacramento. These activities were designed to bridge the gap between the California State University, Sacramento and the community. One was the Chicanito Science Project which was to attract young Chicanos to science. Action anthropology activities extended to other courses and nutrition and art programs.

Rios, Sam. 1978. An Approach to Action Anthropology: The Community Project, C.S.U.S. *Grito del Sol, a Chicano Quarterly* (Year three-Book one, January-March 1978).

- **National Study of Native American Education**
  United States, 1968

The National Study of Indian Education was begun to review, in global terms, the state of the education system which served American Indian communities. The massive project benefited by the participation of a substantial number of anthropologists. These included John Chilcott, Bryan Michener, John Collier, Jr., Margaret Knight, and John H. Peterson, Jr.

Aurbach, Herbert A., and Estelle Fuchs. 1970. *The Status of American Indian Education.* Interim report of NSAIE. Pennsylvania State University.

Fuchs, Estelle and Robert J. Havighurst. 1970. *To Live on This Earth: American Indian Education.* New York: Doubleday.

- **Local Indian Reservations Served by University of San Diego**
  United States, 1970

The University of San Diego initiated the Continuing Education for Community Development for Indian Reservations in San Diego County Program under the direction of anthropologist Florence C. Shipek. This experimental program provided direct educational services to native American people of San Diego County. The program served as liaison between Indian groups and various colleges and universities in the area.

Shipek, Florence C. 1972. *Final Summary Report.* University of San Diego Program of Continuing Education for Community Development for Indian Reservations.

- **Headstart Follow Through Evaluation**
  United States, 1970

The Hopi Tribe of Arizona initiated a Headstart "Follow Through Program" in 1968. This program was studied by Murray L. Wax and Robert G. Breunig who focused upon identifying how Hopi parents defined formal education. They concluded that Hopis viewed schools as white institutions and that this conception did not change as a result of parental involvement programs.

Wax, Murray L. and Robert G. Breunig. 1973. *Study of the Community Impact of the Hopi Follow Through Program.* (Final Report, Project No. 2-O647) U. S. Department of Health, Education and Welfare, Office of Education, National Institute of Education.

- **Curriculum Developed in Ethnically Diverse Areas**
  Canada, 1970

Project Canada West represented a major attempt to develop school curriculum appropriate to the needs of the ethnically diverse western portion of Canada. The project made substantial use of anthropology. Participating anthropologists provided information to curriculum development specialists on various ethnic groups.

Sabey, Ralph H. 1973. The Preparation of Culturally Sensitive Curriculum Material for Canadian Schools: An Overview. *Council on Anthropology and Education Newsletter* 4(2):7-10.

- **Kamehameha Elementary Education Project Started**
  United States, 1970

Throughout its long history the Kamehameha Elementary Education Project (KEEP) has made use of the research of educational anthropologists to address the problem of academic underachievement of students of Polynesian-Hawaiian ancestry. KEEP is a research and development organization with action goals focused upon "discovering ways for improving the educational achievement of Hawaiian and part-Hawaiian children" and to "influence public schools on their behalf." Anthropologists at KEEP function as researchers for action concerned with achieving cultural compatibility in the schools. This involves ethnographic studies of community and classroom and the translation of these data into school practice and program development.

Au, Kathryn H. and Cathie Jordan. 1981. Teaching Reading to Hawaiian Children: Finding a Culturally Appropriate Solution. In *Culture and the Bilingual Classroom: Studies in Classroom Ethnography.* Henry Trueba, Grace P. Guthrie, and Kathryn H. Au. Rowley, MA: Newbury House.
Jordan, Cathie. 1985. Translating Culture: From Ethnographic Information to Educational Program. *Anthropology and Education Quarterly* 16(2):105-123.
_____. Cultural Compatibility and the Education of Hawaiian Children: Implications for Mainland Educators. *Educational Research Quarterly* 8(4):59-71.
_____. 1981. The Selection of Culturally Compatible Classroom Practices. *Educational Perspectives* 20(1):16-19.
_____. 1978. Teaching/Learning Interactions and School Adaptation: The Hawaiian Case. In *A Multidisciplinary Approach to Research in Education: The Kamehameha Early Education Program.* Technical Report No. 81. Honolulu: Kamehameha Center for the Development of Early Education.

- **Action Method Stresses Community Consciousness**
  Brazil, 1970

Using concepts derived from anthropology, Paulo Freire developed what he referred to as the conscientizacion method of inducing change. He attempted to diffuse technical skills to illiterate and passive peasants in northeastern Brazil and Chile. As part of these efforts he worked to increase the peasant's capacity for critical judgments. Freire focused upon the concept of culture as he notes "Culture, as an interiorized product which in turn conditions men's subsequent acts, must become the object of men's knowledge so that they can perceive its conditioning power" (1970: 16).

Freire, Paulo. 1970. Cultural Action for Freedom. *Harvard Educational Review and Center for the Study of Development and Social Change.* Monograph No. 1.
_____. 1972. *Pedagogy of the Oppressed.* New York: Herder and Herder.
_____. 1973. *Education for Critical Consciousness.* New York: The Seabury Press.

- **Ethnography in Education Explored**
  United States, 1971

Frederick Gearing, anthropologist at State University of New York-Buffalo, developed a training program in ethnographic observation for teachers and principals from secondary schools. This project was supported by the Office of Education.

Gearing, Frederick O. and B. Allan Tindall. 1973. Anthropological Studies of the Educational Process. *Annual Review of Anthropology* Vol. 2, B. Siegel, ed. Stanford, CA: Annual Reviews.
Gearing, Frederick, Wayne Hughes with Thomas Carroll, Walter Precourt and Allen Smith. 1975. *On Observing Well: Self Instruction in Ethnographic Observation for Teachers, Principals, and Supervisors.* Amherst, NY: Center for Studies of Cultural Transmission, SUNY-Buffalo.

- **High School Study in New York**
  United States, 1972

The High School Social Organization study program was initiated by Francis A. J. Ianni. The project had both theoretical and applied orientations and used a variety of data gathering techniques. Out of these research efforts come information useful for school programs. The project dealt with various types of schools in the New York metropolitan area.

90

Calhoun, Craig Jackson. 1974. General Status: Specific Role. *Council on Anthropology and Education Quarterly* 5(2):16-20.

Iaani, Francis A. J. 1974. Social Organization Study Program: An Interim Report. *Council on Anthropology and Education Quarterly* 5(2):1-8.

Varenne, Herve. 1974. From Grading and Freedom of Choice to Ranking and Segregation in an American High School. *Council on Anthropology and Education Quarterly* 5(2) 9-15.

- **Rural Schools Evaluated**
United States, 1972

Anthropologists were evaluation researchers for United States Office of Education rural school development projects. Much of this work was carried out through the Cambridge, Massachusetts, consulting firm, Abt Associates, Inc.

Burns, Allan. 1975. An Anthropologist at Work: Field Perspectives on Applied Ethnography. *Council on Anthropology and Education Quarterly* 6(4):28-33.

Clinton, Charles A. 1975. The Anthropologist as Hired Hand. *Human Organization* 34(2):197-204.

_____. 1975. *A Social and Educational History of Hancock County, Kentucky.* Hawesville, Kentucky: Bruner Printing Company.

_____. 1976. On Bargaining with the Devil: Contract Ethnography and Accountability in Fieldwork. *Council on Anthropology and Education Quarterly* 8(2):25-28.

_____. 1977. A Social and Education History of Hancock County, Kentucky. In *Rural America: A Social and Educational History of Ten Communities.* Stephen J. Fitzsimmons, Peter C. Folff, and Abby J. Freeman, eds. New York: Basic Books.

Everhart, Robert B. 1975. Problems of Doing Fieldwork in Educational Evaluation. *Human Organization* 34(2):205-215.

Fitzsimmons, Stephen J. 1975. The Anthropologist in a Strange Land. *Human Organization* 34(2):183-196.

Richen, Marilyn C. 1980. Observation Research: Usable Information for School District Evaluation? *Practicing Anthropology* 3:(1)15-16, 65-67.

- **Curriculum Development Project**
Canada, 1973

The Hobbema Curriculum project was designed to bring about locally controlled change among four native Canadian groups in Alberta. The project was calculated to produce new and appropriate curriculum materials. The project made use of the concepts of devolution and deconcentration.

Aoki, T. 1973. Toward Devolution in the Control of Education on a Native Reserve in Alberta. The Hobbema Curriculum Story. *Council on Anthropology and Education Newsletter* 4(2):1-6.

- **Chicago School Evaluation Projects**
  United States, 1974

Anthropologists as well as other behavioral scientists come to be involved in various evaluation projects as associates of the Center for New Schools in Chicago. The primary effort was the Documentation and Technical Assistance in Urban Schools Project. This was based on a $4.5 million dollar contract with the National Institute of Education. The project was exploratory and based on the "observed day-to-day realities of urban public school life." Research was being carried out in a number of sites in New York City, Los Angeles, Louisville, San Jose, Washington, D.C., and Minneapolis.

Center for New Schools. 1977. *DTA Project, Overview 1977.* Chicago: Center for New Schools.

- **Cleveland Heights School Program Evaluated**
  United States, 1976

The Center for New Schools organized a project to evaluate an innovative education project in Cleveland Heights, Ohio. The approach was consistent with traditional ethnography in that it relied heavily on participant observation.

Wilson, Stephen. 1977. The Use of Ethnographic Methods In Educational Evaluation. *Human Organization* 36(2):200-203.

- **Hartford Research and Training Project Carried Out**
  United States, 1979

In the 1970s there was very rapid growth in the number of Puerto Rican students in the public school system of Hartford, Connecticut. Studies carried out by a community group demonstrated that the school system was not meeting the needs of students. Litigation followed, which forced the system to address these needs. University of Connecticut educational anthropologists advocated that the community groups seek funding for a federal grant to train community groups to do educational research in order to monitor and shape educational programs so that community needs could be better served. The program, as it was funded and implemented, resulted in a two course sequence taught over a three year period for community members. The course of study emphasized ethnographic research methods used in action research settings.

Borrero, Maria, Jean J. Schensul and Roberto Garcia, 1982. Research, Training and Organizational Change. *Urban Anthropology* 11(1):545-569

Schensul, Jean J., Maria Gonzalez Borrero and Roberto Garcia. 1985. Applying Ethnography in Educational Change. *Anthropology and Education Quarterly* 16(2): 149-164.

- **Ponca Adult Education Needs and Resources Assessed**
  United States, 1979

Carried out at the request of the Ponca Tribal Business Committee, the survey determined educational content areas that were of high interest to Ponca clientele while it identified resources for adult education in the community. The project was carried out by anthropologist Donald N. Brown and education researcher Kenneth H. McKinley of Oklahoma State University. Research instruments were developed on the basis of consultation with representatives of the Tribe.

Brown, Donald N. and Kenneth H. McKinley. 1979. *Ponca Adult Education Survey.* Prepared for Ponca Tribal Business Committee.

- **Alaskan Bilingual and Bicultural Curriculum Developed**
  United States, 1980

The Northwest Arctic School District, working in association with anthropologist Helen R. Roberts developed an integrated bilingual and cross-cultural curriculum for eleven village schools with an Eskimo student body. The schools were committed to encouraging community control.

Roberts, Helen R. 1978. The Development of an Integrated Bilingual and Cross-cultural curriculum in an Arctic School District, Presented at Congress on Education, Canadian School Trustees Association, Toronto, Ontario.

- **Chicago Public School Drop-out Rate Examined**
  United States, 1985

In order to better understand the Chicago Public Schools drop-out rate, the Chicago Panel on Public School Finances, a consortium of private-sector agencies concerned with improving education, developed and applied an improved method for analysis of this important problem. The research produced a number of interesting results. Analysis revealed that the drop-out rate for one class was 43 percent. The most vulnerable students were overage males with low reading scores. Almost half of the males entering the Chicago School system dropped out. Students who transfer from school to school are more likely to drop-out. The research team was directed by G. Alfred Hess, Jr.

Hess, G. Alfred, Jr. and Diana Lauber. 1985. *Dropouts from the Chicago Public Schools, An Analysis of the Classes of 1982-1983-1984.* Chicago, IL: Chicago Panel on Public School Finances.

- **Government Funded Programs in Chicago Schools Examined**
  United States, 1986

G. Alfred Hess researched whether Federal categorical assistance grants were being spent on the students for whom the assistance was intended, that is, whether state, Federal and local guidelines were being adhered to. The programs included those classified as enrichment, bilingual/bicultural, early childhood, special education and vocational education. The data were provided by the Chicago School System and primarily consisted of information about the relationship between expenditures and the location of the students that were to be supported through the special programs. The research revealed that generally program expenditures were being made in a way that was consistent with guidelines but that early childhood education programs were not as concentrated in low income areas as they should have been because of the lack of space in schools in these areas and insufficient resources to support all needed programs.

Greer, James L., G. Alfred Hess, Jr., Peter Carlson and Diana Lauber. 1986. *Who Gets Extra Staff? A Review of Government Funded Programs.* Chicago, IL: Chicago Panel on Public School Finances.

- **Chicago School Drop-out Rate Assessed**
  United States, 1989

Drop-out studies have been of considerable interest to the Chicago Panel for some time. This particular study was oriented toward identifying students "early in the elementary grades" who are more likely to drop out. The data were Board of Education records on attendance, grades, conduct evaluations, and certain test scores. The researchers concluded that they were able to determine potential drop outs at an accuracy of 87 percent

94

when absence records and academic scores were both used to determine potential to drop-out.

Hess, G. Alfred, Jr., Arthur Lyons, Lou Corsino, Emily Wells. 1989. *Against the Odds: The Early Identification of Dropouts*. Chicago: Chicago Panel on Public School Policy and Finance.

EMPLOYMENT AND LABOR

- **Sioux Employment Study Carried Out**
  United States, 1942

The Rosebud Sioux Employment Project, sponsored by the U.S. Office of Indian Affairs and the University of South Dakota, was to determine the nature of the Sioux participation in the regional economy.

Useem, John, Gordon MacGregor and Ruth Hill Useem. 1943. Wartime Employment and Cultural Adjustments of the Rosebud Sioux. *Applied Anthropology* 2(2):1-9.

- **Impact of Military Base Employment Assessed**
  United States, 1953

Anthropologists studied the human environment in the region around the Arctic Research Laboratory of the Navy at Point Barrow, Alaska. The Navy was concerned about the long term impact on Inuit of employment at the Naval Petroleum Reserve IV base. The anthropologist concluded that the Inuit would be able to return to their previous economic pattern if employment opportunities at the base declined.

Criswell, Joan H. 1958. Anthropology and the Navy. In *Anthropology in the Armed Services, Research in Environment, Physique, and Social Organization*. Louis Dupree, ed. University Park, PA: Pennsylvania State University, Social Science Research Center.

- **Research Done for Union of African Workers**
  Northern Rhodesia, 1955

The African Railway Workers Union requested that the Rhodes-Livingstone Institute make a study of the organization of the union. The project was carried out by Parkinson Nwewa in association with A. L. Epstein.

Mwewa, Parkinson B. 1958. *The African Railway Workers Union Mdola, Northern Rhodesia.* (Rhodes-Livingstone Communication Number Ten). Lusaka: Rhodes-Livingstone Institute.

▪ Anthropologists in Federal Employment Studied
United States, 1958

Margaret Lantis, herself employed in the federal government carried out a study of the experiences of anthropologists working in the federal government in 1958. She estimated that there were about 175 employed in various agencies. She interviewed ten individuals about their experiences. Most frequently they cited area specialization or language competency as an important reason for being hired. Many felt that their training was inadequate, suggesting that anthropologists need more skills.

Lantis, Margaret. 1961. Anthropologist in the Federal Government. *Human Organization* 20(1):36-41.

▪ Health Careers' Program Evaluated in Pennsylvania
United States, 1968

A team which included anthropologist Ira E. Harrison evaluated the effects of a health careers program for 8th graders in Harrisburg, Pennsylvania. The program was intended to increase health career selection through hospital visitation and other special educational activities. Concomitantly the evaluation studied the role of family support in these career choices. The research showed that the program participants were three-times more likely to express interest in a health career.

Crawford, Charles O., George W. Schelzed, Phyllis T. Flemining and Ira E. Harrison. 1975. Effects of a Health Careers Program and Family Support for a Health Career on Eight Grader's Career Interest. *Public Health Reports* 90(2):168-172.

▪ Migrant Farm Workers Studied in the Stream
United States, 1969

Anthropologist Ira E. Harrison directed a research project intended to provide cultural background to an evaluation of the Pennsylvania Migrant Health Project. The research was intended to improve understanding of the health behavior of participants in the East Coast migrant stream through data collected using participant-observation and key informant interviewing. The researchers entered the migrant stream in Florida, selecting crews which were scheduled to arrive in a five county area in Pennsylvania. Observations were made in Virginia and Maryland. Interviews and observations among crews were done by black staff while interviews done with community officials were done by southern whites. The research resulted in a set of recommendations and was funded by the U.S. Public Health Service.

Harrison, Ira E. 1970. *The Pickers: Migratory Agricultural Farm Worker's Attitudes Toward Health.* Pennsylvania Health Council.
_____. 1972. *The Migrant Papers.* Behavioral Science Working Paper, 72- 73. Pennsylvania Department of Health.

- **Planning to Reduce Unemployment**
  Jamaica, 1972

Adam Kuper was employed as a planner by the National Planning Agency in the Office of the Prime Minister, Jamaica. His main concern was to combat urban unemployment as well as to raise rural productivity.

Kuper, Adam. 1974. Critical Applied Anthropology: Urban Unemployment and Rural Productivity in Jamaica. *Ethnos* 39:7-29.

- **Network-Focused Examination of Employment**
  United States, 1972

The concept of social network seems to have developed primarily within anthropology. Unfortunately its use in applied situations is infrequently documented. One example of its use was a study done by Alvin W. Wolfe on the effects of social network on employment. The study compared social networks of those successfully employed and those who weren't and did not find significant differences between the two groups.

Wolfe, Alvin W. with Linda Whiteford Dean. 1974. *Social Network Effects on Employment.* Report submitted to the Manpower Administration, U. S. Department of Labor.

- **Native Pipeline Employment Researched in Alaska**
  United States, 1975

Larry Naylor contracted with the Bureau of Indian Affairs to research Alaska Native employment on the Trans-Alaska Oil Pipeline. The support of this project was later expanded to include other government agencies and private sector groups such as Alyeska (Trans-Alaska Oil Pipeline Service Company).

Naylor, Larry L. 1976. *Native Hire on Trans-Alaska Pipeline*. Report prepared for Arctic Gas Pipeline Company, Department of Anthropology, University of Alaska.

- **Native American Manpower Training Project Started**
United States, 1976

The Native American Manpower Training Project at Oklahoma State University was funded by the Department of Labor to provide training for administrative staff in Native American CETA programs. The core of the project were seven training workshops and the related training manuals. The project planning process included site visits to CETA sponsors to assess needs for training and to develop case studies for use in the training programs. The project was directed by Donald N. Brown.

Brown, Donald N. 1977. *Services to Participants*. Stillwater, OK: Native American Manpower Training Project, Oklahoma State University.
_____. 1977. *Classroom Training*. Stillwater, OK: Native American Manpower Training Project, Oklahoma State University.
_____. 1977. *Client-Oriented Effectiveness Evaluation*. Stillwater, OK: Native American Manpower Training Project, Oklahoma State University.

- **Welfare and Employment Program Studied in Minnesota**
United States, 1976

The Minnesota Work Equity Program was done to demonstrate an approach to Welfare reform involving required participation in work or work training programs. The evaluation of this social experiment was done with the participation of three anthropologists as field workers. Trend notes, "We tried to steer a middle course between having the field-workers do free-form, 'lone wolf' ethnography and making them into mere data gatherers, the go-fers of the economists and survey analysts (1978:399)."

Trend, M. G. 1978. Research in Progress: The Minnesota Work Equity Project Evaluation. *Human Organization* 37(4):398-399.

- **Anthropologist Directs AAAS Native Americans in Science Project**
United States, 1976

Rayna Green served as Director of the Project on Native Americans in Science of the American Association for the Advancement of Science. The project attempted to identify factors which limit Native American participation in science careers. The project produced recommendations concerned with overcoming the identified constraints.

Brown, Janet W. 1975. Native American Contributions to Science, Engineering and Medicine. *Science* 189:38-40. (July 4, 1975).

Green, Rayna and Shirley Mahaley Malcom. 1976. AAAS Project on Native Americans in Science. *Science* 597-98 (November 5, 1976).

Green, Rayna and Janet Welsh Brown. 1977. Recommendations for the Improvement of Science and Mathematics Education for American Indians. *BIA Educational Research Bulletin* 5:1 (January 1977).

Green, Rayna and Shirley Mahaley Malcom. 1977. Native American Project Finds Some Barriers Breaking Down. *Science* 195:54, 56 (January 7, 1977).

_____. 1977. Conference on American Indian Science and Health Education. *Science* 196:46-47 (April 1, 1977).

- **Distribution of Mental Health Professionals in the South Assessed**
United States, 1979

The Southern Regional Education Board initiated a research project entitled Distribution of Mental Health Professionals in the South. Anthropologists Margaret A. Eisenhart and Joe R. Harding were involved in project design and implementation. The project attempted to answer questions about the influence of mental health training programs on graduate's choice of practice. The research techniques used include in-depth interviews, on-site observation and survey questionnaire.

Eisenhart, Margaret A. and Teresa C. Ruff. 1980. *Retention and Recruitment of Staff in Rural and Urban Mental Health Facilities in the South. The Implication of Staff Organization and Utilization for Retention and Recruitment Success, (Draft) Final Report.* Atlanta, GA: Southern Regional Education Board.

- **Naval Weapons Center Employment Practices Evaluated**
United States, 1981

Karen L. Buehler researched the general characteristics of the Hispanic employees of the Naval Weapons Center, China Lake, California. The data used consisted of analysis of already existing personnel record data, supplemented by interviews with a random sample of Hispanic employees.

Buehler, Karen L. 1981. *Perceptions of Hispanic Employment.* Management Division, Office of Finance and Management, Naval Weapons Center, China Lake, CA.

- **Small Business Hiring Studied in Philadelphia**
United States, 1981

Karen A. Curtis and Elaine L. Simon studied the impacts on small businesses of federal government incentives for the hiring of youth from poor families into entry level jobs in Philadelphia. This work, done for the Philadelphia Private Industry Council, attempted to use a cognitive approach that described the hiring decision making process used by a number of small businesses. This effort was related to a more general attempt to improve the performance of employment training programs focused on small businesses.

Simon, Elaine L. and Karen A. Curtis. 1981. *Small Business Hiring Practices and Implications for Employment and Training.* Final Report for Public/Private Ventures. Philadelphia, PA: Philadelphia Private Industry Council.

- **Kentucky CETA Program Evaluated Statewide**
United States, 1981

Anthropologist David B. Rymph participated in the evaluation of the federally funded Concentrated Employment and Training Act (CETA) programs in Kentucky. One aspect of the evaluation reported on program participant satisfaction. This aspect of the study was based on telephone interviews with over 600 participants.

Rymph, David B. and James G. Hougland. 1981. *An Analysis of Client Satisfaction with CETA Program Activities and Outcomes.* Submitted to the Bureau for Manpower Services, Department for Human Resources, Commonwealth of Kentucky. Lexington, KY: Survey Research Center, University of Kentucky.

- **South African Anthropologist Researched Black Gold Miners**
South Africa, 1982

Anthropologist H.P. Connoway, employed by the Chamber of Mines of South Africa, researched religious behavior of Black gold mine workers in terms of its implications for mine management. The research identified a wide range of religious behaviors used by mine workers as means of protection. Miners consulted magical specialists, made offerings, used special medicine, and wore amulets. Connoway speculated that some more hazardous jobs were associated with higher amulet use. He recommended that management respect these cultural practices.

100

Connoway, H.P. 1982. *Contemporary Religious Customs of Black Mine Workers: Implications for Management.* Pretoria: Chamber of Mines.

- **Oil Rigworkers studied for the Department of the Interior**
  United States, 1983

Using employee records provided by Getty Oil, anthropologist Linda L. Lampl analyzed travel and residency patterns of oil rigworkers for the Minerals Management Service of Department of the Interior. The Minerals Management Service handles the federal oil and gas leasing process.

Herbert, Thomas A. and Linda L. Lampl. 1984. Permitting Against the Toughest, Getty's East Bay Project. *Drilling* June, pp. 67-74.
_____. 1983. *The Travel and Residency Patterns of Rig Workers: The Getty Oil Company East Bay Project, Santa Rosa County, Florida.* Tallahassee, FL: T.A. Herbert and Associates.

- **Coal Miner X-ray Program Participation Rates Examined**
  United States, 1984

Anthropologist Launa Mallet carried out a research project to discover and document reasons for the extremely low participation rates in the Coal Miner Health Surveillance Program of the National Institute for Occupational Safety and Health (NIOSH). This federally mandated program calls for operators of underground coal mines to make chest x-rays available to their miners. If the x-rays find evidence of black lung, the law gives the miner the right to transfer to a less dusty work area with no initial loss of pay. Mallet collected data through key informant interviewing focused on the reasons why miners did or did not take part in the government sponsored program. She interviewed miners, retired miners, members of unions, mine superintendents, mine operators and other company personal.

Mallet, Launa. 1985. Miner Use of the NIOSH X-ray Program: Behavioral Aspects. *IMMR Highlights* 4(5):2
Mallet, Luana, Arthur Frank and Thomas Garrity. 1986. *Utilization of the Working Miner X-Ray Program, Behavioral Aspects.* Lexington, KY: University of Kentucky, Institute for Mining and Minerals Research/BRASH R86-O1.

- **National Institute of Rural Development**
  Researches Leather Workers
  India, 1986

The National Institute of Rural Development is the research and training arm of the Department of Rural Development of the Ministry of Agriculture, Government of India. Anthropologist R.R. Prasad directed a project to study the scheduled caste leather worker and the market for his products. The study also attended to the impact of special government programs for improving the circumstances of the leather workers. The data were collected in three districts of Uttar Pradesh, all heavily involved in carcass flaying, tanning hides and the production of leather sandals and other products. The study documented the decline in the number of scheduled caste persons working in this industry at a time when the leather industry as a whole appears to be flourishing. The success of the organized sector of the leather industry drove up prices, and as a result, small scale producers were driven out of production because of reduction of profit margins and raw material supply.

Prasad, R.R. 1986. *Change and Continuity Among the Scheduled Caste Leather Workers.* Rajendranagar, Hyderabad: National Institute of Rural Development.

- **Training for Employment Programs Studied**
  United Kingdom, 1987

The British government Youth Training Schemes have the goal of reducing unemployment. Ianthe MacLagan, a researcher in the Community Schemes Unit, National Council for Voluntary Organisations, researched reasons why young people left this program. The research took a qualitative approach, focusing on one region of this national program. They interviewed program participants, managers, and staff using a checklist of interview topics. The researcher made an effort to fully understand the program participants in context rather than to explain participants positions away as was done in some earlier studies.

MacLagan, Ianthe. 1989. Early Leavers from YTS. *BASAPP NewsLetter No. 3.*

ENERGY EXTRACTION

- ### Solar Cooker Technology R and D Carried Out in Oaxaca
  Mexico, 1962

Hendrick Serrie carried out a field project in Teotitlan del Valle for the University of Wisconsin Solar Energy Lab that had four basic goals. These were, (1) the development, based on Wisconsin models, of very low cost solar cookers and a solar water boiler; (2) manufacture of the cooker in the community with the participation of community members; (3) introduction of these cookers to a sample of families and; (4) determination of their acceptability and utility in this Zapotec community 25 kilometers from Oaxaca City. The team was able to develop a technically effective, low cost version of the prototype cooker built in Wisconsin. The cooker, manufactured locally, consisted of a frame and a parabolic reflector surfaced with a mosaic of small mirrors. The cookers, actively sought after by members of the community, were useful for preparing corn in anticipation of grinding and cooking atole. The cooker was found to be unsuitable for cooking tortillas and any frying. Tortilla preparation consumed a large portion of fuel used for cooking. Perhaps the most attractive use was the preparation of hot water for washing and bathing. It was apparent that low cost useful cookers could be produced, but that the applicability in the setting was somewhat limited.

Serrie, Hendrick. 1962. *Final Report of the Social Use of Solar Energy Field Project in Teotitlan del Valle, Oaxaca, Mexico.* Madison, WI: Solar Energy Laboratory, University of Wisconsin.

- ### Oil Development Policy Challenged
  Canada, 1973

An oil company consortium, called Panarctic Oils, LTD., began seismic surveying in an area of Bathurst Island used by an Inuit community for caribou hunting. The search for oil had a significant negative impact on wildlife resources. This caused representatives of the community to petition the Ministry of Indian and Northern Affairs to reexamine their policies concerning oil exploration. Anthropologist Milton M. R. Freeman worked as an advisor to the Inuit community.

Freeman, Milton M. R. 1977. Anthropologists and Policy-Relevant Research the Case for Accountability. In *Applied Anthropology in Canada*. Proceedings No. 4, of the Canadian Ethnology Society. Hamilton, Ontario: Canadian Ethnology Society.

- **Boom Town Impacts**
  United States, 1975

The Wyoming Human Services Project was created to deal with the human problems which have developed in Wyoming communities as a result of the rapid development of energy resources in the state. The project, which was multidisciplinary, attempted to provide "human service teams" in the coal communities of Gillette and Wheatland. These teams have worked in public administration, legal services, public health nursing, recreation services, community mental health, youth services, gerontology services and community education.

Uhlman, Julie M. 1977. The Delivery of Human Services in Wyoming Boomtowns. In *Socio-Economic Impact of Western Energy Development*. Berry Crawford and Edward H. Allen, eds. Ann Arbor: Science Publishers.
Uhlman, Julie M., Robert Kimble and David Throgmorton. 1976. A Study of Two Wyoming Communities Undergoing the Initial Effects of Energy Resource Development. In *The Powder River Basin: Buffalo and Douglas, Wyoming -- 1975*. Report prepared for the Wyoming Department of Economic Planning and Development.

- **Alaska Pipeline Information Center Established**
  United States, 1978

Fairbanks, Alaska was subject to certain impacts due to the construction of the Trans-Alaska Pipeline. In response to impact problems the Impact Information Center was established. The staff included anthropologist Mim Dixon.

Dixon, Mim. 1978. *What Happened to Fairbanks? The Effects of the Trans-Alaska Oil Pipeline on the Community of Fairbanks, Alaska*. The Social Impact Assessment Series, No. 1. Boulder, CO: Westview Press.

- **Solar Energy Project Evaluated**
  Upper Volta, 1980

Anthropologist Allen F. Roberts initiated the final assessment of a U.S. Agency for International Development funded project that was to

104

demonstrate the potential for using solar energy as a power source for common village tasks such as grain milling and water pumping at Tangaye, Upper Volta. Roberts' final assessment was preceded by a baseline study finished in 1978 and a social impact study done in 1979. It was hoped that the installed photovoltaic system would ease the work load of women and allow them to redirect their labor to productive tasks other than pumping water and grinding grain. The core of the evaluation was a post-test comparison group study of water drawing, water use, grain grinding, and grain-milling services use.

Burrill, G. and R. Popper. 1978. *Evaluation Planning for the Tangaye Solar Energy Demonstration.* Practical Concepts Inc. for USAID/UV contract, AID/ta-c-1469.

Roberts, A. 1978. *Mid-term Evaluation: Social Impact, Tangaye Solar Energy Demonstration.* USAID/UV contract AID/afr-c-1602.

_____. 1980. *A Final Evaluation of the Social Impact of the Tangaye (Upper Volta) Solar Energy Demonstration.* AID contract AID- 686-089-80, Center for Afroamerican and African Studies, University of Michigan.

_____. 1981. *The Social Impact of the Tangaye (Upper Volta) Solar Energy Demonstration: A Summary Report.* Contract # AID/Afr-0000- 00-1045-00 Center for Afroamerican and African Studies.

- **Village Energy Project Needs Assessment Designed**
  Bolivia, 1980

Practical Concepts, Inc., a Washington, D.C. consulting firm, assisted the U.S. Agency for International Development and the Bolivian Government in planning village level energy projects. As part of this process, a needs assessment survey instrument was developed. The methodology was capable of providing data on energy uses in rural areas, local energy resources, socio-cultural and environmental condition, and village level energy needs. The team that developed the methodology included anthropologist Sylvia Forman.

Practical Concepts, Incorporated. 1980. *Planning Rural Energy Projects: A Rural Energy Survey and Planning Methodology for Bolivia.* Washington, DC: Practical Concepts Inc.

- **Geothermal Energy Development's Impact Assessed**
  United States, 1981

Puna Hui Ohana, is an organization of Hawaiian people that received a grant from the U.S. Department of Energy to assess the social and cultural effects of the development of geothermal energy sources in this area. The assessment project was unusual in that it was carried out by the community rather than an external consultants. The process was assisted by Jerry Johnson and Craig Severance. An unusual assessment strategy used in the project involved sending community leaders to a similar project in New Zealand and evaluating their responses.

Puna Hui Ohana. 1982. *Assessment of Geothermal Development Impact on Aboriginal Hawaiians.* U.S. Department of Energy Contract No. DE-FC03- 79ET 27133.

- **Base-line Study of Ethanol Production Project**
  Honduras, 1984

Anthropologist Sara E. Alexander served as field director of a socio-economic baseline study completed to provide a reference for evaluating the impact of an newly installed ethanol production plant on a small sugar-producing village in Northern Honduras. The project was developed by Baylor University to assist farmers, in a group of cooperatives, find an alternative market for their sugar cane. The local sugar mill could no longer provide reliable demand because of the depressed world market price for refined sugar. Data was collected on socioeconomic characteristics of co-op and non co-op households, domestic energy consumption, and agricultural practices. The research paid close attention to the various ways that the ethanol plant might influence household economies. These data were used to formulate some alternative scenarios of social change.

Alexander, W. Merle, Arthur D. Murphy, C. Ronald Carroll, Sara E. Alexander, Chandra S. Balachandran and Barbara L. Patton. 1987. *An Ethanol Production Project to Aid Socioeconomic Development in a Northern Honduran Village.* Waco, Texas: Institute of Environmental Studies, Glasscock Energy Research Center, Baylor University.

- **Hydro Power Project Evaluated**
  Sri Lanka, 1988

The Development Studies Unit of the University of Stockholm provided consultancy services in conjunction with an evaluation of the Kotmale Hydro Power Project focused on the plight of the persons displaced by the project. The Swedish aid organization [SIDA] contracted with a expatriate anthropologist and a Sri Lankan geographer for a study of the Kotmale Evacuees to determine how the project had affected their lives. The study, which consisted of a large scale survey, determined that many of the relocated persons had to transform their agricultural practice substantially in their new environments. Typically during the pre-construction period they used a mixed farming system focused on production for home consumption centered on a highly adapted wet-rice cultivation. In the new areas some went from wet-rice to highland tea cultivation while others had to shift from subsistence to market production.

Softestad, Lars T. 1990. On Evacuation of People in the Kotmale Hydro Power Project: Experience from a Socio Economic Impact Study. *Bistandsantropogen* [Development Anthropologist] 15:22-32.

ENVIRONMENT

- **National Environmental Policy Act Passed**
  United States, 1969

The National Environmental Policy Act (P.L. 91-190) obligated federal agencies to prepare an environmental impact statement for every major federal action which affects the human environment. This included both the cultural and physical environments and consequently constitutes the most important legislation offering protection to archaeological resources. The Archaeological and Historic preservation Act of 1974 (P.L. 93-291) extended this protection to all remains which might be lost as a result of federal construction or other federally licensed or aided activities, and provided that up to one percent of the project funds could be used for this purpose.

Lipe, W. D. and A. J. Lindsay, Jr., eds. 1974. *Proceedings of the 1974 Cultural Resource Management Conference.* Flagstaff, AR: Museum of Northern Arizona (Technical Series 14).
McGimsey, Charles R., III. 1972. *Public Archaeology.* New York: Seminar Press.

- **Migration and Environment in Oregon Studied**
  United States, 1971

A Rockefeller Foundation funded research project was initiated in order to provide research results to the Oregon State government and legislature. Entitled "Man's Activities as Related to Environmental Quality," one of the projects carried out was done by anthropologist John A. Young, who investigated the motivations and adaptations of in-migrants to the

Willamette Valley using a series of focused interviews. A factor analysis allowed the classification of the respondents in various categories, e.g., restless Californian, Drifters, Working Class, Mavericks, etc.

Young, John A. 1975. *Migrants in Three Willamette Valley Towns: Why They Move and How They Adapt.* Prepared for the Rockefeller Foundation Project "Man's Activities as Related to Environmental Quality." Corvallis: Oregon State University.

- **DOD Experiments Resisted**
  Micronesia, 1972

The United States Department of Defense planned to carry out seismic testing on the island of Enewetak. This island had been the home of a native population prior to atomic weapons testing carried out in 1947. The seismic testing was to further disturb the natural environment. The seismic testing program referred to as PACE (Pacific Cratering Experiments) was actively resisted through the legal use of provisions of the National Environmental Policy Act (NEPA). Anthropologist Robert C. Kiste, who had considerable experience in Micronesian ethnography was requested by the Micronesian Legal Services Corporation to serve as a witness in the hearings. Kiste's activities very clearly advocated the interests of the Enewetak people and contributed to their successful resistance.

Hines, Neal O. 1962. *Proving Ground: An Account of the Radiobiological Studies in the Pacific, 1946-1961.* Seattle: University of Washington Press.
Kiste, Robert C. 1976. The People of Enewetak Atoll vs. The U.S. Department of Defense. In *Dilemmas in Fieldwork, Ethics and Anthropology.* Michael A. Rynkiewich and James P. Spradley, eds. New York: Wiley.

- **Native Latin American Resource Management Studied for the World Wildlife Fund**
  Latin America, 1980

A team of consultants, including anthropologist Leslie Ann Brownrigg, produced a report for the World Wildlife Fund on the relationship between native peoples and management of the environment. This consultantship placed the anthropologists and their coworkers as brokers between the rich body of knowledge and experience relating to resource management possessed by indigenous peoples to those in the international community that are concerned with the progressive deterioration of the environment, world wide. A primary goal of this activity was the transmission of knowledge from native to technician. The knowledge was

108

taught to the consultants by native people in Peru, Bolivia, Ecuador, Mexico, Panama, and Colombia.

Brownrigg, Leslie Ann. 1986. *Al Futuro Desde La Experiencia, Los Pueblos Indigenas y el Manejo del Medio Ambiente.* Quito: Ediciones ABYA-YALA.

- **Environmental Assessment Manual Developed**
  United States, 1980

Operating with the support of a U.S. Agency for International Development contract, Harza Engineering developed a manual which was "intended to assist A.I.D. field officers, development consultants and most country planners in identifying potential societal benefits and undesirable environmental effects that may accompany small rural projects." The manual focused on design considerations for roads, electrification, water supply and sanitation, irrigation and on-farm water management and small industries. The project was executed by a team that included anthropologist William L. Partridge. The manual presents a concrete and specific project impact assessment technique which includes the social, biological and physical environment impact analysis categories. The impact analysis approach is based on a "Project Planning Checklist" which combines an impact-no impact question set with a multi-category impact weighting scheme. These impacts are then displayed on a project impact matrix. The impact matrix divides the project into planning and design, construction and operation phases.

Harza Engineering Company. 1980. *Environmental Design Considerations for Rural Development Projects.* Washington, DC: United States Agency for International Development.

- **Radioactive Waste Siting Process Informed by Ethnography**
  United States, 1987

The State of California sought a site for storage of low level radioactive waste within their borders following Nuclear Regulatory Commission guidelines. Anthropologist Richard W. Stoffle sought to identify concerns of native Americans affected by the selection of the various sites as part of the planning process. The concerns of Native Americans were initially identified from previous environmental impact statements, comments by Native Americans at public hearings, and the Native American who was appointed to the citizen's advisory committee. Data were also collected by interviewing persons from affected Native American groups at their homes and at the potential sites. The concerns of these native people were reported and became part of the public discussion of the siting alternatives.

Stoffle, Richard W., Michael J. Evans, Florence V. Jensen. 1987. *Native American Concerns and State of California Low-Level Radioactive Waste Disposal Facility: Mohave, Navajo, Chemehuevi, and Nevada Paiute Responses*. Menlo Park, CA: Cultural Systems Research.

EVALUATION

- ## Indian Personality and Administration Project
United States, 1941

The Indian Personality and Administration Research Project was organized by the Bureau of Indian Affairs to evaluate the impact of its administrative policies on Native American populations and to identify effects on personality. The project made early use of action research techniques. It produced a number of interesting publications, but had little effect on policy.

Collier, John. 1945. The United States Indian Administration as a Laboratory of Ethnic Relations. *Social Research* 12:265-303.

Joseph, Alice, Rosamond B. Spicer and Jane Chesky. 1949. *The Desert People: A Study of the Papago Indians*. Chicago: University of Chicago Press.

Kluckhohn, Clyde and Dorothea C. Leighton. 1946. *The Navaho*. Cambridge: Harvard University Press.

Leighton, Dorothea C. and John Adair. 1946. *People of the Middle Place: A Study of the Zuni Indians*. New Haven: Human Relations Area Files.

Leighton, Dorothea C. and Clyde Kluckhohn. 1947. *Children of the People*. Cambridge: Harvard University Press.

MacGregor, Gordon. 1946. *Warriors Without Weapons*. Chicago: University of Chicago Press.

Thompson, Laura. 1950. Action Research Among American Indians. *Scientific Monthly* LXX:34-40.

_____. 1951. *Personality and Government*. Ediciones del Instituto Indigenista Interamericano. Mexico: D.F.

_____. 1970. Exploring American Indian Communities in Depth. In *Women in the Field: Anthropological Experiences*. Peggy Golde, ed. Chicago: Aldine.

Thompson, Laura and Alice Joseph. 1944. *The Hopi Way*. New York: Russell Sage.

- **Early Development Anthropology Evaluations**
  United States, 1951

Staff members of the Institute of Social Anthropology, Smithsonian Institution, carried out research projects that evaluated various United States government technical assistance projects in Brazil, Columbia, Mexico, and Peru. Field analyses were carried out by Charles Erasmus, Isabel Kelly, Kalervo Oberg, George Foster, and Ozzie Simmons.

> Foster, George. 1951. *A Cross-Cultural Anthropological Analysis of a Technical Aid Program.* Washington, DC: Institute of Social Anthropology, Smithsonian Institution.

- **Firth Evaluates Colonial Reform Plan**
  United Kingdom, 1951

Raymond Firth evaluated the so-called Colombo Plan which intended to reform British colonial administration and accelerate colonial development. Firth warned of unforeseen social consequences.

> Firth, Raymond W. 1951. Some Social Aspects of the Colombo Plan. *Westminster Bank Review* (May).
> Mair, Lucy. 1969. *Applied Anthropology and Development Policies in Anthropology and Social Change.* London School of Economics, Monographs on Social Anthropology, No. 38. New York: Humanities Press.

- **Oscar Lewis Evaluates Plans for Ford Foundation**
  India, 1952

Oscar Lewis was hired as a consultant for the Ford Foundation in India. He was requested to work with the Program Evaluation Organization of the Planning Commission to review a plan of evaluation of the rural reconstruction program. This program served as a pilot for community development in India.

> Lewis, Oscar. 1958. *Village Life in Northern India.* New York: Vintage.

- **Evaluation of Development Efforts**
  United States, 1955

Anthropologist Louis Miniclier's organization of three teams reviewed early community development in such countries as India, Pakistan,

Philippines, Egypt, the Gold Coast, Puerto Rico and others. George Foster headed up one team, Isabel Kelly another.

Adams, Harold S., George M. Foster and Paul S. Taylor. 1955. *Report on Community Development Programs in India, Pakistan and the Philippines.* Washington, DC: International Cooperation Administration.

Carley, Verna A. and Elmer A. Starch. 1956. *Report on Community Development Programs in Jamaica, Puerto Rico, Bolivia and Peru.* Washington, DC: International Cooperation Administration.

- **Special Multi-purpose Tribal Blocks Scheme Evaluated**
  India, 1959

Special Multi-purpose Tribal Blocks were established jointly by the Ministry of Home Affairs and the Ministry of Community Development and Co-operation to coordinate development in areas where tribal people were in the majority. Subsequent to this a committee, including anthropologists Verrier Elwin and L.P. Vidyarthi, was formed to evaluate the Block program and to make recommendations to the government. Termed the Elwin Committee, the group made recommendations concerning staff of tribal service programs, land alienation and landlessness, agricultural development, and health and education services. Specific attention to shifting cultivation was paid. In a general sense, their recommendations came to be expressed as government policy.

Elwin, Verrier. 1960. *Report of the Committee on Special Multipurpose Tribal Blocks.* New Delhi: Ministry of Home Affairs.

_____. 1977. Growth of a 'Philosophy'. In *Anthropology in the Development Process.* Hari Mohan Mathur, ed. New Delhi: Vikas Publishing House.

Bhowmick, P. K. 1984. Reports on Scheduled Tribes: An Appraisal. In *Applied Anthropology in India (Principles, Problems and Case Studies).* L. P. Vidyarthi, ed. 2nd Edition. Allahabad: Kitab Mahal.

Vidyarthi, L. P. 1984. Nehru's Approach to Tribal Culture. In *Applied Anthropology in India: (Principles, Problems and Case Studies).* L. P. Vidyarthi, ed. 2nd Edition. Allahabad: Kitab Mahal.

Mathur, Hari Mohan. 1977. Anthropology, Government and Developmental Planning in India. In *Anthropology in the Development Process.* Hari Mohan Mathur, ed. New Delhi: Vikas Publishing House.

- **Bottom-up or Top Down, Rhodesian Development Evaluated**
  Northern Rhodesia, 1961

Working under assignment to the Agency for International Development, George M. Foster made an independent study of community development activities and possibilities in Northern Rhodesia. The study, carried out over about five months, was based on field observation and interviewing. The evaluation concluded that there were certain defects in the approach used. Among other things, the Community Development program seemed to have been carried out on a "top-down" planning basis and had little continuity of staff. The report included a number of recommendations that stressed community participation in development implementation and planning. The involvement of the anthropologist in this process was stimulated by Louis Miniclier.

Foster, George M. 1962. *Report to the Chief Secretary of the Northern Rhodesia Government of the Consultant on Community Development of the Agency for International Development.* Washington, DC: Agency for International Development.

- **Health Project Evaluated**
  Ethiopia, 1962

Working under the auspices of the United States Agency for International Development, Simon D. Messing served in a public health demonstration and evaluation team which conducted research in rural Ethiopia. The team dealt with various groups including the Amhara, Galla, Tigre, Somali, Kambatta, Wollamo, Anauk, and Nuer. The team's primary goal was to measure the effects of new health care centers.

Messing, Simon D. 1965. Application of Health Questionnaires to Pre-Urban Communities in a Developing Country. *Human Organization* 24(3).
_____. 1964. Base-Line Health Culture Research in a Developing Country, Public Health Research in Ethiopia for USAID. *American Behavioral Scientist* 7(8).

- **OEO Programs Evaluated in Kentucky**
  United States, 1965

The Center for Developmental Change at the University of Kentucky contracted with the Office of Economic Opportunity to evaluate Community Action Programs in rural Kentucky. The multidisciplinary team included anthropologists Art Gallaher, Jr. and Stephen R. Cain.

Cain, Stephen R. 1968. A Selective Description of a Knox County Mountain Neighborhood Unit 3. In *An Appraisal of the "War on Poverty" in a Rural Setting of Southeastern Kentucky.*

- **Tribal Development Programmes Evaluated**
  India, 1966

P. Shilu Ao served as chairman of a group that was to evaluate tribal development programmes carried out as part of the Fourth Five Year Plan for the welfare of the scheduled tribes. This effort was to provide some perspective on the work done for tribal people during the First, Second and Third Five Year Plans. The charge to the committee expressed concern for making recommendations for increasing tribal groups access to the benefits of development and improving functioning of administrative organization. The Plans tend to express goals as concrete targets such as numbers of schools constructed, school books distributed and bullocks supplied, etc.

Bhowmick, P. K. 1984. Reports on Scheduled Tribes. In *Applied Anthropology in India: (Principles, Problems and Case Studies)* L. P. Vidyarthi, ed. 2nd Edition. Allahabad: Kitab Mahal.

- **OEO Programs Evaluated**
  United States, 1967

Various anthropologists were hired to evaluate component programs of the Office of Economic Opportunity. In one such case, John L. Sorenson and Larry L. Berg evaluated the Indian Community Action Programs at Arizona State University, University of South Dakota and the University of Utah. The evaluation design involved extensive interviewing. The Indian Community Action Programs were depicted as sensitive to the needs of Indian communities.

Sorenson, John L. and Larry L. Berg. 1967. *Evaluation of Indian Community Action Programs at Arizona State University, University of South Dakota, and University of Utah.* General Research Corporation, Santa Barbara, California.

- **Arizona Anthropologists Evaluate Indian Programs**
  United States, 1971

The Gila River Indian Community, consisting largely of Pima and Maricopa Indians, engaged a research team from the Bureau of Ethnic Research to make recommendations to improve operations in the government of the community. Anthropologists involved included Thomas Weaver, project director and B. Alan Kite as co-investigator.

114

Weaver, Thomas et al. 1971. *Political Organization and Business Management in the Gila River Indian Community.* (Research Report Series, June, 1971) Tucson: Bureau of Ethnic Research, University of Arizona.

- **Science Museum of Minnesota Researched as Class Project**
  United States, 1978

Students, from Cynthia A. Cone's Hamline University class, researched visitor behavior in the anthropology hall of the Science Museum of Minnesota. The study focused on "movement and interaction of family groups." It made use of two data collection methods: direct observation of randomly selected parent-child groups and visitor interviews. The interviews took place with the observed family members after they left the Hall.

Cone, Cynthia A. and Keith Kendall. 1978. Space, Time, and Family Interaction: Visitor Behavior at the Science Museum of Minnesota. *Curator* 21(3): 245-258.

- **Ethnographic Evaluation of Career Intern Program Carried Out**
  United States, 1980

David Fetterman evaluated an experimental alternative high school for drop outs called the Career Intern Program (CIP). The evaluation had four components: program implementation; statistical evaluation of students test outcomes; ethnography of the program; and comparison to similar programs. Fetterman was responsible for the ethnography; identifying interrelationships between program components and student outcomes. Ethnography documented high expectations of CIP participants, importance of rituals and rites of passage culminating in graduation, and quantifiable measures of program success in attendance, graduation, and placement. Recommendations included improved management personnel screening and staff pay to decrease turnover, and change in treatment-control design of admittance policy.

Fetterman, David M. 1987. A National Ethnographic Evaluation of the Career Intern Program. In *Anthropological Praxis: Translating Knowledge Into Action.* R. Wulff and S. Fiske, eds. Boulder: Westview.

- **Anthropologist Aids Evaluation of CARE Projects**
  Peru, 1980

Using existing data sources and some interviews, Charlotte I. Miller provided a U.S. Agency for International Development evaluation team with a summary of information on socio-cultural and economic patterns in the highland portions of two provinces of Peru. The report included recommendations for the evaluation study. The research was carried out in a short period of time.

Miller, Charlotte I. 1980. *Socio-cultural and Economic Characteristics of Conditions in Ancash and La Libertad, Peru with Special Emphasis on the Callejones de Huaylas and Conchucos: Questions to be Considered in an Evaluation of Care-Sponsored Water, Sewage and Health Projects.* Washington, DC.

- **Washington State Evaluates Impact of AFDC Program Termination**
  United States, 1981

Based on a random sample of 738, a research team, including anthropologist Hal Nelson of the Washington Department of Social and Health Services, identified adaptations of recipients to termination of the Aid to Families with Dependent Children - Employable Program. Data were collected by telephone supplemented by face-to-face interviews and case file review. The project reported on residential mobility, subsequent use of public assistance, employment status, and apparent effect on marriages.

Fiedler, Fred P. and Hal Nelson. 1982. *Follow-up Study of Assistance Cases Closed as a Result of AFDA-E Program Termination Final Report.* Olympia, Washington: Department of Social and Health Services.

- **Anthropologist Evaluates A.I.D. Evaluations**
  World, 1985

Barbara Pillsbury analyzed the FY 1985 evaluation studies of the Asia and Near East Bureau of the Agency for International Development. The study resulted in a collection of 54 project summaries and provided an overview of the Agency's efforts in Asia. Many of the projects studied were manifestations of A.I.D.'s basic human needs orientation that guided project planning in the late 1970's and early 1980's and had institution building as a goal. Pillsbury's analysis revealed a number of consistently appearing themes relating to personnel quality, project design factors, beneficiary participation, and training.

Pillsbury, Barbara. 1986. *Executive Summaries of Evaluations and Special Studies Conducted for A.I.D. in Asia in Fiscal Year 1985.* Washington, DC: Bureau for Asia and the Near East, Office of Development Planning, Agency for International Development.

FISHERIES AND OTHER MARINE ECONOMIES

- **Evaluation of Fishing Cooperatives**
  Vietnam, 1963

Anthropologist Howard K. Kaufman, employed by U.S. Agency for International Development, was temporarily assigned the duty of evaluating the success of a Vietnamese fishing cooperative in Khanh Hou Province. During this time, Kaufman was employed by Commissioner General of Cooperatives of the Republic of Vietnam.

Kaufman, Howard K. 1974. Culao: A Vietnamese Fishing Cooperative and Its Problems. In *Social Organization and the Applications of Anthropology, Essays in Honor of Lauriston Sharp*. Robert J. Smith, ed. Ithaca: Cornell University Press.

- **Anthropological Perspectives Included in Sea Grant Program at University of Oregon**
  United States, 1971

Oregon State University was one of the first Sea Grant Programs funded by the Federal Government. Sea Grant trains students to work on marine problems, researches a variety of marine issues, and disseminates information to the public. Among the scientists participating in the Oregon State University Sea Grant Program was anthropologist Courtland L. Smith. Smith's work has had two policy-relevant foci. First is public education, and with this goal in mind OSU Sea Grant published a popular history of commercial fishing in Oregon entitled *Fish or Cut Bait* (1977) and an account of public conflict over fishing called *Oregon Fish Fights* (1974). Both these publications were intended to educate the Oregon public. The second aspect of Smith's policy-relevant work was the construction of a computer simulation of the interacting factors in a fishery: fish, fishermen and community. The model is called NETS or Northwest Educational Trawler Simulation. The model is of interest because it includes both social and biological data.

Smith, Courtland L. 1974. *Oregon Fish Fights*. Corvallis, OR: Oregon State University (#ORESU-T-74-004).
_____. 1977. *Fish or Cut Bait*. Corvallis, OR: Oregon State University, (#ORESU-T-77-006).

- **Oyster Fishery Improvement Project Evaluated**
  United States, 1977

Marcus J. Hepburn, working as part of a multi-disciplinary team, assisted in the evaluation of an oyster transplanting project at Cedar Key, Florida done under contract with the state Bureau of Marine Science and Technology. Anthony Paredes assisted the project. The evaluation made use of a wide variety of historical, biological, economic and social data. The social and economic components were addressed in six weeks of observation and interviewing. Interviewing was done with a "purposeful sampling of local residents" without the use of structured interview schedule. These data were supplemented by questionnaires administered to students at the local high school. These research components identified local perceptions of benefits and costs of the project. Oyster transplanting involves the relocation of immature oysters to a location more favorable to growth and resource replenishment.

Hepburn, Marcus J., et al. 1977. *The Cedar Key Oyster Relocation and Demonstration Project - 1977.* Final Report Submitted to the Florida Department of Natural Resources in Fulfillment of Bid Number 5006-77. Gainesville, FL: University of Florida, Florida Sea Grant Program.

- **Development of Local Florida Fisheries Law Assessed**
  United States, 1978

The Gulf and South Atlantic Fisheries Development Foundation, Inc. retained Thomas A. Herbert and Linda Lampl to research the history of the development of local fisheries laws in Florida. The Foundation was advocating legal reform in the fisheries laws, with the possible goal of establishing a unifying Marine Fisheries Commission for the state of Florida.

Herbert, Thomas A. and Linda Herbert. 1979. *Documentation of Conflicts Leading to the Enactment of Local Fisheries Laws in Florida.* Tallahassee, FL: Center for Resource Development.

- **Regional Fishery Research Supported**
  United States, 1979

While employed as Social Anthropologist for the National Oceanic and Atmospheric Administration, Michael K. Orbach initiated a project which was to result in the publication of a bibliography and directory of

118

researchers. In part, this effort was to produce materials that would be "of use to the Regional Fishery Management Councils" so as to assist them in making better use of social sciences in development of fisheries management plans. Valerie R. Harper also worked on the project.

Orbach, Michael K. and Valerie R. Harper. 1979. *United States Fisheries System and Social Science: A Bibliography of Work and Directory of Researchers.* Washington, DC: National Marine Fisheries Service, National Oceanic and Atmosphere Administration, U.S. Department of Commerce.

- **Alaska Fishery Permits Studied for State Legislature**
  United States, 1979

In 1973, Alaska's limited entry program for commercial fisheries was established by act of the state legislature. While the limited entry program did not restrict fishing permits to Alaska residents it was the policy of the state to encourage predominance of residents in all of its commercial fisheries. The aspect of the limited entry program that was of most concern to the legislators was the provision for the transfer of fishing permits on the market. Anthropologist Steve Langdon was contracted to analyze permit transfer patterns and to report his findings to the state legislature. They were especially concerned that the various Alaska fisheries were coming to be controlled by nonresidents.

Langdon, Steve. 1980. *Transfer Patterns in Alaskan Limited Entry Fisheries.* Final Report for the Limited Entry Study Group for the Alaska State Legislature. Anchorage, AK: University of Alaska.

- **Wisconsin Sport Fishery Stocking Program Alternatives Studied**
  United States, 1980

A research team led by Richard Stoffle attempted to clarify some policy questions relating to fish stocking for the Lake Michigan Trout and Salmon sport fishery following the announcement of program reductions by the Wisconsin Department of Natural Resources. Angler preferences for fish stocking policies were assessed using a survey instrument amongst a suitable sample. The research identified an alternate means of financing the stocking program, that when implemented protected the livelihood of charter boat crews and the recreation of sport fishermen.

Stoffle, Richard, Florence V. Jansen and Danny L. Rasch. 1981. *Coho Stocking and Salmon Stamps, Lake Michigan Anglers Assess Wisconsin's DNR Policies.*

Working Papers in Applied Anthropology, Case #2 Kenosha, WI: University of Wisconsin-Parkside.

- **A Program to Increase Demand for Underutilized Species**
United States, 1983

As marine recreational fishing becomes more popular in the U.S., increased pressures are being placed on traditionally sought species such as grouper, snapper, and king mackerel. Yet recreational fishermen annually discard millions of pounds of fish that they consider too small, poor eating, or hard to prepare or clean. In 1983, the National Marine Fisheries Service (NMFS) initiated a program to understand sportfishermen's beliefs about saltwater fish and develop educational materials to increase use of underutilized species. Anthropologists Jeff Johnson and David Griffith (East Carolina University) engaged in research and educational materials development to increase demand for underutilized species in the southeast. Based on interviews with sportfishermen in East and West Florida, Texas, and North Carolina, Johnson and Griffith used multidimensional scaling, hierarchical clustering analysis, and item-by-use matrices to model fishermen's beliefs about saltwater fish (Johnson and Griffith 1985). They found that fishermen often reject species because of local myth or misinformation, and some species considered trash fish in one region are highly prized elsewhere. Project personnel have produced a variety of educational materials based on the model. These include a slide/tape program, a series of brochures and posters featuring species such as amberjack, skates and rays, and sea robin, an underutilized species cookbook, and a guide for developing underutilized species fishing tournaments. Project personnel have also sponsored workshops throughout the southeast.

Johnson, Jeffrey and David Griffith. 1985. *Perceptions and Preferences for Marine Fish: A Study of Recreational Fishermen in the Southeast.* UNC Sea Grant Publication UNC-SG-85-01. Raleigh, NC: UNC Sea Grant College Program.

- **Smithsonian King Crab Mariculture Projects Assessed**
Caribbean, 1985

The Smithsonian Institution, Marine Systems Laboratory contracted Richard W. Stoffle to assess the social and cultural factors relevant to the transfer of newly developed technology for raising King Crabs at various Caribbean sites. Reef environments are capable of producing very large quantities of plant material, which in turn serves as a feed for marine species. The technical problem is to economically convert this feed growth potential into a marketable product. The system involved impounding king crabs in marine cages and feeding them with the growth on portable screens. Developed by the Smithsonian in a controlled, experimental setting, it was Stoffle's task to evaluate transferability out of the experimental situation. The assessment project focused on such questions as who were the most appropriate adopters for the technology; how does the system fit local technology; and what will the impact of the system on local society and markets be. The data were collected through participant-observation and key informant interviewing. Stoffle concluded from the research that the Smithsonian-developed king crab mariculture technology presented a useful addition to the economic repertoire of the potential adopters.

Stoffle, Richard W. 1986. *Caribbean Fishermen Farmers, A Social Assessment of Smithsonian King Crab Mariculture.* Research Report Series, Ann Arbor, MI: Institute for Social Research, Survey Research Center.

- **North Carolina Marinas and Marine Manufacturers Researched**
  United States, 1986

A research team, including anthropologist Jeffery Johnson, completed a telephone survey of marinas and marine manufacturers in North Carolina. The survey format was innovative in that it involved mailing an interview worksheet and cover letter to sampled firms and then interviewing a representative of the firm by telephone concerning the content of the worksheet. This process decreased the number of misdirected mail contacts with a positive effect on the response rate. The data collected allowed accurate description of the nature and magnitude of the economic contribution these activities make to North Carolina.

Johnson, Jeffrey C. and Richard R. Perdue. 1986. *Marine Recreational Fishing, Marine Manufacturers and Marinas in North Carolina: An Economic Characterization.* Raleigh, NC: UNC Sea Grant College Program, North Carolina State University.

- **Impacts of Blue Crab Fishery Assessed**
  United States, 1984

A research team, led by anthropologist John Maiolo, investigated aspects of the Blue Crab Fishery under the provisions of the Sea Grant Program. The study team sought to determine the nature of competition between fishermen of different types and the effects of stock abundance on fishermen and women's occupational choice. The design of the research had two phases; first, interviews with a sample of fishermen and women were carried out and second, a series of key informant interviews were done with dealers and processors.

Maiolo, John, Claudia Williams, Ruth Kearns, Hurbert Bean and Hih Song Kim. 1986. *Social and Economic Impacts of Growth of the Blue Crab Fishery in North Carolina.* Raleigh, NC: Sea Grant College Program, North Carolina State.

- ## Anthropologists Investigate Fishery Management Plan Change
  United States, 1989

The researchers implemented a telephone survey of surf clam vessel owners in the Mid Atlantic and New England regions to determine their response to a draft of a major amendment of the surf clam fishery management plan. Fishery management plans are prepared by regional councils established under the provisions of the Magnuson Act [or the Fishery Conservation and Management Act of 1976]. The regional councils include federal and state officials and interested members of the public and function to regulate resource exploitation. The amendment included various alternatives, but basically advocated a shift in the mechanism for allocating the common property resource from a time allocation system to one based on quota issued to boats. The research was supported by the National and New Jersey Sea Grant programs, New Jersey Marine Sciences Consortium and the New Jersey Agricultural Experiment Station.

McCay, Bonnie J. and Carolyn F. Creed. 1990. Social Structure and Debates on Fisheries Management in the Atlantic Surf Clam Fishery. *Ocean and Shoreline Management* 13:199-229.

- ## Social Effects of Turtle Conservation Programs Studied
  United States, 1990

The research investigated how shrimp fishermen in Bayou La Batre, Alabama responded to and resisted the use of turtle excluder devices that they were forced to use by federal law. The devices of various types are designed to eject turtles from the nets of shrimp trawlers to protect these endangered species. The research, carried out under the auspices of the Mississippi-Alabama Sea Grant Program, examined the sources of the resistance to the federal regulations and some of the responses. Responses included; fishermen evaluating and selecting alternative designs of the device, fishermen developing their own data base on the effects of the devices on catch size and costs; changes in the way fishermen dealt with captured turtles and civil disobedience involving ship channel closure. The researchers were able to show, while the fishermen were depicted as irrationally stubborn in their resistance to the innovations by journalists and bureaucrats, they were quite innovative in general and were resisting the use of the devices because these devices increased costs and seemed to have little positive impact on turtle mortality. The research team, including anthropologist Christopher Dyer, were not working for an agency, but were taking a public interest, advocacy stance.

Dyer, Christopher L. and Mark A. Moberg. 1990. *Responses to Forced Innovation: Turtle Excluder Devices (TEDs) and Gulf Coast Fishermen.* Paper presented at the American Anthropological Association.

FORESTRY AND FORESTS

- **Feasibility of Haitian Reforestation Studied**
  Haiti, 1980

Using a research methodology based on key informant interviewing and field observations, Glenn R. Smucker considered the feasibility of various reforestation strategies for Haiti. The project was undertaken for the U.S. Agency for International Development mission and complemented AID's consideration of a Project Identification Document (PID). Smucker collected and reported ethnographic data on the charcoal economy, peasant agriculture and reforestation, and the agencies which had an interest in the issue of reforestation. Specifically, the report addressed the position of charcoal production in the peasant household economy, factors which encourage charcoal making, and the relationship between charcoal production and field cropping systems.

Smucker, Glenn R. 1981. *Trees and Charcoal in Haitian Peasant Economy, a Feasibility Study of Reforestation.* Port-au-Prince: USAID Mission.

- **Reforestation Project Designed**
  Haiti, 1981

Pan American Development Foundation, was funded by the Agency for International Development to develop and run a tree-planting project to deal with deforestation. Gerald Murray devised a plan to replant trees that was different from the approaches used previously, in that he emphasized farmer control of the resource. The project made use of a number of innovations. These included using fast-growing trees as microseedlings for border planting and intercropping, encouraging the use of trees as a cash crop owned by landowner to be harvested when desired rather than "conserved," and involving local private voluntary organizations for seedling delivery thus avoiding extractive government agencies. The project was very successful and resulted in the planting of twenty million trees, quintupling the original four-year goal. It was found that trees were cut more slowly than anticipated, because the trees were kept as a "bank" against crop failure. Local non-governmental development agencies are now using similar reforestation methods.

Murray, Gerald F. 1987. The Domestication of Wood in Haiti: A Case Study in Applied Evolution. In *Anthropological Praxis: Translating Knowledge Into Action.* R. Wulff and S. Fiske, eds. Boulder: Westview.

- **Village Dialogue Method for Participation Developed**
Nepal, 1984

Donald A. Messerschmidt, an anthropologist working for the Resource Conservation and Utilization Project (RCUP) of the government of Nepal, developed a method for increasing local level participation in development projects. The village dialogue method is intended to foster local participation in development, integrate and coordinate resources and to utilize and strengthen present governmental institutions. This method relies on the promotion of present social institutions and a two-way system of communication, i.e. top-down and bottom-up.

Messerschmidt, Donald A. 1984. *Gaun Sallah: The Village Dialogue Method for Local Planning in Nepal.* Kathmandu: South East Consortium for International Development and the Resource Conservation and Utilization Project, Ministry of Forest and Soil Conservation.

(Steve Morin)

- **Anthropologist Serves in Social Forestry Project**
Pakistan, 1985

Michael R. Dove served as senior project anthropologist in a large scale, four year social forestry project carried out by Office of the Inspector General of Forests, Government of Pakistan and Winrock International based on U.S.A.I.D. funding. The project was designed to help small farmers grow trees on their own land to meet their household needs for

124

fuel, fodder, and small timbers for construction and agricultural implements. It was also the goal of the project to supplement income through wood sales and to conserve cow dung for use as manure instead of fuel. The program included provisions for free seedlings, advice, training, guaranteed prices, and demonstration. He supervised research, extension, and policy involving participation of small farmers in this project. The program surveyed over 1,100 farmers in three different agroecological regions about their knowledge, attitude, and practices related to agroforestry. The project included a farmer outreach program which faced an interesting constraint. The forestry department which was attempting to do outreach had in the past frequently arrested farmers for noncompliance with forestry laws.

Dove, Michael R. 1987. *Report #1. Household-Level Factors Affecting Interest in Planting Trees and Operating Nurseries: The Punjab.* Islamabad, Pakistan: Office of the Inspector General of Forests, Forestry Planning and Development Project.

_____. 1987. *Report #2. Household-Level Factors Affecting Interest in Planting Trees and Operating Nurseries: The NWFP.* Islamabad, Pakistan: Office of the Inspector General of Forests, Forestry Planning and Development Project.

_____. 1987. *Report #3. Household-Level Factors Affecting Interest in Planting Trees and Operating Nurseries: Baluchistan.* Islamabad, Pakistan: Office of the Inspector General of Forests, Forestry Planning and Development Project.

_____. 1987. *Report #4. Village-Level Factors Affecting Interest in Farm Forestry: The Punjab, NWFP, Baluchistan.* Islamabad, Pakistan: Office of the Inspector General of Forests, Forestry Planning and Development Project.

_____. 1987. *Report #5. Prospects for Farm Forestry on Rainfed Versus Irrigated Farms: The Punjab, NWFP, Baluchistan.* Islamabad, Pakistan: Office of the Inspector General of Forests, Forestry Planning and Development Project.

_____. 1987. *Report #6. Prospects for Wood-Dung Fuel Replacement through Farm Forestry Development: The Punjab, NWFP, Baluchistan.* Islamabad, Pakistan: . Office of the Inspector General of Forests, Forestry Planning and Development Project.

Dove, Michael R., Nasrullah Khan Aziz, Jamil A. Qureshi. 1988. *Report #7. Farmer Preferences for the Timing of Tree-planting: The Punjab, NWFP, Baluchistan.* Islamabad, Pakistan: Office of the Inspector General of Forests, Forestry Planning and Development Project.

- **Forestry Project Monitoring Methods Revised**
  Nepal, 1986

The Community Forestry Development Project provides technical assistance to a cooperative project between the Government of Nepal and a World Bank forestry development and training project which had as its goals establishment of village forests, management of village level forests, and distribution of tree seedlings for private planting. One component of the project is monitoring local conditions and project progress. Donald A. Messerschmidt, a FAO consultant, was assigned to revise the existing data collection guidelines for the project. The guidelines were developed over a three year period and included a annual schedule for regular monitoring and evaluation, forms for various types of reports, procedures for the determination of certain measures, and some simple statistical procedures.

Bhattarai, Tara N., J. Gabriel Campbell, Donald N. Messerschmidt. 1986. *Data Collection Guidelines for Monitoring and Evaluation of Community Forestry Activities in Nepal.* Field Document No. 12. Kathmandu: Community Forestry Development Project. HMG/UNDP/FAO.

- **Social Science Instruction in Forestry**
  Nepal, 1987

Donald A. Messerschmidt, a consultant for USAID and the Institute of Forestry (IOF) in Nepal, developed recommendations for Nepali IOF staff interested in improving social science training offered by the institute. Content of the curriculum included anthropological theory such as ethnocentrism, the cross cultural approach and holism. His plan included criteria for student evaluation and a section dealing with sources of published materials useful to social scientists.

Messerschmidt, Donald A. 1987. *Working Paper on a Social Science Curriculum for the Institute of Forestry, Nepal.* Kathmandu: U.S. Agency for International Development.

(Steve Morin)

GERIATRIC SERVICES

- **People and Pets Program Researched in Ithaca**
  United States, 1982

Anthropologist Joel Savishinsky and a student team from Ithaca College studied the volunteer-based Cornell Companion Animals Program which provided pets and visitation services to three nursing and geriatric institutions in Ithaca, New York. The research focused on a number of goals tapped through data collected through participant-observation. Topics addressed included the development of the project; assessment of volunteer, residents, and staff feelings about the Companion Animal Program; and assessment of how the project was meeting its goals.

Savishinsky, Joel S., Rich Lathan, Mari Kobayakawa and Andrea Nevins. 1983. *The Life of the Hour: A Study of People and Pets in Three Nursing Homes.* Ithaca, NY: Department of Anthropology, Ithaca College.

- **Needs Assessment in Housing Project for Elderly**
  United States, 1984

At the request of the Chair of the Board of Directors of the Casabe housing project for the well-elderly, the Department of Community Medicine of Mount Sinai Medical School provided technical assistance in doing a needs assessment. The primary goal of the assessment was to, "gather information that could lead to designing specific service projects which could contribute to meeting resident's perceived needs." The housing project provides housing for 135 Hispanic and African American residents at an East Harlem site.

Freidenberg, Judith with Rafael Rivera-Muniz. 1987. *Being Old in East Harlem: The People of Casabe.* New York: Health Services Research and Development Unit, Department of Community Medicine, Mount Sinai School of Medicine.

- **Los Angeles American Indian Elder Needs Assessment**
  United States, 1987

Public hearings, carried out in 1982, indicated that there was little statistical information available on the American Indian elderly population of Los Angeles and that this population had special needs. Mr. Lincoln Billedeaux, the founder of the Los Angeles American Indian Council on Aging, and anthropologist Joan Weibel-Orlando cooperated to develop a proposal to fund a needs assessment and outreach project focused on this population. The project, when funded, was directed by anthropologist Josea Kramer. Needs data were collected from 328 persons using an interview schedule which obtained data on demographics, socio-economic situation, health circumstances, and assessment of functionality. Questions were also asked concerning the types of activities, services, and programs for a planned American Indian senior center. The schedule, developed by Weibel-Orlando, made use of substantial input from community members and agencies. Emphasis was placed on disseminating the research results to agencies serving the needs of American Indian elders in the community and the Los Angeles County Area Agency on Aging incorporated project findings into its planning process. The Project received an Achievement Award from the National Association of Counties. The large Los Angeles data set was expanded to a national perspective in a related project directed by Kramer. The national study of urban elders made use of data from the academic research literature, reports of service providers in urban areas with significant American Indian populations, and federally funded demonstration projects.

Kramer, B. Josea, Donna Polisar and Jeffrey C. Hyde. 1990. *Study of Urban American Indian Aging.* Los Angeles, CA: Public Health Foundation.

Weibel-Orlando, Joan and Josea Kramer. 1989. *Urban American Indian Elders Outreach Project, A Cooperative Needs Assessment Research, Outreach and Linkage Effort.* Final Report, Administration on Aging Demonstration Project. Los Angeles, CA: Los Angeles County Area Agency on Aging.

- **Dementia Sufferers and Care Givers in London**
  United Kingdom, 1987

Joel Savishinsky carried out an applied research project assessing the situation of families trying to care for elderly, demented relatives at home in the London Borough of Islington. Specifically, the goal of the project was to identify the strengths and weaknesses in the existing system of care, and to develop recommendations for improving the supports for dementia sufferers and their caregivers. The data were derived through participant observation and interviews. Those interviewed included staff of public and private agencies and caregivers. The project was done in collaboration with the Centre for Environmental and Social Studies in Ageing at the Polytechnic of North London, and with the advocacy organization, Age Concern.

Savishinsky, Joel S. 1989. *Dementia Sufferers and Their Carers: A Study of Family Experiences and Supportive Services in the London Borough of Islington.* A Report Prepared for the Working Party on Dementia Sufferers and Their Carers, Conceived by Islington Age Concern. Ithaca: Department of Anthropology, Ithaca College.

_____. 1990. *Dementia Sufferers and Their Carers: A Study of Family Experiences and Supportive Services in the London Borough of Islington.* London: PNL Press.

_____. 1990. The Defiance of Hope: Dementia Sufferers and their Carers in A London Borough. In *The Home Care Experience: Ethnography and Policy.* Jay Gubrium and Andrea Sankar, eds. Newbury Park, CA: Sage Publications.

GOVERNMENT AND ADMINISTRATION

- **Foundation for Colonial Administration Laid**
  Cape Colony, 1880

The government of Cape Colony established a "commission of enquiry" which examined the "customs and institutions of the native populations."

Myres, J. L. 1928. The Science of Man in the Service of the State. *Journal of the Royal Anthropological Institute of Great Britain and Ireland* LIX:19-52.

- **Anthropologists Involved in Tribal Affairs**
  Philippines, 1901

David P. Barrows, along with Merton L. Miller and Albert Jenks, organized the Bureau of Non-Christian Tribes. Barrows was named its first Chief. Barrows strongly emphasized the importance of sound ethnology as the basis for effective administration.

Eggan, Fred. 1974. Applied Anthropology in the Mountain Province, Philippines. In *Social Organization and the Applications of Anthropology, Essays in Honor of Lauriston Sharp*. Robert J. Smith, ed. Ithaca: Cornell University Press.
Barrows, David P. 1902. *Report of the Bureau of Non-Christian Tribes of the Philippine Islands for the Year Ended August 31, 1902*. Washington, DC: Philippine Commission, Bureau of Insular Affairs, War Department.

- **Government Anthropologist Hired**
  Nigeria, 1906

The first government anthropologist appointed in Africa was W. Northcote Thomas. He served in Nigeria and later in Sierra Leone. Thomas' appointment was precipitated by a crisis concerning the applicability of indirect rule policies to the Ibo.

Lackner, Helen. 1973. Social Anthropology and Indirect Rule. The Colonial Administration and Anthropology in Eastern Nigeria: 1920-1940. In *Anthropology and the Colonial Encounter*. Talal Asad, ed. New York: Humanities Press.

- **Anthropologist Appointed to the Board of Indian Commissioners**
  United States, 1909

Warren K. Moorehead, an archaeologist from Phillips Academy, was appointed by President Theodore Roosevelt to the Board of Indian Commissioners. He remained on the board until it was dissolved in 1933.

Stewart, Omer C. 1961. Kroeber and the Indian Claims Commission Cases. Alfred L. Kroeber: A Memorial. *Kroeber Anthropological Society Papers.* No. 25 (Fall).

- **Government Anthropologist Hired**
  Gold Coast, 1920

W. S. Rattray was appointed to the newly created post of Government Anthropologist.

Kuper, Adam. 1973. *Anthropologists and Anthropology, the British School, 1922-1972.* London: Allen Lane.

- **Meek Census Commissioner**
  Nigeria, 1921

C. K. Meek was appointed census commissioner. Meek was an administrative officer who had received anthropological training. Meek's work resulted in the gathering of ethnographic data as part of Nigerian census operations.

Hailey, W. H. 1957. *An African Survey.* Revised 1956. London: Oxford University.

- **Government Anthropologist Hired**
  New Guinea, 1921

The first government anthropologist, W. M. Strong was appointed by Sir J. N. P. Murray. Strong was trained in medicine. He was succeeded by F. E. Williams.

Chinnery, W. P. 1933. Applied Anthropology in New Guinea. *Report of the 21st Meeting of the Australian and New Zealand Association for the Advancement of Science.* pp. 163-175.

- **Australian Administrators Use Anthropologists**
  New Guinea, 1922

The first appointment of a staff anthropologist to assist the administrator of the Australian New Guinea Territories led to expanded use of anthropologists in unique functional areas by the Australians. Anthropologists did general ethnography, as well as working on administratively defined problems.

Williams, F. E. 1939. Creed of a Government Anthropologist. *Report of the Australian and New Guinea Association for the Advancement of Science,* Vol. 24.
_____. 1951. *The Blending of Cultures: An Essay on the Aims of Native Education.* Port Moresby, Territory of Papua: Government Printer.

- **Ethnology Apparatus Established for Native Administration**
  Union of South Africa, 1925

The government created an Ethnological section of the Native Affairs Department. Kuper notes, "the work of this body--later much expanded--has never gone much beyond the routine of making ethnological censuses, advising on the claims of various candidates for chiefships, and, more recently, devising pseudo-traditional forms of tribal administration" (Kuper 1973:128).

Kuper, Adam. 1973. *Anthropologists and Anthropology, the British School, 1922-1972.* London: Allen Lane.

- **Meek and Talbot Posted to Study Administration**
  Nigeria, 1927

C. W. Meek and P. Talbot were posted to Southern Nigeria in order to investigate the breakdown of local administration there. According to Kuper, the role of government anthropologists did not become institutionalized in West Africa.

Kuper, Adam. 1973. *Anthropologists and Anthropology, the British School, 1922-1972.* London: Allen Lane.
Meek, C. W. 1937. *Law and Authority in a Nigerian Tribe.* London: Oxford University Press.

- **Administrator-Anthropologist Teams Established**
  Tanganyika, 1928

District officer-anthropologist teams were developed on an experimental basis to improve administration. The anthropologist served as a staff consultant, providing information but not plans for action. The project was carried out by G. Gordon Brown and A. H. Hutt.

Brown, G. Gordon and A. M. Hutt. 1935. *Anthropology in Action.* London: Oxford University Press.

- **John Collier Appointed**
  United States, 1932

John Collier was appointed Commissioner of Indian Affairs in the Roosevelt administration. Through him a very large number of anthropologists were hired.

Spicer, Edward H. 1977. Early Applications of Anthropology in North America. In *Perspectives on Anthropology, 1976.* Anthony F. C. Wallace et al, eds. Washington, DC: American Anthropological Association.

- **Administrators Become Anthropologists**
  Sudan, 1942

In the British Colonies, a large number of administrative officers received training in anthropology. Some of these contributed useful works to the basic ethnographic literature on the administered peoples. One example is P. P. Howell, who not only worked as a District Officer in Anglo-Egyptian Sudan, but ultimately obtained a D. Phil. in anthropology.

Howell, P. P. 1954. *A Manual of Nuer Law, Being an Account of Customary Law, Its Evolution and Development in the Courts Established by the Sudan Government.* London: International African Institute by Oxford University Press.

- **Anthropologist Appointed Advisor to Princely State**
  India, 1944

The anthropologist, Christoph von Furer-Haimendorf, became involved in a variety of social programs when appointed tribal advisor to the Government of Hyderabad.

von Furer-Haimendorf, Christoph. 1944. Aboriginal Education in Hyderabad. *Indian Journal of Social Work* 5(2).

- **Lauriston Sharp Appointed in State Department**
  United States, 1945

Lauriston Sharp served as Assistant Chief of the Division of Southeast Asian Affairs in the Department of State. Sharp's coworkers included Cora Dubois and Raymond Kennedy. Following this experience Sharp developed the program of instruction in applied anthropology at Cornell.

Smith, Robert J. 1974. Introduction. In *Social Organization and the Applications of Anthropology: Essays in Honor of Lauriston Sharp*. Ithaca: Cornell University Press.

- **State Department Hires Anthropologists**
  United States, 1950

The Technical Cooperation Administration of the U.S. Department of State was established. This organization hired anthropologists.

Voegelin, Erminie W. 1953. United States. In *International Directory of Anthropological Institutions*. William L. Thomas, Jr., and Anna M. Pikelis, eds. New York: Wenner-Gren.

- **Anthropologist to Staff Administrative Position**
  American Samoa, 1951

The Samoan Affairs Officer position was created to advise the American civilian government on native affairs. The position was to be filled by a cultural anthropologist.

MacGregor, Gordon. 1955. Anthropology in Government: United States. In *Yearbook of Anthropology, 1955*. William L. Thomas, ed. New York: Wenner-Gren.

- **Government Programs Studied**
  United States, 1953

The Mutual Security Administration of the United States used social scientists, including anthropologists, to study their various programs in Southeast Asia.

McNamara, Robert L. 1953. The Role of a Social Science Adviser to a STEM Mission. *Economic Development and Culture Change* (5):390-393.

■ **Anthropologist on the Frontier**
India, 1954

Verrier Elwin was appointed advisor for Tribal Affairs by the North East Frontier Agency. The efforts in N.E.F.A. were coupled with basic ethnography research programs.

Fuchs, Stephen. 1969. Applied Anthropology in India. In *Anthropology and Archaeology, Essays in Commemoration of Verrier Elwin*. M. C. Pradhan, R. D. Singh, P. K. Misra, and D. B. Sastry, eds. London: Oxford University Press.

■ **Nash Appointed Commissioner of Indian Affairs**
United States, 1961

After an earlier political career as administrative assistant to President Harry S. Truman and Lieutenant Governor of Wisconsin, Philleo Nash was nominated by President Kennedy as U.S. Commissioner of Indian Affairs. This was not done without difficulty as Nash explains, "I have to say to other applied anthropologists that I was confirmed in spite of being an anthropologist, not because of it. The Senate of the United States in those days did not think it wise to have a believer in the worth of indigenous cultures serving as Commissioner of Indian Affairs" (1979:23).

Landman, Ruth H. and Katherine Spencer Halpern, eds. 1989. *Applied Anthropologist and Public Servant: The Life and Work of Philleo Nash*. NAPA Bulletin 7. Washington, DC: National Association for the Practice of Anthropology.
Nash, Philleo. 1979. Anthropologist in the White House. *Practicing Anthropology* 1(3):3,23,24.

■ **Anthropologist Appointed Tribal Commissioner**
India, 1967

Nirmal Kumar Bose was appointed Commissioner for Scheduled Castes and Scheduled Tribes by the President of India. In a general sense his task was to provide an assessment annually, to the President of the Republic, as to whether the constitutional protections for these groups were properly functioning. The three years Bose spent in this post were marked by extensive travel and consultation with the groups he was to

134

serve.   According to Sinha's account, his work was consistent with his Gandhian ideology in that it stressed sympathy to the "weakest of the weak" and emphasis on self-determination and "interdependence with other groups" (Sinha 1986:81).

Bose, Nirmal K. 1968. *Report of the Commissioner for Scheduled Castes and Scheduled Tribes.* New Delhi.
Sinha, Surajit. 1986. *Nirmal Kumar Bose, Scholar Wanderer.* New Delhi: National Book Trust, India.

- **Anthropologist Placed on Advisory Committee for Andaman Islands**
  India, 1976

The Ministry of Home Affairs, in conjunction with the Andaman and Nicobar Island Administration, established a special advisory committee to execute a plan to improve the circumstances of the various hunting and gathering groups of the Andaman Islands. T. N. Pandit was appointed to the Committee in 1976.   The Committee's program involved the development of separate plans for each of the four resident groups: the Onge, Jarawa, Great Andaman and Sentinalese. In spite of these efforts the populations of these groups continued to decline.

Pandit, T. N. 1985. The Tribal and Non-tribal in Andaman Islands: A Historic Perspective. *Journal of the Indian Anthropological Society* 20:111-131.

- **Training of Traditional Leadership Evaluated**
  Swaziland, 1989

Edward C. Green directed an evaluation of the efforts of the USAID supported Swaziland Manpower Development Project. The project trained traditional leaders in an array of content areas tailored to participant needs. Green surveyed a sample of local leaders derived from the attendance lists of "development workshops" stratified by region. Green found that there were more local organizations functioning, local development efforts had increased, chiefs were more directly involved, and people were more willing to contribute money than in the past.

Green, Edward C. 1989. *Local Leaders and Development Training in Swaziland: Evaluation of Traditional Sector Training.* Washington, DC: Swaziland Manpower Development Project, Transcentury Corporation.
_____. 1984. *Traditional Leadership, Community Participation and Development Education.* Mbabane: USAID/Swaziland.

HEALTH AND MEDICINE

- **Early Nurse Anthropologist**
United States, 1936

According to George Foster, Esther Lucille Brown was the first anthropologist to make significant contributions to anthropology and nursing.

Brown, Esther Lucille. 1936. *Nursing as a Profession.* New York: Russell Sage.
_____. 1948. *Nursing for the Future.* New York: Russell Sage.
_____. 1961. *Newer Dimensions of Patient Care, Part 1, The Use of the Physical and Social Environment of the General Hospital for Therapeutic Purposes.* New York: Russell Sage Foundation.
_____. 1962. *Newer Dimensions in Patient Care, Part 2, Improving Staff Motivation and Competence in the General Hospital.* New York: Russell Sage.
_____. 1964. *Newer Dimensions in Patient Care, Part 3, Patients as People.* New York: Russell Sage.

- **Early Public Health Work in Anthropology**
United States, 1944

The Navaho Door was published as an attempt to "educate and influence" the professional staff that provided health care to Navajo people. It argued against the displacement of traditional Navajo curing practices and had an impact on government policy. This represented an important attempt to bring the cultural relativism perspective to health planning.

Leighton, Alexander H. and Dorothea C. Leighton. 1944. *The Navaho Door.* Cambridge: Harvard University Press.
Leighton, Dorothea C. 1972. Anthropology in the Medical Context. *Medical Anthropology Newsletter* 4(1) 1-3.

- **Early Clinical Application of Anthropology**
United States, 1948

A Boston preventative psychiatry group, the Human Relations Service, was established. David F. Aberle served as a staff member researching family cases. This represents an early appearance of the anthropologist working in conjunction with a clinic.

Aberle, David F. 1950. Introducing Preventative Psychiatry into a Community. *Human Organization* 9(3):5-9.

- **Talladega Development Effort**
  United States, 1951

A group of citizens from Talladega, Alabama, approached the University of Alabama to find out the range of health services that might be available to them. This inquiry led to a research group being formed at the University that developed a working relationship with the Talladega community. The group for the most part limited its activities to research, but did consult on various problems. During the two years of the project, a community council was formed, a health inventory, and various development projects were carried out. Anthropologists in the project included Asael T. Hansen, Solon T. Kimball, and Marion Pearsall.

Kimball, Solon T. 1952. Some Methodological Problems of the Community Self-Survey. *Social Forces* 31:160-164.

_____. 1955. An Alabama Town Surveys its Health Needs. In *Health, Culture, and Community.* B. D. Paul, ed. New York: Russell Sage.

Kimball, Solon T. and Marion Pearsall. 1954. *The Talladega Story, A Study in Community Process.* University, Alabama: University of Alabama Press.

Pearsall, Marion. 1955. Community Self-Surveys and Mental Health Programs. *Alabama Mental Health* 7:1-3.

- **INCAP Sponsors Research**
  Guatemala, 1951

The Institute of Nutrition of Central America and Panama (INCAP) sponsored research to discover a means for overcoming resistance to their projects in a predominantly Indian community. Richard N. Adams researched the problem and identified a number of causes. These included defects in communication, political conflict between factions, a counter-productive social welfare program and an array of conflict-generating contrasts between local custom.

Adams, Richard N. 1952. La Antropologia Applicada en Los Programas de Salud Publica de la America Latina. *Boletin de la Oficina Sanitaria Panamericana* 33(4):298-305.

_____. 1953. Notes on the Application of Anthropology. *Human Organization* 12(2):10-14.

- **Health Programs Evaluated in Latin America**
United States, 1952

Anthropologists participated in the evaluation of the Latin American Health Development programs of the Institute of Inter-American Affairs. The Institute was a United States Government venture. The team which evaluated the broad spectrum ten year project included a number of anthropologists; George M. Foster (El Salvador and Chile), Charles Erasmus (Columbia and Ecuador), Isabel T. Kelly (Mexico), Kalervo Oberg (Brazil), and Ozzie Simmons (Peru and Chile).

Foster, George M. 1953. Use of Anthropological Methods and Data in Planning and Operation. *Public Health Reports* 68(9):841-857.
_____. 1976. Medical Anthropology and International Health Planning. *Medical Anthropology Newsletter* 7(3):12-18.

- **Many Farms Project Develops Health Care Techniques**
United States, 1955

The Navajo-Cornell Field Health Project at Many Farms, Arizona, represented an early, sophisticated attempt to improve the quality of western health care delivery to a non-western population through the cooperative research and development efforts of a team of anthropologists and health care professionals. The project was carried out with the cooperation of the Navajo Tribal Government and the United States Public Health Service.

Adair, John. 1960. The Indian Health Worker in the Cornell-Navaho Project. *Human Organization* 19(2):59-63.
Richards, Cara E. 1960. Cooperation Between Anthropologists and Medical Personnel. *Human Organization* 19:64-67.
Rabin, David L., et al. 1965. Untreated Congenital Hip Disease: A Study of the Epidemiology. Natural History, and Social Aspects of the Disease in a Navajo Population. *American Journal of of Public Health* 55(2) Supplement.

- **Half-way House Therapy Modality Based on Anthropological Theory**
United States, 1956

The Rehabilitation Project of the Massachusetts Mental Health Center made use of a culture based therapy strategy. The project, which focused on a halfway house for mentally ill women, viewed the rehabilitation process in terms of socialization into society at large. Although the therapy was based on anthropological theory, it was administered by a

138

social worker. An anthropologist was attached to the project as a researcher.

Landy, David. 1961. A Halfway House for Women: Preliminary Report of a Study. In *Mental Patients in Transaction.* Springfield: Charles C. Thomas.

- **USPHS Anthropologist Studies Hospitalized Natives**
  United States, 1956

The U.S. Public Health Service, as part of its program of tuberculosis treatment and control, contracted with various hospitals in Seattle, Washington to provide treatment to Alaskan Natives. This required that individual patients be hospitalized far from home. Margaret Lantis, who was one of the few anthropologists working for P.H.S. on a direct-hire basis, was requested to study the problems of Inuit hospitalized in Seattle.

Lantis, Margaret L. and Evelyn B. Hadaway. 1957. How Three Seattle Tuberculosis Hospitals Have Met the Needs of Their Eskimo patients. Paper presented to the National Tuberculosis Association, Kansas City, Missouri.

- **Early Medical Anthropology Dissertation**
  United States, 1959

Margaret Clark completed the first medical anthropology doctoral dissertation. George Foster served as her mentor.

Clark, Margaret. 1959. *Health in the Mexican-American Culture.* Berkeley, CA: University of California Press.

- **Nurse-Anthropologist Collaboration**
  United States, 1963

An early example of the benefits of including behavioral science faculty in medical schools is an evaluation study carried out by anthropologist Marion Pearsall, in collaboration with the Department of Nursing of the University of Kentucky. The anthropologist-nurse collaboration led to an effective refocus of nursing services.

Pearsall, Marion and M. Sue Kern. 1967. Behavioral Science, Nursing Services, and the Collaborative Process: A Case Study. *Journal of Applied Behavioral Science* 3(2) 243-270.

- **TB Eradication Program Started**
  United States, 1963

An anthropologist-physician team initiated a program designed to eradicate tuberculosis in Martin County, Kentucky. The strategy involved coordination of health care agencies from within and from outside the community, a combination of both social science and medical expertise, integration of both clinical and public health approaches and the use of action research techniques.

Hochstrasser, Donald. 1966. Community Health Work in Southern Appalachia. *Mountain Life and Work* 42(3):7-16.

_____. 1966. It's All-Out-War on TB in an Appalachian County. *Bulletin National Tuberculosis Association*. 52(1):3-8.

Hochstrasser, Donald., G. S. Nickerson and Kurt W. Deuschle. 1966. Sociomedical Approaches to Community Health Programs. *Milbank Memorial Fund Quarterly* 44(3):345-359.

- **Specially Trained Nurse Anthropologists Graduate**
  United States, 1965

The first Nurse-Anthropologists were graduated. These individuals were the products of federally sponsored programs which provided training in anthropology to registered nurses. In 1969, the Society for Medical Anthropology organized its Committee on Nursing and Anthropology. Madeline Leininger served as the initial chair.

Leininger, Madeline M. 1967. The Culture Concept and its Relevance to Nursing. *The Journal of Nursing Education.* 6(2): 27-39.

_____. 1968. The Significance of Cultural Concepts in Nursing. *Minnesota League for Nursing Bulletin.* 16(3):3-12.

_____. 1970. *Nursing and Anthropology: Two Worlds to Blend.* John Wiley: New York.

- **Society for Medical Anthropology Organizational Meeting**
  United States, 1967

What was later to be called the Society for Medical Anthropology held its first formal organizational meeting at the American Anthropological Association meetings in Washington. The steering committee consisted of Clifford R. Barnett, Donald A. Kennedy, Benjamin D. Paul, Marion Pearsall, Steven Polgar, Norman A. Scotch, Ailoh Shiloh, Hazel H. Weidman, and Paul E. White.

140

1968. Medical Anthropologists Meet. *Fellow Newsletter* 9(2):3.

- **African American Neighborhood Clinic Studied for Pennsylvania Department of Health**
United States, 1968

As a staff researcher of the Pennsylvania Department of Health Ira E. Harrison researched interaction between patients and "non-therapist personnel" at an urban neighborhood clinic that served a largely African American clientele. The data were obtained during clinic hours using relatively unstructured observation supplemented by interviews. The research report made recommendations concerning spatial arrangements, hiring of lay staff and African American professionals, and local needs assessment.

Harrison, Ira E. 1969. *Observations in a Black Neighborhood Clinic, a Progress Report.* Working Paper No. 69-1, Division of Behavioral Science, Bureau of Planning, Evaluation and Research, Pennsylvania Department of Health.

- **Community Health Facilities Planned through Charette Process**
United States, 1970

A charette is a means of organizing public discussions for community problem solving. The process involves general meetings supplemented by small group discussions on special topics aided by outside experts. General sessions are constituted on the basis of problem solutions formulated in the small group sessions. One such charette was carried out in York, Pennsylvania with the goal of improving community health services. Anthropologist Ira E. Harrison, at the time Public Health Behavioral Scientist for the Pennsylvania Department of Health, served as a consultant to the York Charette.

Harrison, Ira E. and Norma Browand. 1970. *Community Health Process and York Charette Action.* Behavioral Science Working Paper, 70-2. Pennsylvania Department of Health.

- **Culture Brokerage Techniques Developed**
United States, 1971

The Health Ecology Project was developed in Miami, Florida, to incorporate anthropological theory and knowledge into "the training of health professionals, the structure of the health care system, and the delivery of health care" (Weidman 1976:106). A key concept in the project is that of culture broker. The culture broker is a collaborating professional member of the health-care delivery team who serves as link and mediator between a cultural group and the health care providers.

Bryant, Carol A. 1975. The Puerto Rican Mental Health Unit. *Psychiatric Annals* 5(8):333-338.

Carroo, Agatha E. 1975. A Black Community in Limbo. *Psychiatric Annals* 5(8): 320-323.

Lefley, Harriet P. 1975. Approaches to Community Mental Health: The Miami Model. *Psychiatric Annals* 5(9):315-319.

Sandoval, Mercedes C. and Leon Tozo. 1975. An Emergent Cuban Community. *Psychiatric Annals* 5(9):324-332.

Weidman, Hazel H. 1971. Trained Manpower and Medical Anthropology: Conceptual, Organizational and Educational Priorities. *Social Science and Medicine* 5(1):15-36.

_____. 1973. Implications of the Culture-Broker Concept for the Delivery of Health Care. Paper presented at the meetings of the Southern Anthropological Society, Wrightsville Beach, North Carolina.

_____. 1974. Toward the Goal of Responsiveness in Mental Health Care. Paper presented at Department of Psychiatry, University of Miami.

_____. 1975. Concepts as Strategies for Change. A Psychiatric Annals Reprint. New York: Insight Communications.

_____. 1976. In Praise of the Double Bind Inherent in Anthropological Application. In *Do Applied Anthropologists Apply Anthropology?* M. Angrosino, ed. Proceedings of the Southern Anthropological Society, No. 10. Athens: University of Georgia Press.

Weidman. Hazel H. and Janice A. Egeland. 1973. A Behavioral Science Perspective in the Comparative Approach to the Delivery of Health Care. *Social Science and Medicine* 7(ll):845-860.

- **Down's Syndrome Children Assessed**
United States, 1972

Physical anthropologist Christine Conk was employed by the Developmental Evaluation Clinic, Children's Hospital, Medical Center in Boston, Massachusetts as a member of a team diagnosing and recommending treatment for mentally retarded children. Using anthroposcopy and anthropometry, she carried out phenotypic and growth assessment of children suspected of mental retardation to determine if they had abnormal phenotypes. In addition, she conducted a longitudinal study of Down's syndrome children, collaborating with a nutritionist in order to monitor their well being and regulate their diet.

Cronk, Christine E. 1976. Statural growth in Down's Syndrome Children, Birth to Three Years. *American Journal of Physical Anthropology* 44:173.
_____. 1976. Physical growth. In *A Manual for Home Training Specialists of the Multihandicapped Child.* Massachusetts Department of Mental Health.

■ **Health Education Courses Examined for Effectiveness**
Sri Lanka, 1974

George M. Foster, working for the World Health Organization, evaluated curricula in behavioral sciences at the University of Sri Lanka, faculty of medicine. The short term consultation made recommendations concerning staffing, curriculum structure, and student aid.

Foster, George M. 1975. *Behavioral Science Research in Sri Lanka.* SEA/HE/75, World Health Organization, South-east Asia Region.

■ **Latina Mother and Infant Project**
United States, 1974

The Latina Mother-Infant Project was developed to serve the needs of Latin mothers in Chicago. It emerged from a coalition of community leaders, mental health professionals, and anthropologists. Anthropologists Gwen Stern and Stephen Schensul participated as researchers and proposal developers. This effort led to an NIMH funded research project to produce a community data base. The approach was collaborative and community members were trained to do the research. The developing data base was used to improve services for community women. The project was able to put together a series of services for women based on the data which they collected. What emerged was the Dar a Luz Program that provided prenatal and health education for women and other community members and post partum visits and other kinds of support.

Stern, Gwen. 1985. Research, Action and Social Betterment. *American Behavioral Scientist* 29(2):229-248.

■ **Therapeutic Anthropology Discussed**
United States, 1975

According to Ailon Shiloh, the first reference to therapeutic anthropology in print was in a discussion of the question, "what is applied anthropology?" developed by Alvin W. Wolfe and published in *Human*

Organization. Shiloh suggested that therapeutic anthropologists receive special training and become a kind of health professional which treats patients.

Anonymous. 1975. What Is Applied Anthropology? *Human Organization* 34:370.
Shiloh, Ailon. 1977. Therapeutic Anthropology: The Anthropologist as Private Practitioner. *American Anthropologist* 79(2):443-445.

- **Feasibility of Hearing Aid Use Determined**
  United States, 1975

The United States Public Health Service contracted Joe R. Harding to assist in developing methodologies for determining the acceptability of hearing aid use at Zuni Pueblo, New Mexico.

Harding, Joe R. and Jefferson Boyer. 1976. *Determination of Zuni Perceptions of Otitis Media Treatments and Attributes: A Methodology and Some Pilot Results.* Chapel Hill, NC: Policy Research and Planning Group.

- **Hispanic Health Council Project Initiated**
  United States, 1976

Puerto Rican Health Task Force was established to deal with a number of problems in health care delivery in Hartford, Connecticut. Consisting of community activists and anthropologists, the group developed a research, action, and proposal development agenda to improve health care delivery to the Hispanic population of the community. Various anthropologists were involved in these activities. Stephen Schensul and Pertti Pelto provided important early leadership. Funds were obtained to support the creation of the Hispanic Health Council. Jean J. Schensul became the associate director.

Backstrand, Jeffrey R. and Stephen Schensul. 1982. Co-evolution in an Outlying Ethnic Community: The Puerto Ricans of Hartford, Connecticut. *Urban Anthropology* 11(1):9-37.
Borrero, Maria G., Jean J. Schensul and Robert Garcia. 1982. Research Based Training for Organizational Change. *Urban Anthropology* 11(1):129-153.
Pelto, Pertti J., Maria Roman, Nelson Liriano. 1982. Family Structures in an Urban Puerto Rican Community. *Urban Anthropology* 11(1):39-58.
Schensul, Jean J. Iris Nieves, and Maria D. Martinez. 1982. The Crisis Event in the Puerto Rican Community. *Urban Anthropology* 11(1):101-128.
Schensul, Stephen L. 1979. Medical Anthropology in the Community. *Medical Anthropology* 3(3):365-382.

Schensul, Stephen L. and Maria Borrero. 1982. Introduction: The Hispanic Health Council. *Urban Anthropology* 11(1):1-8

Schensul, Stephen L. and Jean J. Schensul. 1982. Helping Resource Use in a Puerto Rican Community. *Urban Anthropology* 11(1):59-80.

Schensul, Stephen L., Maria G. Borrero, Victoria Barrera, Jeffery Backstrand, and Peter Guarnaccia. 1982. A Model of Fertility Control in a Puerto Rican Community. *Urban Anthropology* 11(1)81-100.

- **Zuni Otitis Media Concepts Studied for Indian Health Service**
  United States, 1976

The Sensory Disabilities Program of the Indian Health Service (IHS) of the U.S. Public Health Service started a major program to remedy otitis media and the related hearing losses. This type of infection has extraordinarily high incidence on Indian reservations in the United States. In addition there was resistance to the use of hearing aids. Anthropologists Joe R. Harding and Jefferson Boyer contracted with the Program to develop and field test a "concept elicitation instrument" and a "belief elicitation instrument" which could be used to determine people's knowledge of sensory disabilities and other health problems, available services and their feelings toward them, and perceptions of appropriateness of the services for existing health problems.

Harding, Joe R. and Jefferson Boyer. 1976. *Determination of Zuni Perceptions of Otitis Media Treatments and Attributes: A Methodology and Some Pilot Results*. Report to Sensory Disabilities Program, IHS. Chapel Hill, NC: Policy Research and Planning Group.

- **Use Rates of Rural Health Care Facilities Studied**
  El Salvador, 1976

Polly F. Harrison undertook a study of factors influencing use rates of health care facilities in rural settings. The study was motivated by the apparently high availability of health care in the rural countryside and the low use rates. The research focused upon variables which were called "social" and "intellectual distance." This focus was expressed by examining the "quantity and quality of the personnel staffing fixed facilities," appropriateness of role performance of staff to local needs, and user satisfaction. The research also considered certain health-related, non-clinical behaviors.

Harrison, P. F. 1976. *The Social and Cultural Context of Health Delivery in Rural El Salvador: Implications for Programming.* AID Contract 519-127.

- **Maternal and Child Health Program Studied**
  Philippines, 1978

U.S. Agency for International Development carried out a social feasibility study of the Targeted Maternal and Child Health program that was on-going at various sites in the Philippines. The goal of the research was to "obtain an indication of the types of socio-cultural variables which affect people's participation in the program."

Jansen, William H., II. 1978. *Beliefs, Behavior and Perceptions of Participants in a Philippine Nutrition.* National Nutritional Council of the Philippines and U.S. Agency for International Development.

- **Malaria Control Issues Studied by AID Anthropologist**
  India, 1978

U.S. Agency for International Development anthropologist William H. Jansen produced a socio-cultural overview of malaria control issues in India. The analysis noted some of the constraints that India's National Malaria Eradication Program faced in achieving its goals. Some of these constraints are the immense size of the Indian population, the extent of cultural diversity, and issues related to the social acceptance of techniques used in malaria control. This study was based on review of published and unpublished literature.

Jansen, William H. II 1978. *National Malaria Control in India: A Consideration of Some Socio-cultural Variables.* Washington, DC: U.S. Agency for International Development.

- **Foster Consults on Health Education Program**
  Malaysia, 1978

The Public Health Institute of the Ministry of Health of the Government of Malaysia initiated a post-graduate course in health education with some United Nations funding. During later phases of implementation, George M. Foster served as a consultant to the program. His activities included course development and evaluation procedures development.

Foster, George M. 1979. *Assignment Report.* MAA/MCH/00l. Regional Office for the Western Pacific, World Health Organization.

- **Navajo Health Studied**
  United States, 1978

The Mental Health Branch of the Navajo Area Office of the Indian Health Service (NAIHS) hired an anthropologist to conduct applied research in an action setting to deal with relocation of Navajo from the Hopi portion of Federal Joint Use Area (FJUA). The relocation resulted in physical and emotional illnesses. Martin Topper, the anthropologist was to gather data on relocatee problems, study impact on NAIHS of relocatee requests, and provide consultation to NAIHS and other agencies on relocation impact reduction. Background information was gathered through newspapers, legal documents, agency-commissioned studies, agency staff interviews, and Navajo and Hopi statements. The information was used to plan intervention.

Topper, Martin D. 1987. FJUA Relocation: Applying Clinical Anthropology in a Troubled Situation. In *Anthropological Praxis: Translating Knowledge Into Action.* R. Wulff and S. Fiske, eds. Boulder: Westview.

(Steven E. Maas)

- **WHO Immunization Program Evaluated**
  Cameroon, 1979

An Expanded Programme on Immunization (EPI) was established in Yaounde, the national capital, in 1975. An evaluation involving anthropologist Judith Brown, attempted to determine why the project had not achieved its goals. The evaluation examined four general factors which could have affected immunization coverage. These were, target population socio-economic characteristics, the nature of the system for providing immunization, parent's knowledge, and community attitudes. The study made use of data primarily from previously completed health surveys as well as key informant interviews. One neighborhood was surveyed anew.

Brown, Judith et al. 1980. *Identifying the Reasons for Low Immunization Coverage: A Case Study of Yaounde.* United Republic of Cameroon, World Health Organization, EPI/GEN/80/4.

- **Health Education Training Evaluated**
  Ghana, 1979

The Primary Health Training for Indigenous Healers (PRHETIH) Program was initiated. This program had as its goal the improvement of health care in a rural district, through training various types of healers. The project was conceived and designed by a group which included anthropologist Dennis M. Warren. Some of the topics addressed in the training were hygienic preparation and preservation of medicinal herbs, houseflies and the spread of disease, storage of medicinal herbs in a liquid form, weaning foods, basic first aid, and vaccination--indigenous and western.

Warren, D. M. and Mary Ann Tregoning. 1979. Indigenous Healers and Primary Health Care in Ghana. *Medical Anthropology Newsletter* 11(2): 11-13.
Warren, D. M., G. Steven Bova, Mary Ann Tregoning and Mark Kliewer. 1981. Ghanaian National Policy Towards Indigenous Healers: The Case of the Primary Health Training for Indigenous Healers (PRHETIH) Program. Paper presented at Society for Applied Anthropology Meetings, Edinburgh.

- **Integrated Basic Services Project for Children Evaluated**
  Malawi, 1979

UNICEF and the government of Malawi entered into an agreement to establish what was called an Integrated Basic Services Project. The objectives of this project were to "objectively improve the basic living conditions of the children, their families and neighbors" in certain target areas and to deliver services in "an integrated and comprehensive fashion." The project design called for the active participation of beneficiaries. The project was to be directed at four general areas. These are health, environmental sanitation and water supply, primary education, and food storage and nutrition. This project had a monitoring and evaluation component which included anthropologist Bruce T. Williams.

Williams, Bruce T. 1980. *Integrated Basic Services Project: A Baseline Survey.* UNICEF/Malawi, Centre for Social Research, University of Malawi.

- **Washington, DC Infant Death Rate Studied**
  United States, 1979

Margaret Boone, a medical anthropologist funded by the National Science Foundation, researched the sociocultural basis of high infant death rate in

Washington, DC. She worked one and a half years at a public hospital in an attempt to understand the sociocultural basis of poor maternal and infant health among inner-city Blacks. Her hospital activities included supervision of research assistants and collection of data for a case/control study of women with low-weight and women with normal-weight infants. Absence of prenatal care, smoking, alcoholism, psychological distress, violence in personal lives, ineffective contraception, and rapidly-paced child bearing were found to be implicated in low birth weight or death of infants.

Boone, Margaret S. 1989. *Capital Crime: Black Infant Mortality in America.* Newbury Park, CA: Sage.

_____. 1987. Practicing Sociomedicine: Redefining the Problem of Infant Mortality in Washington, D. C. In *Anthropological Praxis: Translating Knowledge Into Action.* R. Wulff and S. Fiske, eds. Boulder: Westview.

_____. 1985. Policy and Praxis: Anthropology and the Domestic Health Policy. In *Training Manual in Medical Anthropology.* Carole E. Hill, ed. Washington, DC: American Anthropological Association.

_____. 1982. A Socio-Medical Study of Infant Mortality Among Disadvantaged Blacks. *Human Organization 41(3):227-236.*

(Steven E. Maas)

- **Oral Rehydration Therapy Project Evaluated**
  Honduras, 1980

Oral rehydration therapy is a treatment for the dehydration associated with diarrhea. Anthropologist Carl Kendall served as the field director of this A.I.D. funded project. ORT consists of an inexpensive, effective solution that can be prepared and administered orally to children at home. The project really focused on increasing acceptance in use through multi-media health education. The field study focused upon communication exposure, diarrhea morbidity, anthropometric assessment, as well as nutritional and medical beliefs. Research was done in 18 rural communities with combined population of 5000.

Kendall, Carl. 1981. *An Ethnographic Evaluation of the Honduran Village Health Worker Program: A Controlled Comparison of Two Villages.* Project No. P-47-81. Tegucigalpa, Honduras: USAID, Integrated Rural Health.

- **Health Education Training Project Examined**
  Cameroon, 1980

The Practical Training in Health Education Project was initiated by the Cameroon Government in 1978 to improve community organization as it related to health promotion and to increase the knowledge of health education by health personnel and others involved in development. This project was assisted by research done by anthropologists Judith E. Brown and Tony L. Whitehead. The research team was charged with identifying the social units which were "meeting basic human needs in the Kadey Department of Eastern Province" and to recommend the social units which should be worked with in the effort to improve health and health knowledge.

Brown, Judith E., Edmond Ndjikeu and Tony L. Whitehead. 1981. *Socio-anthropological Study of Selected Populations of the Kadey Department, Eastern Province, United Republic of Cameroon.* Practical Training in Health Education Project.

- **Traditional Birth Attendant Training Program Evaluated**
  Peru, 1980

Judith Davidson, was contracted by AID and Occidental Petroleum, Peru, to evaluate the Peruvian Ministry of Health traditional birth attendant (TBA) training program aimed at decreasing maternal and infant mortality and morbidity. Her goals were to examine the effectiveness of the program's efforts at upgrading TBA performance and to provide program improvement recommendations. Input of Ministry of Health personnel was requested at each research phase to increase chance of recommendation utilization. The evaluation design was aimed at discovering whether and why TBAs followed training instructions and was divided into three phases.

Davidson, Judith R. 1987. The Delivery of Rural Reproductive Medicine. In *Anthropological Praxis: Translating Knowledge Into Action.* R. Wulff and S. Fiske, eds. Boulder: Westview.

(Steven E. Maas)

- **Mexican-American Folk Remedies that Cause Lead Poisoning Researched**
  United States, 1980

Robert Trotter, funded by numerous state and federal agencies set out to determine the extent that a harmful lead-based folk remedy was used in Mexican-American communities and then create and implement projects to eliminate such use. He carried out ethnography with folk healers and herb shop owners to determine the extent and type of lead use.

150

Development of culturally sensitive health education content encouraged people to switch to harmless remedies. Trotter consulted with the agency concerning the necessity of a nation-wide initiative to solve the problem of lead poisoning.

Trotter, Robert T., II. 1987. A Case of Lead Poisoning from Folk Remedies in Mexican American Communities. In *Anthropological Praxis: Translating Knowledge Into Action.* R. Wulff and S. Fiske, eds. Boulder: Westview.

(Steven E. Maas)

- **Health Education for Sanitation and Water Project Developed**
  Swaziland, 1981

The Academy for Educational Development began a five-year health education project to combat diseases related to impure water and poor sanitation. Swaziland, like many developing countries, suffers from a number of diseases resulting from poor environmental sanitation, improper excreta disposal and contaminated water supplies. The project development process as aided by a knowledge, attitudes, and practices study carried out by anthropologist Edward C. Green. This research project, funded by U.S. Agency for International Development, was intended to provide baseline data for the health education program while it provided guidance for the public health and sanitation engineering components of the project.

Green, Edward. 1982. *A Knowledge, Attitudes, and Practices Survey of Water and Sanitation in Swaziland.* Swaziland: Health Education Unit, Ministry of Health and Water Borne Disease Control Project.

- **Maternal and Child Project Instituted in Hartford**
  United States, 1982

Using a collaborative research model, a team, including anthropologist Jean J. Schensul, developed a project in response to health problems in the Puerto Rican/Hispanic community of Hartford, Connecticut and expressed it in a grant proposal to the federal government. The grant request sought to reestablish a health care role based on the traditional midwife/birth attendant role extant in Puerto Rico, termed the *comadrona*. This process required the reestablishment of other traditional practices, improvement of understanding of the reproductive health care needs of Puerto Rican women, and increasing community based support networks.

Schensul, Jean J., Donna Denelli-Hess, Maria G. Borrero, and Ma Prem Bhavati. 1987. Urban Comadronas: Maternal and Child Health Research and Policy Formulation in a Puerto Rican Community. In *Collaborative Research and Social Change, Applied Anthropology in Action.* Donald D. Stull and Jean J. Schensul, eds. Boulder, CO: Westview Press.

- ### Situation of Traditional Healers Assessed in Swaziland
  Swaziland, 1982

The Ministry of Health of Swaziland requested that the Health Planning and Management Project provide information on traditional healers. The Project obtained the services of Edward C. Green, an anthropologist with an A.I.D. project, and Lydia Makhuba, an administrator at the University of Swaziland, to complete a study. The request grew out of meetings called by the King to discuss royal policy toward traditional medicine. Subsequently, the Ministry of Health developed concern for the availability of manpower in the modern health sector. Green and Makhuba were called upon to examine a number of policy questions relating to traditional healers to be trained as paraprofessionals in the modern sector and potential for developing a professional association for healers.

Green, Edward C. and Lydia Makhuba. 1983. *Traditional Healers in Swaziland: Toward Improved Cooperation Between the Traditional and Modern Sectors.* Swaziland: Ministry of Health.

- ### Community Health Organizations Studied
  Swaziland, 1983

Edward C. Green researched community organization and mobilization for health for the Swaziland Ministry of Health in response to information needs for the U.S.A.I.D. funded Rural Water-Borne Disease Control Project. The project called for the establishment of 200 local sanitation committees, and the research was to help assess the feasibility of this task. This research project could be best described as a base-line study of health related organizations in rural Swaziland villages. The research identified all the different types of committees that related to health. The research also intended to assess the variation in organizational potential in communities and to derive principles of successful project implementation.

Green, Edward C. 1983. *Community Mobilization for Health and Development in Swaziland.* Washington, DC: Academy for Educational Development and the Swaziland Ministry of Health.

- **ORT Community Acceptance Studied**
Haiti, 1984

Jeannine Coreil evaluated community acceptance of oral rehydration therapy in Haiti, on behalf of the Maternal and Child Health Program of the Pan American Health Organization. Oral rehydration therapy makes use of a solution of sugar and salt to replace body fluids lost during diarrheal episodes. It has demonstrable effectiveness in preventing death of young children and others who are suffering severe diarrheal disease. In 1983, UNICEF, WHO/PAHO, AID, and the Haitian Ministry of Health mounted a national campaign to disseminate information and encourage use of rehydration salt packets with the goal of reducing diarrhea-related deaths by one half. The campaign included public education through mass media, community outreach, and other communication channels and commercial sale of the salts. The salts, conforming to WHO standards, were sold for about 15 cents in a foil protected packet. The analysis carried out by Coreil revealed a number of interesting results. The research found that fully a third of the preschool children surveyed had diarrhea during the preceding week. The analysis found that there were no significant cultural barriers to ORT use. In addition, diarrhea, classed as a hot disease, was viewed as being treatable by ORT solutions, seen as cold in this folk classification. The research found that although there was widespread knowledge of the basic recipe for ORT, many did not know the relative amounts of the various ingredients, or added some others.

Coreil, Jeannine. 1985. *Community Acceptance of Oral Rehydration Therapy in Haiti. Final Report, Project No. 107USA4.* Pan American Health Program, Maternal and Child Health Program, CDD Operational Research.

- **Hispanic Health Council Surveys Pediatric Impairments**
United States, 1984

The Hispanic Health Council of Hartford, Connecticut pediatric impairments survey produced baseline data on the prevalence of physical and developmental impairments among Puerto Rican children, 0 to 5 years of age. Also collected were updates on the demography of the Puerto Rican community of Hartford and health service use patterns and related constraints. The survey instruments were based on pilot interviews with selected families and a translation of components of a standard questionnaire used for developmental assessments. The research found that the impairment rate was in the upper range of national comparison data. The director of the project was Jean J. Schensul.

Schensul, Jean J., Nydia Orozco and Lisa Allen. 1985. *Puerto Rican Pediatric Impairments Survey.* Hartford: Hispanic Health Council.

- **Oklahoma Adolescent Health Needs Assessed**
United States, 1984

The Oklahoma Adolescent Health Project undertook to document the need for adolescent clinical services throughout Oklahoma. The Project, funded by the Robert Wood Johnson Foundation to improve and consolidate the health care services of adolescents, was active at a number of sites in Oklahoma. Oklahoma health statistics reveal substantial health problems among adolescents, including substance abuse, sexually transmitted diseases, unintended pregnancies, and many other health problems. Anthropologist Robert F. Hill of the University of Oklahoma Health Services Center consulted with the project to provide a "contextual profile" of each of the adolescent health clinics. These data were complemented by data on program usage in terms of client age strata, health problems presented, and clinic visited. The data were collected from eight clinics and summarized in descriptive profiles. The research demonstrated the high demand for adolescent clinic services.

Hill, Robert F. 1985. *Adolescent Clinic and Community Profile Study. Oklahoma Adolescent Health Project.* A Report to the Robert Wood Johnson Foundation. Oklahoma City, OK.

- **Anthropologist Evaluates Onchocerciasis Control Program**
West Africa, 1985

A multidisciplinary team, including anthropologist Antoinette B. Brown, assessed the mid project impact of the massive, multi-donor Onchoceriasis Control Program (OCP) initiated in 1974. Onchoceriasis or river blindness is a parasitic disease transmitted by the bite of the female blackfly. The Program was to reduce the incidence of the disease through vector control and the subsequent dying out of the parasite by interrupting its life cycle. In the ten years of its existence, OCP has resulted in dramatic reduction in incidence of the disease and opening up 15,000,000 hectares of land in formerly infested areas. It was estimated, for example, that 27,000 cases of river blindness have been prevented in Birkina Faso alone since the start of the project. The impact review took place over a number of weeks. After travel to the headquarters of OCP in Ouagadougou, Birkina Faso, team members interviewed project staff and others and reviewed documents. The team found the project to be a model program.

154

Kelly, Jim, Clive J. Shiff, Howard C. Goodman, Larry Dash, Antoinette B. Brown, Ali Khalif Galaydh. 1986. *Impact Review of the Onchoceriasis Control Program Ouagadougou, August 1985.* AID Project Impact Evaluation Report No. 63. Washington, DC: AID.

■ **Handbook for Operations Research on Community Organization in Health Developed**
World, 1985

The Center for Human Services maintains the Primary Health Care Operations Research (PRICOR) project to promote operations research as a practice useful to program managers and policy makers in "designing and operating primary health care (PHC) programs." As part of this commitment, PRICOR developed a series of five monographs on OR to better transfer the knowledge of OR practice to development personnel working in the developing world. Anthropologist Barbara L. Pillsbury participated in the development of the monograph on Community Organization. Working with a team that included a committee of consultants, Pillsbury and her coauthors provided a text on the use of OR in community organization as it relates to primary health care. Operations research as conceived by PRICOR consists of three phases. These are, "1) systematic analysis of the operational problem, 2) application of the most appropriate analytical methods to identify the best solution(s) to the problem; and 3) validation of the solutions(s)" (Goldsmith, Pillsbury and Nicholas 1985:2).

Goldsmith, Arthur, Barbara Pillsbury and David Nicholas. 1985. *Operations Research Issues, Community Organization.* Chevy Chase, MD: Primary Health Care Operations Research, Center for Human Services.

■ **Mixe Traditional Medical Treatment Compiled for Community Use**
Mexico, 1986

A team of anthropologists and health professions worked with a number of Mixe consultants, trained in traditional medical treatment procedures, to compile a guide to certain traditional remedies for use by the people of the Municipio de San Juan Guichicovi. The pamphlet focused on diseases such as diarrhea, dysentery, susto, evil eye as well as others and was published by the Instituto Nacional Indigenista. Done as part of the Instituto's Program for Redemption of Traditional Medicine, the work encouraged use of herbal remedies. Interestingly the plants mentioned in the text were made available as seed or propagation stock through a cooperating botanic garden. Involved in the project were anthropologists Michael Heinrich (University of Freiburg) and Paloma Escalante (Metropolitan Autonomous University).

Instituto Nacional Indigenista. 1986. *Remedios Caseros Mixes.* San Juan Guichicovi, Oaxaca: Subdireccion de Bienestar Social, INI.

- **Child Health Baseline Data Compiled**
  Central America and Panama, 1986

The baseline was compiled with the support of USAIDs Regional Office on Central American Programs as a part of a multi-donor "Child Survival Program." Its purpose is to provide country-level and regional baseline data for use in subsequent evaluations. Related to this effort were attempts to improve the quality of the information systems and to establish specific sites for un-going monitoring. Anthropologist Elizabeth Burleigh, who compiled the baseline, traveled to Belize, Guatemala, El Salvador, Honduras, Costa Rica, and Panama to obtain data on demography, health personnel, health facilities, oral rehydration projects, immunization, mortality, and morbidity.

Burleigh, Elizabeth. 1987. *Child Survival Baseline 1985 for Central America and Panama.* Guatemala: Regional Office on Central American Programs, USAID.

- **Public Health Project Evaluated**
  Belize, 1987

A multidisciplinary team, including anthropologist Donald A. Messerschmidt, assessed interim progress in project implementation of the Improved Productivity Through Better Health (IPTBH) project funded by U. S. Agency for International Development. This $7,000,000 project was directed at malaria control, mosquito control, potable water delivery, and sanitation. Health education, community participation, and training were important aspects of the project. The data were collected through formal and informal interviews with government officials, A.I.D. mission and contractor staff, and field trips. The evaluation team found that the project, while technically sound, did not place sufficient emphasis on community participation and the goals in health education were not being met. As a formative evaluation the project team was concerned with redirecting the project to decrease its shortfalls. This concern was shown in the fact that three quarters of the evaluation report consisted of recommendations directed at the government officials, A.I.D. mission and contractor staff, as appropriate.

Barbiero, Victor K., Robert A. Gearheart, Donald A. Messerschmidt. 1987. *Evaluation Report, Increased Productivity for Better Health.* (Project 505-0018). Arlington, VA: Vector Biology and Control Project.

- **AIDS Researched in Community Setting**
United States, 1987

The Community Outreach Prevention Program [COPE] of Hartford, CT worked with IV drug users and their sex partners to educate at-risk persons and help prevent AIDS. The project interviewed and served large numbers of individuals who were referred to AIDS prevention programs in the community. The goal of the project is to provide culturally appropriate AIDS prevention services through education, group counseling, crisis intervention, referrals, and limited case management. Anthropologist Jean J. Schensul was involved in project design and implementation. The project was funded by the Centers for Disease Control and local sources.

AIDS Community Research Group. 1989. *AIDS Knowledge, Attitudes and Behaviors Survey in a Multi-ethnic Neighborhood of Hartford.* Hartford: Institute for Community Research.

- **Syphilis Ethnography Done for Health Department**
United States, 1990

In order to improve Oregon's Multnomah County government's understanding of a regional syphilis epidemic, Martha Balshem and her associates Deborah van Rooyen and Kathy Girod, completed an ethnographic study which focused on the relationship between syphilis transmission and the use of illegal drugs, especially crack cocaine. The County was especially concerned with low compliance with syphilis testing and treatment. The research team interviewed service providers and persons at risk. High risk interviewees were recruited through various agencies and networking. Some standard questions were asked of each interviewee on gender, age, ethnicity, residence, education, and employment. Questions were also asked about whether the interviewee was a professional sex worker or if they used the services of such workers. Questions were also asked about drug use and trading sex for drugs. The data analysis/presentation included use of extended quotations and frequency tabulations of structured questions and interview narrative as well as the research team's analytical narrative. The analysis showed the differences between expert theories and folk theories of the cause of this disease and produced a series of recommendations.

Balshem, Martha, Deborah van Rooyen, Kathy Girod. 1990. *Final Report: Syphilis Ethnographic Study.* Submitted to Multnomah County Health Department, Portland, OR.

HOUSING

- ## Women's Anthropological Society of Washington Supports Muckraking Housing Research
United States, 1896

Founded in 1885 as an alternative to the then all-male Washington Anthropological Society, the Women's Anthropological Society of Washington showed a commitment to dealing with pressing social issues. In 1896 the Women's Anthropological Society's Committee on Housing the People supported research into housing conditions in the District of Columbia. The research was carried out by Clara de Graffenried who was employed by the Department of Labor. The Society soon sponsored the creation of the Washington Sanitary Housing Improvement Company which provided improved housing to the poor.

Helm, June. 1966. *Pioneers of American Anthropology.* Seattle: University of Washington Press.
Kober, George M. 1927. *The History and Development of the Housing Movement in the City of Washington, 1897-1927.* Washington, DC: Washington Sanitary Housing Company.
Schensul, Stephen L. and Jean J. Schensul. 1978. Advocacy and Applied Anthropology. In *Social Scientists as Advocates, Views from the Applied Disciplines.* George H. Weber and George J. McCall, eds. Beverley Hills: Sage.

- ## Anthropologist as Housing Advocate
United States, 1966

Urban Planning Aid, an advocacy planning group in Boston, was created to serve an advocacy function in planning for certain lower income Boston neighborhoods. The organization made use of anthropologists in advocacy planning roles.

158

Peattie, Lisa R. 1968. Reflections on Advocacy Planning. *American Institute of Planners* 34:80-87.

- **Appropriate Housing Planning Techniques Explored**
  United States, 1970

Under contract with the Public Health Service, research was conducted on the Papago reservation to measure the impact of improved housing of the Department of Housing and Urban Development on health and work productivity, and evaluate the architectural and proxemic design of housing preferred by the Papago. Anthropologist Robert M. Wulff was site director with a project team that included public health personnel and Papago interviewers and translators.

Wulff, Robert M. 1972. *Housing the Papago: An Analytical Critique of a Housing Delivery System.* International Housing Productivity Report, University of California, Los Angeles.
_____. 1973. Papago Architecture and Modernization: Style and Proxemic Preferences. *Southwestern Anthropology Association Newsletter* (October)

- **Housing Needs Evaluated**
  Canada, 1971

The Manitoba Metis Federation engaged an anthropologist to evaluate their housing needs. J. N. Kerri evaluated the housing development efforts of the Remote Housing Project, in particular. The RHP, as it was called, was to provide houses and create jobs. The field work and survey covered 48 communities.

Kerri, James N. 1977. A Social Analysis of the Human Element in Housing: A Canadian Case. *Human Organization* 36(2):173-185.

- **Housing on the Border Studied**
  United States, 1973

The Bureau of Ethnic Research, Department of Anthropology, University of Arizona initiated a comprehensive survey of housing conditions of Douglas, Arizona under a Bureau of Community and Environmental Management, U. S. Public Health Service contract. The project was directed by Thomas Weaver. Data analysis was under the supervision of Theodore Downing.

Weaver, Thomas and Theodore Downing, eds. 1975. *The Douglas Report: The Community Context of Housing and Social Problems.* Tucson: Bureau of Ethnic Research, University of Arizona.

- **Housing Allowance Program Evaluated**
  United States, 1973

Anthropologists working in conjunction with Abt Associates, Inc., a Cambridge, Massachusetts consulting firm, were part of a team which carried out an evaluation of components of a so-called housing allowance program instigated by the Department of Housing and Urban Development. The component focused upon was the administrative agency experiment, that evaluated a model administrative structure.

Chambers, Erve J. 1977. Working for the Man: The Anthropologist in Policy Relevant Research. *Human Organization* 36(3):258-267.

- **Anthropologist Serves as Kaibab Planner**
  United States, 1978

The Kaibab Paiute Indian Reservation was awarded a HUD 701 Planning Assistance Grant. Southern Utah State College contributed expertise in research and development in exchange for student and faculty learning through participation in tribal and community affairs. Allen C. Turner designed and implemented a planning process through restored communal decision-making in order to improve the quality of reservation life. Turner attended meetings with the community planning committee where HUD grant terms were converted to Paiute concepts. Two basic principles were identified: change should be based on Paiute cultural patterns and change should be broadly beneficial to the community.

Turner, Allen C. 1987. Activating Community Participation in a Southern Paiute Reservation Development Program. In *Anthropological Praxis: Translating Knowledge Into Action.* R. Wulff and S. Fiske, eds. Boulder: Westview.

(Steven E. Maas)

- **Housing Development Planning Assisted by Anthropologist**
  Botswana, 1979

John Mason carried out a research project in response to the needs of planners and others, to help establish "minimal, acceptable national site and service standards" for low-income housing in Botswana. The study, which was carried out in Botswana's urban areas, was funded by the U.S.

Agency for International Development and implemented by FCH International, Inc. The research took the form of a needs assessment executed through a sample survey in four different settlement areas. The interview schedule items focused upon knowledge of, desire for and willingness to pay for urban services.

Mason, John. 1979. *Social Research of Resident Preference, Need and Ability to Pay: Towards a Framework for Physical Planning Standards in Botswana's Self Help Housing in Site and Service Areas.* Washington, DC: FCH International Inc.

■ **Limitations in Memphis Home Weatherization Program Identified**
United States, 1982

Four applied anthropologists from the Center for Voluntary Action Research (CVAR) at Memphis State University, worked with Memphis Light, Gas and Water (MLG&W) Division of the City of Memphis, in a two year project to develop an effective communication system between MLG&W and low-income residents. The primary goal was to increase participation in a no-interest, long-term home weatherization loan program. The project team included CVAR members and two MLG&W managers. Participant observation and unstructured interviewing in the target neighborhood uncovered prevalent grassroots beliefs about MLG&W and identified communication networks which helped inform the action program. Anthropologists from four other agencies with identifiable neighborhood interests joined the team to form an action coalition. Research results, that became the basis for development of an action agenda, were presented to agencies and neighborhood groups. Because of the research information provided, resources were reallocated and activities redirected in agencies. The coalition, through anthropologists' mediation role, brought about a twenty fold increase in number of weatherized units. More neighborhood units were weatherized in the first half of 1984 than in the previous seven years. Also, neighborhood associations were formed to work with public agencies for neighborhood improvements.

Hyland, Stanley, Bridget Ciaramitaro, Charles Williams, and Rosalind Cottrell. 1987. Redesigning Social Service Delivery Policy: The Anthropologist as Mediator. In *Anthropological Praxis: Translating Knowledge Into Action.* R. Wulff and S. Fiske, eds. Boulder: Westview.

■ **Native American Housing Researched**
United States, 1989

Working on behalf of the non-profit organization, Common Profits, Cynthia Cone's Hamline University class in applied anthropology researched housing problems of Native Americans in Minneapolis and St. Paul. They did this by interviewing ten Native Americans about housing and other aspects of their life. About half these people were from reservations and the rest were raised in the city. The analysis consisted of the construction of a narrative about various aspects of the housing problems of these people.

Cone, Cynthia, Diane Ledo, Linda Cartee and Bruce Larson. 1989. *In My Family's Moccasins, Issues in Native American Housing in Minneapolis and St. Paul.* St. Paul, MN: Department of Anthropology, Hamline University.

HUMAN RIGHTS, RACISM AND GENOCIDE

- **Conference on Racial Differences Established**
  United States, 1928

Franz Boas was one of the founding members of the Conference on Racial Differences sponsored by the National Research Council and the Social Science Research Council.

Stocking, George W., Jr. 1979. Anthropology as Kulturkampf: Science and Politics in the Career of Franz Boas. In *The Uses of Anthropology.* Walter Goldschmidt. ed. Washington, DC: American Anthropological Association.

- **Work Done on Human Rights Declaration**
  France, 1949

Anthropologists participated in early UNESCO attempts to develop the Universal Declaration of Human Rights.

Metraux, Alfred. 1951. UNESCO and Anthropology. *American Anthropologist* 53(2):294-300.
_____. 1953. Applied Anthropology in Government: United Nations. In *Anthropology Today.* A. L. Kroeber, ed. Chicago: University of Chicago Press.

- **Anthropologists Involved in UNESCO Anti-racism Program**
  France, 1949

UNESCO convened a scientific board in Paris, "to consider the desirability of initiating and recommending the general adoption of a program of disseminating scientific facts designed to remove what is generally known

162

as racial prejudice" (UNESCO 1961:491-494). A Declaration of Race was issued in 1950. This statement was developed by a group which included anthropologists.

> Comas, Juan. 1978. The International Fight Against Racism: Words and Realities. *Human Organization* 37(4) 334-344.
> UNESCO. 1961. *Race and Science. The Race Question in Modern Science.* New York: Columbia University Press.

- **Second Conference on Racism Held**
  France, 1951

UNESCO convened a second conference on racism to improve the document titled "A Declaration on Race and Racial Differences" published in 1950.

> Ashley-Montagu, M. F. 1951. *Statement on Race. An Extended Discussion in Plain Language of the UNESCO Statement by Experts on Race Problems.* New York: Henry Shuman.
> Comas, Juan. 1978. The International Fight Against Racism: Words and Realities. *Human Organization* 37(4):334-344.

- **Houston Racial Discrimation Researched by Art Gallaher**
  United States, 1961

The Houston Council on Human Relations and the Southern Regional Council cosponsored research into job discrimination toward Blacks in Houston, Texas. The project, which was directed by Art Gallaher, Jr., found extensive racial discrimination. The resulting report was concluded with the following statement, "How long can a major city of the United States continue to undertrain a sizable segment of its young people, limit their opportunities for entry into the labor market, hamper and restrict their employment advance, underutilize their professional skills, deprive them of job security, without serious consequences to the city's own economic and social advance?"

> Southern Regional Council. 1961. *The Negro and Employment Opportunities in the South.* Atlanta, GA: Houston Council on Human Relations and Southern Regional Council.

- **IWGIA Established in Denmark**
  Denmark, 1968

The International Work Group for Indigenous Affairs was established by a group of anthropologists from a number of countries. The initial impetus for this group were reports on "crimes and abuses" against various Indian populations which took place in a number of South American countries. Lars Person and Helge Kleivan acted in leadership roles initially. IWGIA's program includes monitoring the status of various native groups, international advocacy, publication on problems and abuses, and public education.

International Work Group for Indigenous Affairs. 1971. IWGIA, its work and experiences 1968-71. *IWGIA Newsletter* August 1971.

- **Conditions of Indians in Paraguay Investigated**
  Paraguay, 1978

David Maybury-Lewis was requested by the U.S. Agency for International Development to investigate the conditions of Indians in Paraguay and to determine if development funds could assist them. He visited various Indian sites. This survey dealt with a number of issues including accusations of Paraguayan government complicity in the raiding and murder of Indians there.

Cultural Survival, Inc. 1979. Paraguayan Update. *Cultural Survival Newsletter* 3(2):1-2.

- **Race Relations Certificate Program Approved**
  at York University
  Canada, 1989

Anthropologists and Sociologists at York University developed a certificate program in race relations in response to a series of racist incidents in the community, a needs assessment, and faculty concerns. The program of theoretical and practical study involved the development of sustained relationship between the community and the school.

Yawney, Carole D. 1990. Campus and Community: The Race Relations Certificate at York University. *Proactive* 9(1):3-12.

164

INDUSTRY AND BUSINESS

- **Early Industrial Anthropology**
New Guinea, 1921

The anthropologist, W. P. Chinnery, was appointed labor administrator in a New Guinea copper mine. This represents an exceptionally early use of anthropology in an industrial setting. His primary goal was maintaining a healthy and stable work force.

Chinnery, W. P. 1933. Applied Anthropology in New Guinea. *Report of the Twenty-First Meeting of the Australian and New Zealand Association for the Advancement of Science.* Sydney, New South Wales: Australian and New Zealand Association for the Advancement of Science.

- **Early Business Research in Anthropology**
United States, 1946

Along with W. Lloyd Warner, Burleigh B. Gardner established Social Research, Inc. to engage in consultation work with businesses. The organization was also staffed by psychologists and sociologists. The company did work in market research, business relations, and social change. One of the earliest clients was Sears, Roebuck and Company for which Social Research. Inc. developed an employee attitude survey scheme as part of a management information system.

Gardner, Burleigh B. 1978. Doing Business with Management. In *Applied Anthropology in America.* Elizabeth M. Eddy and William L. Partridge, eds. New York: Columbia University Press.

- **Anthropologist Studies Impact of Steel Plant Construction**
India, 1968

The Government of India started the planning of the Rourkela Steel Plant in Southern Orissa in the 1950s. This was part of their strategy of decentralized industrial development. As part of the applied research program of the Office of the Registrar General of India, B. K. Roy Burman carried out an assessment of the impact of the massive Rourkela Steel Mill project. Focused on the adaptive strategies of the displaced villagers, he showed how village coherence across caste lines increased as the resistance to resettlement increased. At first, resistance was activated by middle and small farmers, the wealthier and landless agriculturalists were initially much less resistant. When individual villages came to be specifically threatened, resistance became consolidated. Resistance took the form of non-cooperation and resulted in the Mill having trouble hiring workers.

Roy Burman, B. K. 1968. *Social Processes in the Industrialization of Rourkela (with reference to displacement and rehabilitation of tribal and other backward people)*. Mimeograph Series, Office of the Registrar General of India. New Delhi. Vol. 1.
_____. 1987. Political Anthropology of Displacement, Relocation and Future of Transfer of Technology: An Overview and Issues. In *Anthropology, Development and Nation Building*. A.K. Kalla and K.S. Singh, eds. New Delhi: Concept Publishing Company.

- **Industrialization Potential Determined in Arkansas**
  United States, 1971

Anthropologists participated in a multi-disciplinary research team which evaluated the potential for industrial development in a rural region of Arkansas. Government policy makers expressed concern that the local labor force manifested characteristics which would preclude effective industrial development. The Grinstead study revealed a high potential for success for potential workers.

Davis, R. N., B. L. Green and J. N. Redfern. 1975. *Low-Income Rural People in East Central Arkansas Face Roadblocks to Jobs*. Washington, DC: Agricultural Economic Report No. 200.
Grinstead, M. J. 1976. Poverty, Race and Culture in a Rural Arkansas Community. *Human Organization* 35(1):33-34.
Grinstead, M. J., B. L. Green and J. M. Redfern. 1974. *Social and Labor Adjustment of Rural Black Americans in the Mississippi Delta: A Case Study of Madison Arkansas*. Washington, DC Agricultural Economic Report, No. 274.
_____. 1975. *Rural Development and Labor Adjustment in the Mississippi Delta and Ozarks of Arkansas: A Summary Report*. Fayetteville, AR: Agricultural Experiment Station Bulletin 795.

- **HUD Study of Business Practices in Tribal Governments**
  United States, 1973

Under contract to the Department of Housing and Urban Development, anthropologists Theodore Downing and Thomas Weaver served as

166

researchers in a project to assess the business management practices and political organization of seven Arizona Indian reservations. The groups were Cocopah, Ak Chin, Fort McDowell, Camp Verde, Hualapai, Payson-Apache, and Havasupai.

Weaver, Thomas and Theodore Downing. 1974. *Office Procedures Manual for Seven Arizona Indian Reservations, Report of the Seven Reservations Project.* Tucson: Bureau of Ethnic Research, University of Arizona.
———. 1974. *The Tribal Management Procedures Study Report of the Seven Reservations Project.* Tucson: Bureau of Ethnic Research, University of Arizona

- **International Career Paths Studied at General Motors**
  United States, 1986

Elizabeth K. Briody of General Motors Research Laboratories and Marietta L. Baba of Wayne State University researched the development of individual career paths of those General Motors employees that have worked internationally for the firm. More specifically they addressed the issue of ease of repatriation of employees returning from international posts within General Motors. The data which they used were of two general types. The first, derived from GM publications, was directed at understanding what might be called the corporate ethnohistory of international operations and staffing. The second, derived from semi-structured interviews with GM employees returned from international assignments as well as their families and supervisors, focused on selection and repatriation experiences. Ease of repatriation was examined in terms of a measure of job satisfaction.

Baba, Marietta L. 1986. *Business and Industrial Anthropology: An Overview.* NAPA Bulletin 2. Washington, DC: National Association for the Practice of Anthropology.
Briody, Elizabeth K. and Marietta L. Baba. 1988. *Multiple Organizational Models and International Career Pathing at General Motors Corporation.* GMR-6161. Warren, Michigan: General Motors Research Laboratories.

LAND USE AND LAND CLAIMS

- **Omaha Lands Allotted**
  United States, 1885

The Omaha Allotment Act, which was a pilot for the General Allotment Act of 1887 (The Dawes Act), was passed. Alice Fletcher, who served as allotting agent to the Omaha and other tribes, lobbied for both acts. The promotion of the act was based on certain basic understandings of cultural dynamics, that is, private ownership would lead to assimilation. The act proved a tragedy for Native Americans, in spite of the planners' good intentions and the use of primitive culture change theory.

Lurie, Nancy O. 1966. Women in Early American Anthropology. In *Pioneers of American Anthropology: the Uses of Biography.* J. Helm, ed. Seattle: University of Washington Press.

- **Policy Study on Native Lands Carried Out**
United States, 1899

Charles C. Royce's comprehensive study entitled *Indian Land Cessions in the United States* was published by the Bureau of American Ethnology. Hinsley cites this as a, "continuation of Powell's earlier involvement in Indian policy" at the Bureau. He also suggests that it marks the "withdrawal from public concerns" of the Bureau.

Hinsley, Curtis M., Jr. 1979. Anthropology as Science and Politics: the Dilemmas of the Bureau of American Ethnology, 1879 to 1904. In *The Uses of Anthropology.* Walter Goldschmidt, ed. Washington, DC: American Anthropological Association.

- **Policy Concerns Motivate Early Research on Algonquian Hunting Territory**
Canada, 1910

Frank G. Speck carried out ethnographic research that allowed conceptualization of the idea of hunting territory among Algonquians. Speck presented this research in the larger political arena of Canada and the Province of Quebec. He was in support of establishing Algonquian land claims as having legal substance in a modern sense. Working in association with John M. Cooper, Speck attempted to influence the Hudson's Bay Company as well as federal and provincial governments to legally recognize native hunting territories and to give exclusive use to natives. They distributed a master map of hunting territories of Quebec and portions of Ontario and the Maritimes to the Hudson's Bay Company and Government of Canada. Quebec did establish exclusive use areas which forced the Company and Ottawa to do the same. Speck's basic research had the explicit purpose of improving native claims on their lands. Speck continued arguing his case through the 1940's. Feit argues that historically

168

there has be been a close relationship between theoretical and applied interests in the work of Canadian anthropology. This linkage, he also argues, has been largely unrecognized.

Feit, Harvey A. 1986. Anthropologists and the State: The Relationship Between Social Policy Advocacy and Academic Practice in the History of the Algonquian Hunting Territory Debate, 1910-50. Paper for the 4th International Conference on Hunting and Gathering Societies, London School of Economics and Political Science.

- **Homesteading Researched for Territorial Government**
  United States, 1935

Felix Keesing investigated aspects of Hawaiian homesteading patterns for the Hawaiian Legislature.

Kessing, Felix M. 1947. Applied Anthropology in Polynesia. *Applied Anthropology* 6:(2):22-25.

- **Southwest Land Use Studied for USDA**
  United States, 1935

The organization of the Rio Grande Socioeconomic Survey by the United States Department of Agriculture was completed. Directed at Native American, Mexican American, and Anglo-American residents of the Southwest, research focused on the cultural factors that had influenced land use. The concept of land use community was identified. This work was done under the aegis of the Soil Conservation Service established under the New Deal.

Kimball, Solon T. and John H. Provinse. 1942. Navaho Social Organization in Land Use Planning. *Applied Anthropology* 1(4):18-25.
Provinse, John H. 1942. Cultural Factors in Land Use Planning. In *The Changing Indian*. Oliver La Farge, ed. Norman: University of Oklahoma Press.

- **Papago Place Names Studied**
  United States, 1937

Ruth Underhill was employed by the so-called TC-BIA research group to study various aspects of Papago life. This was an early policy research activity of the Bureau of Indian Affairs. One facet which was selected for study was Papago place names. In early 1938, the TC-BIA submitted a report to the Office of Indian Affairs on place names. The report stimulated controversy because it was based on a minimal amount of field study. Papago Agency staff did the whole project over again with a greater emphasis on the Papago's viewpoint.

Papago Agency. n.d. *Place Names on the Sells, Gila Bend and San Xavier Indian Reservations.* Sells: Papago Agency, Department of the Interior.

- **Landholding Studied for Government Body**
  Mexico, 1940

As part of the research program of the Department of Native Affairs, a number of general studies of Indian communities were carried out. These studies focused on Mestizo relations. Spicer suggests that one of the "most successful" of these studies was done by Alfonso Fabila in Yaqui communities in northwest Mexico. Based on this research, a new form of landholding was recommended.

Fabila, Alfonso. 1940. *Las Tribus Yaquis y su Anhelada Auto-Determinación.* Mexico: Departmento de Asuntos Indigenes.

- **Oberg Appointed to Soil Conservation Board**
  United States, 1941

Anthropologist Kalervo Oberg was employed as Associate Coordinator of the Middle Rio Grande Board of the Soil Conservation Service of the United States Department of Agriculture. This organization served to coordinate various Federal Conservation and Development programs in that area of the Southwest.

Oberg, Kalervo, Allan G. Harper and Andrew R. Cordova. 1943. *Man and Resources in the Middle Rio Grande Valley.* Albuquerque: University of New Mexico Press.

- **Early Land Claims Cases Litigated**
  United States, 1944

Prior to the litigation stimulated by the Indian Claims Commission Act of 1946 there were many Indian tribes which filed suit against the American government for lost land. Stewart suggests that the number of anthropologists contributing to the preparation of these cases was quite limited. One case that was assisted by an anthropologist was filed by the Indians of California. These people were aided by C. Hart Merriam, a biologist turned ethnologist.

Stewart, Omer C. 1961. Kroeber and the Indian Claims Commission Cases. Alfred L. Kroeber: A Memorial. *Kroeber Anthropological Society Papers No. 25.*

- **Land Tenure Studied**
  Northern Rhodesia, 1945

Working as an auxiliary to the Native Land Tenure Committee a group of researchers from the Rhodes-Livingstone Institute undertook a survey of the Plateau Tonga of Mazabuka District of Northern Rhodesia. The team included anthropologist Max Gluckman. This research was directed at providing information concerning "proposals to establish a system of controlled and improved land-usage among the Tonga." The government had expressed concern that a class of large land owners was developing which was going to inevitably displace the subsistence farmer. The submitted report suggested that these concerns were unfounded. The large land owners were shown to represent less than one percent of the population and that they derived their land through customary law.

Allen, W., Max Gluckman, D. U. Peters, and C. G. Trapnell. 1948. *Land Holding and Land Use Among the Plateau Tonga of Mazabuka District.* Rhodes-Livingston Papers No. 14. Rhodes Livingstone Institute: Livingstone.

- **Land Claims Legislative Hearings**
  United States, 1946

The hearings, organized concerning the legislation that created the Indian Claims Commission, had few participating anthropologists. These were A. V. Kidder and Gene Weltfish, they testified for the American Civil Liberties Union.

Stewart, Omer C. 1961. Kroeber and the Indian Claims Commission Cases. Alfred L. Kroeber: A Memorial. *Kroeber Anthropological Society Papers No. 25.*

- **Indian Claims Commission Established**
  United States, 1946

The establishment of the Indian Claims Commission created many opportunities for ethnohistoric, archaeological, and ethnographic research for professional anthropologists. The commission, created in response to the Indian Claims Act of 1946, was to resolve issues associated with Indian land title, use, and occupancy. The act allowed most native groups in the United States to sue for compensation for lost lands.

Baerreis, David A. 1974. *Anthropological Report on the Chippewa, Ottawa, and Potowatomi Indians in Northeastern Illinois and the Identity of the Mascoutens.* New York: Garland.

Beals, Ralph L. and James A. Hester. 1974. *Indian Land Use and Occupancy in California.* New York: Garland.

Bell, Robert E. 1974. *Wichita Indian Archaeology and Ethnology: A Pilot Study.* New York: Garland.

Dobyns, Henry F. 1974. *Prehistoric Indian Occupation Within the Eastern Area of the Yuman Complex: A Study in Applied Archaeology.* New York: Garland.

Dobyns, Henry F. and Robert C. Euler. 1974. *Socio-Political Structure and Ethnic Group Concept of the Pai.* New York: Garland.

Ellis, Florence H. 1974. *Anthropological Data Pertaining to the Taos Land Claim.* New York: Garland.

Grosscup, Gordon L. 1974. *Northern Paiute Archaeology.* New York: Garland.

Gussow, Zachary. 1974. *An Anthropological Report on the Sac, Fox and Iowa Indians.* New York: Garland.

Hackenberg, Robert A. 1974. *Papago Indians: Aboriginal Land Use and Occupancy.* New York: Garland.

_____. 1974. *Aboriginal Land Use and Occupancy of the Pima-Maricopa.* New York: Garland.

Harvey, Herbert R. 1974. *The Luiseno--Analysis of Change in Patterns of Land Tenure and Social Structure.* New York: Garland.

Heizer, Robert F. 1974. *Indians of California.* New York: Garland.

Jablow, Joseph. 1974. *Illinois, Kickapoo and Potawatami Indians.* New York: Garland.

Kroeber, A. L. 1974. *Basic Report on California Indian Land Holdings.* New York: Garland.

Lurie, Nancy Oestrich. 1955. Anthropology and Indian Claims Litigation: Problems, Opportunities, and Recommendations. *Ethnohistory* 2:357-375.

Manners, Robert A. 1974. *An Ethnographic Report on the Hualapai (Walapai) Indians of Arizona.* New York: Garland.

Steward, Julian H. 1974. *Aboriginal and Historical Groups of the Ute Indiana of Utah; an Analysis with Supplement.* New York: Garland.

Stout, David B., Erminie W. Voegelin and Emily J. Blasingham. 1974. *Indians of E. Missouri, W. Illinois, and S. Wisconsin, from the Proto-Historic Period to 1804.* New York: Garland.

Taylor, Herbert C., Jr. 1974. *Anthropological Investigation of the Tillamook Indians.* New York: Garland.

United States Indian Claims Commission. 1974. *Commission Findings on the Sac, Fox and Iowa Indians.* New York: Garland.

_____. 1974. *Commission Findings on the Chippewa Indians.* New York: Garland.

172

Voegelin, Erminie W. and E. J. Blasingham. 1974. *Anthropological Report on the Indian Occupancy of Royce Areas 77 and 78*. New York: Garland.
Voget, Fred W. 1974. *Osage Research Project.* New York: Garland.

- **Alaska Native Land Use Researched for Bureau of Indian Affairs**
  United States, 1946

Walter R. Goldschmidt and Theodore H. Haas researched patterns of historic and contemporary land use among various natives of Southeastern Alaska. This research was done in response to proposed hearings "on possessory rights of the natives." The results of their research were submitted to the Commissioner of Indian Affairs. The research and hearings were carried out to resolve uncertainties concerning land occupancy amongst groups like the Tlingit and Haida.

Goldschmidt, Walter R. and Theodore H. Haas. 1946. *A Report to the Commissioner of Indian Affairs, Possessory Rights of the Natives of Southeastern Alaska.* mimeograph.

- **Kroeber as Expert Witness in Indian Claims**
  United States, 1952

A. L. Kroeber was retained as expert witness by the attorneys for "Indians of California" in their case before the Indian Claims Commission. Kroeber worked in this endeavor with the assistance of Robert F. Heizer, Edward W. Gifford, Samuel A. Barrett, S. F. Cook, and Donald Cutter. Kroeber developed an up-dated linguistic map of California for his testimony. *The Handbook of California Indians* produced by Kroeber was used in evidence. The government hired anthropologists to support their case. These persons included Julian H. Steward, William D. Strong, Harold Driver, Erminie Voegelin, Walter R. Goldschmidt, Abraham Halpern, and Ralph L. Beale.

Stewart, Omer C. 1961. Kroeber and the Indian Claims Commission Cases. *Kroeber Anthropological Society Paper No. 25.*

- **James Bay and Northern Quebec Agreement Negotiated**
  Canada, 1975

The James Bay and Northern Quebec Agreement (JBNQA), signed in 1975, was developed as a means to resolve legal injunctions against a massive hydro-electric project announced by the government of Quebec in

Indigenous people of Northern Quebec strongly opposed the project because of its impact on hunting and fishing resources. In response to the impasse caused by the injunction, the parties to the dispute entered into negotiation. The agreement was the product of the lengthy negotiation and represents the first modern aboriginal rights agreement in Canada. Provisions of the Agreement included: an income security program for persons who live by hunting, fishing and trapping; establishment of consultative bodies on subsistence and environmental provisions that included Cree and Inuit experts; writing of policy controlling wildlife and environment; legal allocation of wildlife to indigenous people as well as increases in Cree and Inuit control of social services. Indigenous communities were aided in the presentation of their case by anthropologist Harvey A. Feit. He was employed as advisor to Cree organizations during the negotiations that produced the JBNQA and also served as an appointee of the Cree Regional Authority to two government boards established to administer aspects of the agreement.

Feit, Harvey A. 1979. Political Articulations of Hunters to the State: Means of Resisting Threats to Subsistence Production in the James Bay and Northern Quebec Agreement. *Etudes/Inuit/Studies* 3(2):37-52.

_____. 1980. *The James Bay and Northern Quebec Native Harvesting Research Project: The Basis for Establishing Guaranteed Levels of Harvesting by Native Peoples of Northern Quebec.* Montreal: Cree Regional Authority.

_____. 1980. Negotiating Recognition of Aboriginal Rights: History, Strategies and Reactions to the James Bay and Northern Quebec Agreement. *Canadian Journal of Anthropology/Revue Canadienne d'Anthropologie* 1(2):159-172.

_____. 1982. Protecting Indigenous Hunters: The Social and Environmental Protection Regime in the James Bay and Northern Quebec Land Claims Agreement. In *Indian SIA: The Social Impact Assessment of Rapid Resource Development on Native Peoples.* Charles C. Geisler, Daniel Usner, Rayna Green and Patrick West, eds. University of Michigan Natural Resources Sociology Lab, Monograph No. 3. Ann Arbor.

_____. 1985. The Power and the Responsibility: Implementation of the Wildlife and Hunting Provisions of the James Bay and Northern Quebec Agreement. In *The James Bay and Northern Quebec Agreement, Ten Years After.* Sylvie Vincent, ed. Montreal.

Feit, Harvey A. and A. F. Penn. 1975. *Guaranteed Harvests for the People of Eastmain and Paint Hills Possibly Affected by the Project.* Montreal: Grand Council of the Crees. Mimeographed.

- **Land Use in Alaska Investigated**
  United States, 1975

Development in Alaska stimulated various types of policy studies. These include Nancy Yaw Davis's research on land use. Her efforts were intended to increase understanding of rural Alaskan culture change as this related to policy issues identified by the Federal-State Land Use Planning Commission. These issues included change and stability in subsistence activities, effects of cash-jobs, intra village and village government communication and social change.

Davis, Nancy Yaw. 1976. *Steps Toward Understanding Rapid Culture Change in Native Rural Alaska.* Federal-State Land Use Planning Commission for Alaska Study Number 16.

- **Aboriginal Land Rights Act passed by Australian Parliament**
  Australia, 1976

This legislation provided a means for native Australians to claim certain types of land, such as "unalienated crown land," for future use. These claims were filed through the Northern Land Council and included large amounts of linguistic and cultural data. The claims attempted to reestablish "traditional ownership" rather than obtaining compensation. In this way, the claims were different from the claims filed for compensation under the Indian Claims Commission Act in the United States. The research methodology included extensive interviewing with various claimants.

Toohey, John. 1981. *Alligator Rivers Stage II Land Claim.* Report by the Aboriginal Land Commissioner, Mr. Justice Toohey to the Minister for Aboriginal Affairs and to the Administrator of the Northern Territory. (Interim Edition).
Layton, Robert and Nancy Williams. 1980. *The Finniss River Land Claim: A Claim on Unalienated Crown Land in the Adelaide River-Batchelor-Wagart Reserve Area of the Northern Territory.* Darwin, Northern Land Council.

- **PNG Land Reform Commission Conducts Research**
  Papua New Guinea, 1979

The Law Reform Commission of Papua New Guinea conducted a Customary Law Project directed by Richard Scaglion. The project, funded by a National Public Expenditure Program Development Grant, was designed to gather information on customary legal systems in order to help develop a self-reliant national legal system based on indigenous customs and practices. Extensive archival research formed the basis for a bibliography of customary law in PNG. Field research, supervised by Bospidik Pilokos and Richard Scaglion, was conducted by some thirty researchers in all provinces. This research resulted in a large corpus of extended customary law cases which formed the basis for a summary of principles of customary law in a monograph. Specific problem areas, including homicide compensation, family law, and land law, were also investigated and draft legislation was prepared for submission to the National Parliament.

Law Reform Commission of Papua New Guinea. 1980. *Customary Compensation.* Report No. 11, Port Moresby.
Richard Scaglion. 1979. Formal and Informal Operations of a Village Court in Maprik. *Melanesian Law Journal* 7:116-129.
_____. 1981. Samukundi Abelam Conflict Management: Implications for Legal Planning in Papua New Guinea. *Oceania* 52:28-38.
_____. 1981. *Homicide Compensation in Papua New Guinea: Problems and Prospects.* Law Reform Commission of Papua New Guinea Monograph No. 1, Port Moresby.

- **Cultural Survival, Inc. Supports Land Demarcation Project**
  Ecuador, 1980

Cultural Survival, Inc. of Cambridge, Massachusetts assisted Ecuadorian agencies and various Huaroni, Siona-Secoya and Cofan Indians in a land demarcation project. The project was intended to assure an adequate land base for these three native groups. This was done in the face of encroachments of colonists and natural resource extraction. The Ecuador Land Demarcation Project was oriented toward the use of a mixed subsistence and cash economy.

Cultural Survival, Inc. 1980. Ecuador: Land Documentation. *Cultural Survival Newsletter* 4(4):10-11.

- **Action Research Undertaken with Big Mountain Navajo Community**
  United States, 1981

In order to settle the land conflict between the Hopi and Navajo, the Navajo and Hopi Indian Relocation Commission was established. This organization administered a plan to relocate both Navajos and Hopis from different areas under dispute. One such area was the Big Mountain community. Anthropologists John J. Wood and Walter M. Vannette were asked by the Director of the Navajo-Hopi Land Dispute Commission to investigate the human costs of relocating the Navajo Big Mountain Community. This analysis emphasized the cultural significance of sacred sites interpreted in terms of the American Religious Freedom Act. Data were collected through participant-observation and key informant interviewing and were presented at Senate hearings.

Wood, J. J. and W. M. Vannette. 1979. *A Preliminary Assessment of the Significance of Navajo Sacred Places in the Vicinity of Big Mountain, Arizona.* Flagstaff: Navajo and Hopi Indian Relocation Commission.

LANGUAGE AND ACTION

- **Linguist Leads Alphabetization Program**
  Mexico, 1939

Maurice Swadesh became the director of a national program for the introduction of alphabets and written materials in various languages. Swadesh took specific responsibility for the Tarascan program. Primers and other instructional materials were developed.

Spicer, Edward H. 1977. Early Applications of Anthropology in North America. In *Perspectives on Anthropology, 1976.* Anthony F. C. Wallace et al, eds. Washington, DC: American Anthropological Association.
Swadesh, Mauricio. 1940. *La Nueva Filologia.* Coleccion "Siglo XX" Mexico, D. F.: Biblioteca del Maestro.

- **Bilingual Education Training Grant Awarded**
  United States, 1977

The Cross-Cultural Resource Center of California State University, Sacramento was established under the Bilingual Education Act (PL 93-380). This project, developed by Steven F. Arvizu, was to "support training to improve the likelihood of success in programs of bilingual education" in a region that included Arizona, California, Nevada and some Pacific Territories.

Arvizu, Steven F. 1978. Home-School Linkages: A Cross Cultural Approach to Parent Participation. In *A Cultural Approach to Parent Participation.* Sacramento: Cross Cultural Resource Center.
Arvizu, Steven F. and Warren A. Snyder with Paul T. Espinosa. 1978. *Demystifying the Concept of Culture: Theoretical and Conceptual Tools Monograph I.* Sacramento: Cross Cultural Resource Center.
Gibson, Margaret A. and Steven F. Arvizu. 1978. *Demystifying the Concept of Culture: Theoretical and Conceptual Tools Monograph II.* Sacramento: Cross Cultural Resource Center.

Gil, Abjandra. 1978. The Changing Role Definition among Chicanas Revealed Through Life History Technique. In *A Cultural Approach to Parent Participation.* Sacramento: Cross Cultural Resource Center.

Guzman de Velasco, Isabel. 1978. A Guide for Effective Parent and Community Participation in Bilingual Bicultural Education. In *A Cultural Approach to Parent Participation.* Sacramento, CA: Cross Cultural Resource Center.

Ogbu, John U. 1978. *Cross Cultural Resource Center Institute on Parent Participation: An Evaluation Report.* Sacramento: Cross Cultural Resource Center.

Rich, George W. and Margaret A. Gibson. 1978. *Demystifying the Concept of Culture: A Teacher's Guide to the Cross-cultural Study of Games and Play, Monograph IV.* Sacramento: Cross Cultural Resource Center.

- ## Action Research Started with Kickapoo
United States, 1978

Using what he refers to as an action anthropology approach, Donald D. Stull started a project with the Kansas Kickapoo. The project produced linguistic research data that may be used in bilingual-bicultural programs in the future. This was supplemented by general research on Kickapoo ethnography. These activities are supported by the Tribal Council and have resulted in tangible benefits for the tribe. The ethnographic component of the research has resulted in a multimedia exhibit on traditions and change, improved historical documentation for the tribe and various planned publications.

Stull, Donald D. 1979. Action Anthropology among the Kansas Kickapoo, Paper presented at the Society for Applied Anthropology meetings at Philadelphia.

- ## Literacy Programs Evaluated
United States, 1980

U.S. Agency for International Development sponsored an evaluation of their efforts in the area of "non-formal adult literacy programs in AID" from the standpoint of their relation to their sociolinguistic context. The research was carried out by Susan J. Hoben. It included a literature review on language use and planning in emerging nations with emphasis on countries in which there were AID projects. There was also an analysis of project and evaluation documents from twenty literacy projects, of which seven were examined more closely. The process resulted in a series of recommendations concerning the integration of sociolinguistic information into AID literacy programs.

Hoben. S. J. 1980. *The Sociolinguistic Context of Literacy Programs: A Review of Non-formal Adult Literacy* AID Contract 147-PE-70.

■ **TV Station Call Letter Similarity Examined**
United States, 1982

Anthropological linguist J. Jerome Smith evaluated linguistic and semantic aspects of a set of new call letters for a Tampa, FL television station. The station claimed that the call letters proposed by another station were too similar to their own in a complaint to the Federal Communications Commission. The law firm of the complainant contracted with Smith to examine the similarity between the proposed call letters and the existing set, in anticipation of the FCC Hearings on the issue. When confronted with Smith's technical assessment, the station withdrew its application for new call letters.

Smith, J. Jerome. 1982. *Form and Meaning Relationships in Broadcast Station Call Letters: WFTS and WFTB Compared.* Tampa, FL: Department of Anthropology, University of South Florida.

■ **Feasibility of Reviving the Use of Kickapoo in Kansas Assessed**
United States, 1984

The Kansas Kickapoo Technical Assistance Project (KKTAP) carried out a study of the feasibility of reviving the use of Kickapoo among Kansas Kickapoo. The feasibility study was based on literature review and some previously collected field data. Kickapoo was no longer spoken in Kansas, although it remained in wide use in Oklahoma. The Kansas Kickapoo speak mostly English although a sizable minority are able to speak Potawatomi, a related language. The feasibility study identified a number of alternative approaches to linguistic revival including simple language appreciation workshops, incorporation of language courses in the Kickapoo Nation School and fully developed community-wide attempt to revive the language. In support of these alternatives resources were identified, including extant grammars, texts, and classrooms. KKTAP had developed a pilot project plan for implementing grade school and summer language camp instruction. This organization had participated in a number of development efforts on the Kickapoo Reservation. KKTAP was directed by Donald D. Stull. The feasibility study reported here was done by Liess Vantine.

Vantine, Liess. 1984. *Native American Language Instruction at the Kickapoo Nation School: A Feasibility Study.* Lawrence, KS: Center for Public Affairs, University of Kansas.

- **Hualapai Bilingual/Bicultural Education Program**
  United States, 1975

The Hualapai Bilingual/Bicultural Education Program was started to document these people's language and culture. Linguistic anthropologist, Akira Y. Yamamoto, extended the basic task collaboratively in many interesting ways. Many of the research products of the project were made available for use in Hualapai Schools. In addition he trained native-speakers to become researchers. In this way the relationship between Yamamoto and the community was transformed to a complex and productive collaboration.

Watahomigie, Lucille J. and Akira Y. Yamamoto. 1987. Linguistics in Action: The Hualapai Bilingual/Bicultural Education Program. In *Collaborative Research and Social Change, Applied Anthropology in Action.* Donald D. Stull and Jean J. Schensul, eds., Boulder, CO: Westview Press.

LAW AND REGULATION

- **Research into Native Law Carried Out**
  Bechuanaland, 1933

Anthropologist Isaac Schapera was hired to document native law and customs as a guide to the administration.

Schapera, Isaac. 1939. Anthropology and the Native Problem. *South African Journal of Science* 36:89-103.

- **Indonesian Traditional Law Documented**
  Netherlands, 1933

Van Vollenhoven's classic compilation of Indonesian customary law, adat, was published. The Dutch administration was highly committed to the use of indirect rule, hence they used adat as the basis of civil law in these territories. Van Vollenhoven's studies facilitated Dutch control.

van Vollenhoven, C. 1933. *La Decouverte du Droit Indonesien.* Paris.

- **Redfield Serves as Expert Witness**
  United States, 1950

Robert Redfield served as an expert witness in Sweatt v. Painter, as it was argued before the United States Supreme Court. This case, which dealt with a legal attack on segregated law school facilities at the University of Texas, anticipated Brown v. Board of Education. Redfield indicated that no rational foundation for segregation was to be found in the social science literature.

Kluger, Richard. 1976. *Simple Justice: The History of Brown v. Board of Education and Black America's Struggle for Equality.* New York: Knopf.

- **Regulations for Federal Acknowledgment of Indian Tribes Established**
  United States, 1978

Based on federal law and regulation, Indian groups can petition to be recognized as Indian Tribes by the federal government. In 1978 a set of formal procedures were established that regularized the petition process. Petitions are submitted to the Branch of Federal Acknowledgment of the Bureau of Indian Affairs. This organization, staffed by anthropologists, historians and other researchers, evaluates these petitions and makes recommendations. The primary basis of the federal response to the petition is ethnohistoric research directed at determining whether an Indian group meets certain criteria. The data, used for both petitions and the evaluations of petitions, includes informant interviews, censuses, treaties, court records, tribal rolls, annuity rolls, scientific publications, and maps as well as many others.

Bureau of Indian Affairs. 1982. *Regulations, Guidelines and Policies of Federal Acknowledgement as an American Indian Tribe, 25 CFR 54.* Washington, DC: Bureau of Indian Affairs, Branch of Acknowledgment and Research.

- **BIA Recommends Acknowledgment of Grand Traverse Band of Ottawa and Chippewa**
  United States, 1980

Ethnohistoric, archival, and legal research resulted in the recommendation that the federal trust relationship be established with this northern Michigan group of Native Americans who petitioned for recognition by the

Federal government. The acknowledgement process is based on a number of criteria that are part of Federal regulation [as mentioned above]. Research found that the Grand Traverse Band was an amalgamation of several groups that entered the region at different times, the earliest before 1800.

Federal Acknowledgement Branch, Bureau of Indian Affairs. 1979. *Anthropological Report on the Grand Traverse Band of Ottawa and Chippewa of Michigan.* Washington, DC: Bureau of Indian Affairs.
_____. 1979. *Demographic Report on the Grand Traverse Band of Ottawa and Chippewa.* Washington, DC: Bureau of Indian Affairs.
_____. 1979. *Report on Genealogy of Members of the Grand Traverse Band of Ottawa and Chippewa Indians of Michigan.* Washington, DC: Bureau of Indian Affairs.

- **Lower Muskogee Creek Tribe Not Acknowledged**
  United States, 1981

Following appropriate regulations a group, claiming to be the Lower Muskogee Creek Indians, applied for recognition by the Federal Government as a legal tribe. This particular group claimed that they were descendants from southeastern Creeks that were remnant following the Removal to Oklahoma in the early 19th century. The Government reported that the organization dates from 1972 when they had purchased 102 acres west of Cairo, Georgia.

Bureau of Indian Affairs. 1981. *Recommendation and Summary of Evidence for Proposed Finding Against Federal Acknowledgment of the Lower Muskogee Creek Tribe-East of the Mississippi, Inc. of Cairo, Georgia, pursuant to 25 CFR 54.* Washington, DC: U.S. Department of the Interior.
_____. 1981. *Genealogical Report on the Lower Muskogee Creek-Tribe East of the Mississippi, Inc. (Cairo, Georgia).* Washington, DC: U.S. Department of the Interior.
_____. 1981. *Historical Report on the Lower Muskogee Creek Tribe-East of the Mississippi, Inc.* Washington, DC: U.S. Department of the Interior.

- **Snohomish Tribe Petition for Federal Recognition Rejected**
  United States, 1983

The Branch of Acknowledgement and Research of the Bureau of Indian Affairs rejected the petition of the Snohomish Tribe of Indians that they be recognized as an Indian Tribe. In the case of the Snohomish group, the Branch took the position that the group was derived in part from a group

182

that had been organized in the 1920's to file an Indian claims case. Members of this population were descendants of pioneer-Indian marriages that dated from the period 1856 to 1875. The Branch found the group did not meet all of the necessary criteria by which groups are recognized as tribes and therefore did not recommend recognition.

Bureau of Indian Affairs. 1983. *Recommendation and Summary of Evidence for Proposed Finding Against Federal Acknowledgement of the Snohomish Tribe of Indians, Inc. Pursuant to 25 CFR 83.*
_____. 1983. *Evaluation of the Snohomish Petition by the Criteria in part 83 (Formerly Part 54) of Title 25 of the Code of Federal Regulations.*

- **San Juan Southern Paiute Tribe Acknowledged**
United States, 1989

The San Juan Paiute Tribe petitioned for acknowledgement in 1980. In the case of the San Juan Paiute Tribe, the initial petition with its related ethnographic and ethnohistorical documentation was prepared by anthropologists Robert Franklin and Pamela Bunte working in conjunction with legal counsel and, of course, reviewed by the San Juan Paiute council of elders. Bunte and Franklin had been doing linguistic and cultural research with San Juan Paiute community members as early as 1979. In 1982 they were asked by the San Juan Paiutes and their attorneys to research and prepare reports relating to the acknowledgement process. Their involvement in the process continued beyond the original submission to include responding to requests of additional information from the government and various interventions from other groups, such as the Hopi and Navajo. The San Juan Paiute petition, researched by Franklin and Bunte, was successful, resulting in acknowledgement. Acknowledgement was contested by the Navajo Tribe. Information provided by Franklin and Bunte was important to the development of the response to the Navajo opposition. The need for applied research and consultation will continue because of the need to respond to legal challenges.

Branch of Acknowledgement and Research, Bureau of Indian Affairs. 1989. *Summary Under the Criteria and Evidence for Final Determination for Federal Acknowledgement of the San Juan Southern Paiute Tribe.* Washington, DC: Bureau of Acknowledgement and Research, Bureau of Indian Affairs.

MEDIA AND BROADCASTING

- **Honigmann Does Evaluation**
  Pakistan, 1952

American anthropologist John J. Honigmann was hired by an agency of the U. S. Department of State to evaluate the effects of U. S. information films on rural audiences. Honigmann concentrated his efforts on three villages in different linguistic areas of what was then West Pakistan.

Honigmann, John J. 1953. *Information for Pakistan, Report of Research on Intercultural Communication through Films.* Chapel Hill: Institute for Research in Social Science, University of North Carolina.

- **Media Anthropology in the Tucson Market**
  United States, 1969

Public Television-Radio in Tucson, Arizona, KUAT developed Project Fiesta which was calculated to attract, entertain, and inform Mexican-Americans. The project used anthropological research techniques in program planning and development and in the ultimate evaluation. The project was funded by the Ford Foundation and directed by anthropologist E. B. Eiselein.

Eiselein, E. B. and Wes Marshall. 1976. Mexican-American Television: Applied Anthropology and Public Television. *Human Organization* 35(2):147-156.
Eiselein, E. B. and Wes Marshall. 1971. Fiesta--An Experiment in Minority Audience Research and Programming. *Educational Television* 3(2):11-15.
Marshall, Wes, E. B. Eiselein, J. T. Duncan and P. Gomez. 1974. *Fiesta: Minority Television Programming.* Tucson: University of Arizona Press.

MILITARY

- **USAF Flight Crew Efficiency Studied**
  United States, 1951

The Human Resources Research Center at Randolph AFB, San Antonio, Texas, hired anthropologists Alan R. Beals and Walter Goldschmidt to use participant-observation research techniques to identify factors related to B-29 bomber crew efficiency. The research focused upon three issues, these included; the crew formation process, the effect of the aircraft on the crew as social unit, and the relations between the crew and the rest of the Air Force. The research produced reports which were, in the end, suppressed.

Beals, Alan R. 1976. Flying the Big'uns: Ethnography of a B-29 Crew. in *Paths to the Symbolic Self, Essays in Honor of Walter Goldschmidt*. J. P. Loucky and J. R. Jones, eds. *Anthropology, UCLA.* 8(1 and 2).

- **Air Crew Survival Studied through Participant-Observation**
  United States, 1956

Using participant-observation techniques, anthropologist Louis Dupree evaluated U. S. Air Force bailed-out flight crew survival techniques. These evaluations were carried out in Panamanian rain forests, Libyan deserts, and off the coast of Puerto Rico. Test groups were randomly selected from B-52 crews and accompanied by an anthropologist. Each day the observer recorded information on prepared data cards. This included information on physical condition, equipment use and improvision, leadership, morale and reactions to the environment. The results of the research revealed a number of significant deficiencies in Air Force survival training. The role of the commander was revealed to be very important.

Dupree, Louis. 1956. *The Jungle Survival Field Test.* Maxwell AFB, Alabama, ADTIC Publ. T-lOl.
_____. 1956. *The Desert Survival Field Test.* Maxwell AFB, Alabama, ADTIC Publ. D-lO4.
_____. 1958. *The Water Survival Field Tests.* Maxwell AFB, Alabama, ADTIC Publ. G-lO7.

- **Ethnic Guides for Crashed Crew Members**
  United States, 1958

By 1958, the U. S. Air Force had published 150 ethnic group guides for downed air crew members. Each guide consists of a set of 5 by 8 inch cards which fit in a flight suit packet. Each set contains information on population, range, environment, physical appearance, language, religion, social organization, economy, diet, transportation, and tendency to be hostile. Most of the studies were prepared by Air Force anthropologists.

Nesbitt, Paul H. 1958. Anthropology and the Air Force. In *Anthropology in the Armed Services: Research in Environment, Physique, and Social Organization*. Louis

185

Dupree ed., University Park, PA: Pennsylvania State University, Social Science Research Center.

MISSIONS

- **Missionary Anthropology Promoted**
United States, 1926

The Catholic Anthropological Conference was organized at an informal meeting held at the Catholic University of America, Washington, DC. The chief aims of the Conference were the advancement of anthropological science through the promotion of research and publication by missionaries and professional anthropologists as well as anthropological training among candidates for missionary work. The Conference published the journal entitled *Primitive Man,* which later became *Anthropological Quarterly.*

Luzbetak, Louis J. 1961. Toward an Applied Missionary Anthropology. *Anthropological Quarterly* 34:165-176.
Miller, Elmer S. 1970. The Christian Missionary, Agent of Secularization. *Anthropological Quarterly* 43:14-22.

NUTRITION

- **Committee on Food Habits Established**
United States, 1940

The Committee on Food Habits was created by the National Research Council to obtain scientific data on American nutritional levels and to ascertain how American nutritional levels could be improved. The plan of action of the committee included general guidelines for action. The anthropologists associated with the committee included Ruth Benedict, Rhoda Metraux, Allison Davis, and Carl Guthe. Margaret Mead served the committee as Executive Secretary.

Bennett, John W., Harvey L. Smith and Herbert Passin. 1942. Food and Culture in Southern Illinois, A Preliminary Report. *American Sociological Review* 7:645-660.
_____. 1943. Dietary Patterns and Food Habits. *Journal of the American Dietetics Association* 19:1-5.
_____. 1943. The Problem of Changing Food Habits: with Suggestions for Psychoanalytic Contributions. *Bulletin of the Menninger Clinic* 7:57-61.
_____. 1943. The Problem of Changing Food Habits. in *The Problem of Changing Food Habits.* Washington, DC: National Research Council.

Montgomery, Edward and John W. Bennett. 1979. Anthropological Studies of Food and Nutrition: The 1940s and the 1970s. In *The Uses of Anthropology.* Walter Goldschmidt, ed. Washington, DC: American Anthropological Association.

National Research Council, Committee on Food Habits. 1943. *The Problem of Changing Food Habits.* Washington, DC: National Research Council.

_____. 1945. *Manual for the Study of Food Habits.* Washington, DC: National Research Council.

Passin, Herbert and John W. Bennett. 1943. Social Process and Dietary Change. In *The Problems of Changing Food Habits.* Washington, DC: National Research Council.

Powdermaker, Hortense. 1943. Summary of Methods of a Field Work Class Cooperating with the Committee on Food Habits. In *The Problem of Changing Food Habits.* Washington, DC: National Research Council.

- **Dietary Component Added to On-farm Research Project**
  Ecuador, 1980

For a number of years CIMMYT (International Center for the Improvement of Maize and Wheat) has maintained socio-economic research programs that were calculated to improve the responsiveness of their plant breeding programs to farmers' needs and constraints. While this has included baseline farming systems research, CIMMYT has also invested in various kinds of on-farm plant breeding research. As part of an attempt to improve on-farm research operations, CIMMYT made efforts to include a dietary data gathering component in their on-going, on-farm research project established in conjunction with the National Agricultural Research Institute of Ecuador. The dietary research was carried out by CIMMYT anthropologist, Robert Tripp. Tripp used 24-hour recall procedures, secondary data sources and key farmer interviews. Among Tripp's findings was the fact that hard endosperm maize that had been developed in the breeding program was not useful in certain frequently prepared dishes. Dietary information was used to redirect the objectives of the plant breeders.

Tripp, Robert. 1982. *Including Dietary Concerns in On-farm Research: An Example from Imbabura, Ecuador.* Mexico: Centro International de Mejoramiento de Maiz y Trigo.

- **U.S. Food Aid to Peru Evaluated**
  Peru, 1982

U.S. Agency for International Development set about to evaluate the effects of PL 480 Title I Food Assistance in Peru. Internationally, PL 480 represented the largest AID program and consisted of authorization for the U.S. government to sell agricultural commodities produced in the U.S. on highly concessional terms to certain developing countries. Commodities sold through this program generate income to the recipient country government that can be used for development projects. PL 480 has a number of purposes, these include surplus disposal, foreign policy aims, economic development, and market development. The evaluation team, led by anthropologist Twig Johnson, conducted the field study component of the evaluation during July and August of 1982. Data collection consisted of key informant interviews and review of documents. Data collection was focused on a number of dimensions of the PL 480 program in Peru. These included impact on balance of payments, food production incentives, agricultural price policy, and income-distribution. Also considered were impacts on diet and nutrition.

Johnson, Twig, Linn Hammergren, Elizabeth Berry, Robert Landman, Judy Cohen and Robert Adler. 1983. *The Impact of PL 480 Title I in Peru: Food Aid as an Effective Development Resource.* A.I.D. Project Impact Evaluation No. 47. Washington, DC: U.S. Agency for International Development.

- **Socio-cultural Factors Affecting the Safety of Food Discussed**
  Thailand, 1982

A conference on socio-cultural factors affecting the safety of food was organized and held by the World Health Organization and the School of Public Health, Mahidol University, Bangkok. Participants from various disciplines attended, including sociology, microbiology, nutrition, anthropology, environmental health, planning, public health administration, and sanitary science. The conference was, in part, intended to prepare materials on socio-cultural factors which affect food safety for a FAO/WHO Expert Committee on Food Safety. The role of behavioral scientists in food safety programs was discussed.

Foster, George M. 1982. *Socio-cultural Factors Affecting the Safety of Food.* Report on Informal Discussions between Behavioral Scientists and Food Scientists, School of Public Health, Mahidol University. Bangkok: World Health Organization.

- **Food Consumption Aspects of Farming Systems Research Assessed**
  United States, 1985

Timothy R. Frankenberger developed a set of recommendations for effectively incorporating food consumption considerations in the process

188

of the development of new farm technology. This research was carried out for the Nutrition Economics Group, Office of International Cooperation and Development, United States Department of Agriculture. Frankenberger's analysis focused upon what he referred to as production/consumption linkages. These include; seasonality of production, crop mix and minor crops, income, role of women in production, crop - labor requirements, and market prices and their seasonality. In the case of each linkage, the analysis produced a number of "possible strategies" for dealing with the effects of production on consumption. These strategies included research, development and extension recommendations. Suggestions for incorporating these considerations into the various stages of FSR were made, including target area selection, diagnostic baseline studies, formulating recommendation domains, and evaluating project performance. In 1987, teams at the Universities of Arizona and Kentucky entered into an agreement with the Nutrition Economics Group, Office of International Cooperation and Development of USDA to provide technical and research support "to promote and assist the incorporation of nutritional considerations in agricultural development programs and projects." The co-principal investigators were Frankenberger and Kathleen DeWalt. Project activities include development of methods for incorporating food consumption and nutritional concerns in AID development projects, developing training materials, presenting workshops, writing case studies and disseminating this information through the Nutrition and Agriculture Network.

DeWalt, Kathleen M. 1987. *Case Studies in Nutrition and Agriculture.* Report No. 2. Nutrition in Agriculture Cooperative Agreement. Tucson, Arizona: University of Arizona and University of Kentucky.

Frankenberger, Timothy R. 1987. *Food Consumption and Farming Systems Research: A Summary.* Nutrition in Agriculture Cooperative Agreement. Tucson, Arizona: University of Arizona and University of Kentucky.

_____. 1985. *Adding a Food Consumption Perspective to Farming Systems Research.* A Report for Nutrition Economics Group, Technical Assistance Division, Office of International Cooperation and Development, United States Department of Agriculture.

Harrison, Gail G. 1988. *Nutritional Status Indicators: Their Use in Applied Agricultural Development.* Report No. 4. Nutrition in Agriculture Cooperative Agreement. Tucson, Arizona: University of Arizona and University of Kentucky.

Mack, Maura D. and Sandra Saenz de Tejada. 1988. *Nutrition in Agriculture Annotated Bibliography.* Volume No. 1. Nutrition in Agriculture Cooperative Agreement. Tucson, Arizona: University of Arizona and University of Kentucky.

O'Brien-Place, Patricia. 1987. *Evaluating Home Garden Projects.* U.S. Department of Agriculture, Office of International Cooperation and Development, Nutrition Economics Group.

O'Brien-Place, Patricia and Timothy R. Frankenberger. 1988. *Food Availability and Consumption Indicators.* Report No. 3. Nutrition in Agriculture Cooperative Agreement. Tucson, Arizona: University of Arizona and University of Kentucky.

- **Nutritional Status Surveyed**
  Mauritania, 1988

Claire Monod Cassidy, working with the support of the A.I.D.-funded Nutrition in Agriculture Cooperative Agreement, surveyed nutritional status of children under four and their mothers during winter time in four villages along the Senegal River. The research found both children and their mothers were undernourished. The analysis revealed a number of risk factors.

Cassidy, Claire Monod. 1988. *A Survey of Nutritional Status in Children Under Four and Their Mothers in Four Villages in the Regions of Brakna, Guidimaka and Gorgol.* Tucson: Nutrition in Agriculture Cooperative Agreement, University of Arizona.

- **Food Consumption Researched Using RRA Techniques**
  Zaire, 1988

Using rapid rural assessment techniques, Elizabeth Adelski directed a team which surveyed forty-four villages in the central Bandundu region for the Agricultural Production and Marketing Project (PROCAR). This research was supported by U.S. Agency for International Development through USDA and the Nutrition in Agriculture Cooperative Agreement. A major objective of the study was to collect information on the regional system of economic production and fish farming, animal husbandry, off-farm employment and marketing. The researchers used separate interview guides for men and women so as to clearly determine their respective economic roles. In doing, this male and female responses to questions about the development goals of the villages were differentiated and compared. The research also focused on household provisioning as well as agricultural production.

Adelski, Elizabeth, Sita Lumbuenamo and Kebemba Mayomba. 1989. *Rapid Rural Appraisal in Central Bandundu, Zaire. Part II. Summary Reports on the Eleven Collectivites Surveyed in the RRA.* Report No. 7. Nutrition in Agriculture Cooperative Agreement. Tucson, Arizona: University of Arizona and University of Kentucky.

POLICY MAKING

- **Indian Tribal Isolation Policy Advocated**
  India, 1939

Anthropologist Verrier Elwin's monograph on the Baiga laid out a policy framework for tribal administration in India that was thought to increase the levels of isolation of tribal groups and slow processes of development. An important feature of his policy stance was the reduction of tribal peoples contact with missionaries. His views were present in various publications and were ultimately endorsed by Prime Minister Jawaharlal Nehru. In its developed form, Elwin's isolationist perspective was expressed as a proposal for a National Park to serve as a refuge for the Baiga Tribe and others. The position taken by Elwin, came to be labeled pejoratively as isolationist by social welfare professionals and the Indian National Congress. In Nehru's preface to Elwin's *A Philosophy for NEFA* a somewhat modified "isolationist" orientation is expressed.

Elwin, Verrier. 1939. *The Baiga.* London: John Murray.
_____. 1957. *A Philosophy for NEFA.* Shillong: Government of Assam.
_____. 1977. Growth of a 'Philosophy'. In *Anthropology in the Development Process.* H. N. Mathur, ed. New Delhi: Vikas Publishing House.

- **Political Organizations Investigated**
  Northern Rhodesia, 1943

As director of the Rhodes-Livingstone Institute, Max Gluckman developed a major applied anthropology research project which examined government policy as it related to the political organization of the Barotse.

Gluckman, Max. 1943. *Administrative Organization of the Barotse Native Authorities.* Communication I, Northern Rhodesia: Rhodes-Livingstone Institute.
_____. 1955. *The Judicial Process Among the Barotse of Northern Rhodesia.* Manchester: University of Manchester Press.

- **Termination Policy Examined in Wisconsin**
  United States, 1955

The Wisconsin Legislative Council's Menominee Indian Study Committee, that investigated the impact of "Termination" on the Menominees included anthropologists.

Ames, David W. and Burton R. Fisher. 1959. The Menominee Termination Crisis: Barriers in the Way of a Rapid Cultural Transition. *Human Organization* 18(2):101-111.

Lurie, Nancy O. 1972. Menominee Termination: From Reservation to Colony. *Human Organization* 31(3).

- **International Cooperation Administration**
Development Policy Studied
Afghanistan, 1957

On assignment to the United States Operations Mission to Afghanistan of the International Cooperation Administration, George M. Foster evaluated various rural development alternatives and make recommendations for future ICA rural development policy. In this evaluation, the anthropologist found substantial competition between the international development agencies and very limited staff resources. The report raised questions about the utility of so-called pilot projects in countries like Afghanistan.

Foster, George M. 1957. *Terminal Report.* Kabul, Afghanistan: United States Operations Mission to Afghanistan. International Cooperation Administration.

- **Philleo Nash and Jim Officer**
Appointed to Task Force on Indian Affairs
United States, 1961

John F. Kennedy appointed Philleo Nash and James E. Officer to a task force to examine federal Indian Policy. Their general orientation was toward increasing self-determination in American Indian communities.

Spicer, Edward H. 1977. Early Applications of Anthropology in North America. In *Perspectives on Anthropology, 1976.* Anthony F. C. Wallace, et al, eds. Washington, DC: American Anthropological Association.

- **Policy Oriented Survey of Native Canadians Completed**
Canada, 1964

Harry B. Hawthorn and Marc-Adelard Tremblay directed a comprehensive examination of Native Canadian conditions of life involving fifty Canadian researchers. According to Price, the report "became a baseline of data and policy ideas for all subsequent critiques of Canadian Indian Policy."

Included in the text were 151 recommendations that "were sophisticated enough to take into account the very complex panorama of different kinds of native cultures, communities, and conditions for future participation in Canadian development" (Price 1987:2).

Hawthorn, Harry B., ed. 1966-67. *A Survey of the Contemporary Indians of Canada.* 2 Vols. Ottawa: Indian Affairs.

Price, John A. 1987. *Applied Anthropology: Canadian Perspectives.* Downsview, Ontario: SAAC/York University.

- **In-Up-Out Personnel Policy for Peace Corps**
United States, 1965

The Peace Corps Act of 1961 was amended at the suggestion of Sergeant Shriver. The change specified that above the grade of GS-9 no person could be employed by the Peace Corps for more than five years. This provided legal sanction for the so-called In-Up-Out policy developed by Robert B. Textor. This policy controlled staffing of Peace Corps Washington offices to returned volunteers who worked for a limited amount of time.

Textor, Robert B. 1966. Conclusions, Problems and Prospects. In *Cultural Frontiers of the Peace Corps.* R. B. Textor, ed. Cambridge, MA: M.I.T. Press.

POPULATION AND DEMOGRAPHY

- **Family Planning Association Set Up**
Mauritius, 1957

One of the first anthropologists to assist organizations concerned with birth planning was Burton Benedict. He was asked by the International Planned Parenthood Federation to give advice on how to implement the recommendations of the Committee on Population in Mauritius. Benedict went on to help set up the Mauritius Family Planning Association.

Benedict, Burton. 1970. Controlling Population Growth in Mauritius. Paper presented to the meetings of the American Anthropological Association.

- **Census of India Hires Anthropologists**
  India, 1961

The Census of India retained anthropologists to do a special series of village studies. These studies resulted in good quality data on microdevelopment.

Adelman, Irma and George Dalton. 1971. A Factor Analysis of Modernization in Village India. In *Economic Development and Social Change*. George Dalton, ed. New York: Natural History Press.

Mathur, H. M. 1976. Anthropology, Government and Development Planning in India. In *Development from Below, Anthropologists and Development Situations*. David C. Pitt, ed. The Hague: Mouton Publishers.

- **Anthropologist Research Director for Planned Parenthood**
  United States, 1963

Steven Polgar was hired as Director of Research at the Planned Parenthood Federation of America.

Polgar, Steven. 1977. Anthropologists and Birth Planning-1935 to 1975. unpublished paper.

- **WHO meets on FRMs**
  Switzerland, 1972

The World Health Organization Task Force on the Acceptability of Fertility Regulating Methods was organized. Among the participants were three anthropologists, Haydee Seijas, Masri Singaribun, and Steven Polgar.

Polgar, Steven and J. F. Marshall. 1976. The Search for Culturally Acceptable Fertility Regulating Methods. In *Culture, Natality and Family Planning*. Steven Polgar and J. F. Marshall, eds. Carolina Population Center Monograph 21, Chapel Hill, NC.

- **IUD Acceptability Studies Carried Out**
  Korea, 1973

Joe R. Harding designed research on the acceptability of certain fertility regulating methods under a contract from the Population Council. The research focused upon perceptions of different fertility regulating methods with the purpose of determining if, and by what process, IUDs could be introduced to a maximum number of Korean women.

194

Harding, Joe R., et al. 1973. *Population Council Copper - T Study.* Berkeley CA: Policy Research and Planning Group.

- **Fertility Beliefs Studied for Development Effort**
Bangladesh, 1977

With Clarence J. Maloney acting as Director, a research team at the Institute of Bangladesh Studies, Rajshahi University, undertook a study on "beliefs and fertility in Bangladesh" for U.S. Agency for International Development. Maloney was assisted by Bangladeshi anthropologists, K.M. Ashraful Aziz and Profulla C. Sarker. The research resulted in an extensive compilation of ethnographic content on fate and God as these concepts relate to the number of children, rituals effecting fertility, purdah, childbearing, intercourse, contraception, abortion, and infanticide.

Aziz, K.M.A. 1980. *Sex Socialization and Philosophies of Life in Relation to Fertility Behavior: An Anthropological Approach.* Ph.D. dissertation, Rajshahi University.
Maloney, Clarence, K.M.A. Aziz and Profulla C. Sarker. 1980. *Beliefs and Fertility in Bangladesh.* Rajshahi, Bangladesh: Institute of Bangladesh Studies, Rajshahi University.

- **Aspect of Teenage Pregnancy Program Evaluated**
United States, 1988

The Teen Initiative Center was formed to delay the initiation of sexual activities among teenagers in a low income housing project of Lexington, Kentucky. The specific objectives were to provide education on life choice decisions and family life, to build self-esteem, and to provide after-school professional drop-in counseling. A team, consisting of Doraine Bailey, Kathleen Fluhart and Laura von Harten from the Department of Anthropology, University of Kentucky, carried out a multi-faceted evaluation of the program which had ties to both city government and Planned Parenthood. The goals of the evaluation were to describe the activities of the Teen Center and to evaluate the effectiveness of the Center's program in terms of levels of participation, appropriateness of curriculum and participant's attitudes toward the center. The evaluation was done as a term project in a research methods course.

Doraine Bailey, Kathleen Fluhart, Laura von Harten. 1988. *Evaluation of the Teen Initiative Center, Bluegrass-Aspendale Housing District, Lexington, Kentucky.* Lexington: Department of Anthropology, University of Kentucky.

- **Teenage Pregnancy and the Chicago Public Schools**
United States, 1988

"About one-third of the female student body of the Chicago public schools will become mothers before they reach their twentieth birthday." The circumstances reported by this statement motivated a research team from the Chicago Panel on Public School Policy and Finance to examine the relationship between teen pregnancy and dropping out. Surprisingly there is little research on this relationship. An ethnically-stratified sample of eighty-seven teen mothers from the Chicago School System were interviewed. The research found that about half of these women were still "on-track" toward graduation and about 40 percent of the drop-outs were proceeding with alternate routes for education such as the GED. The research found that schools did not provide much support for these pregnant students nor did they refer these women to community agencies. In this regard about one third of these women reported that the school did not know they were pregnant and two-thirds never visited a school nurse.

Hess, G. Alfred, Jr. Denise O'Neil Green, Anne Elliot Stapleton and Olga Reyes. 1988. *Invisibly Pregnant, Teenage Members and the Chicago Public Schools.* Chicago: Chicago Panel on Public School Policy and Finance.

RECREATION

- **Recreational Use of Daniel Boone National Forest Studied**
United States, 1979

A team of anthropologists from the University of Kentucky, researched recreational uses of the Red River Gorge area of the Daniel Boone National Forest, Kentucky. The team, led by Eugenie C. Scott and Billie R. DeWalt, provided research data to National Forest personnel so as to improve their management capabilities. The research obtained data from over 3200 recreational visitors as well as members of conservation and recreational groups and landowners. Among the analytic concepts used in the research were density tolerance and recreational niche. The niche concept allowed the analysis to more clearly focus on different user types and their needs. The project produced a series of management recommendations for the Forest Service.

Scott, Eugenie C., Billie R. DeWalt, Elizabeth Adelski, Sara Alexander and Mary Beebe. 1982. *Landowners, Recreationists, and Government: Cooperation and Conflict in Red River Gorge.* Lexington, KY: University of Kentucky, Water Resources Research Institute, Research Report No. 134.

RELIGIOUS EXPRESSION

- **Testimony Concerning Religious Freedom and Peyote**
  United States, 1951

Various anthropologists provided testimony in a number of trials dealing with the use and possession of peyote by members of the Native American Church. The case was based on the view that peyote was sacramental in nature and its use should be allowed on Constitutional grounds.

La Barre, Weston, David P. McAllester, J. S. Slotkin, Omer C. Stewart and Sol Tax. 1951. Statement on Peyote. *Science* 114:582-583.

- **Anthropologist Acts as Expert Witness in Amish Case**
  United States, 1971

As part of their struggle to maintain the appropriateness of their education system, the Old Order Amish of Wisconsin resisted public school consolidation and compulsory secondary education. The resistance efforts of the Amish benefited from data supplied by anthropologist John Hostetler. Hostetler had carried out a basic research project focused on Old Order Amish socialization and education. He testified before the Supreme Court.

Hostetler, John A. 1972. Amish Schooling: A Study in Alternatives. *Council on Anthropology and Education Newsletter* 3(2):1-4.
Hostetler, John A. and G. E. Huntington. 1971. *Children in Amish Society: Socialization and Community Education.* New York: Holt, Rinehart and Winston.

RESETTLEMENT

- **AFS Resettlement Project Aided by Anthropologist**
  United States, 1937

The Penncraft Resettlement Project, sponsored by the American Friends Service Committee, used an anthropologist as a consultant to create an independent community. Among other innovations the project made use of "mutual self-help" housing techniques.

Richardson F. L. W., Jr. 1941. Community Resettlement in a Depressed Coal Region. *Applied Anthropology* l(l):24-53.
_____. 1942. Community Resettlement In a Depressed Coal Region II, Economic Problems of the New Community. *Applied Anthropology* 3(3):32-6l.
Richardson, F. L. W., Jr. and R. C. Sheldon. 1948. Community Resettlement in a Depressed Coal Region III. The Problem of Community Change: From Company Town to Planned Resettlement. *Human Organization* 7(4):l-27.

- **Resettlement Project Staffed by Anthropologists**
  Mexico, 1947

The Papaloapan Resettlement Project was made necessary by the construction of a large scale hydrological project of the Mexican government. Although the project would result in significant positive impact on food production, it would also result in the displacement of large numbers of Mazatec, Chinantec, and Popoloca Indian villages. The resettlement program was the responsibility of Instituto Nacional Indigenista. The project strategy called for thorough base-line research, cooperative, non-coercive planning of the project by anthropologists and local leadership, and the maintenance of a significant number of pre-migration life ways.

Villa-Rojas, Alfonso. 1955. *Los Mazatecos y al Problema Indigena da la Cuenca del Papaloapan.* Mexico D.F. Memorias del Instituto Nacional Indigenista, Vol. 7.

- **Forced Relocation at Bikini Examined**
  Micronesia, 1948

Emergency investigation into the causes of and solutions to the problems associated with the forced relocation of the Bikini atoll population to Rongerik was started. The Bikinians were forced to relocate because their home atoll was selected as an atomic test site in 1946. The move caused traumatic effects.

Kiste, Robert C. 1974. *The Bikinians: A Study in Forced Migration.* Menlo Park: Cummings Publishing Company.
Mason, Leonard. 1950. The Bikinians: A Transplanted Population. *Human Organization* 9(1):5-15.

_____. 1958. Kili Community in Transition. *South Pacific Commission Quarterly Bulletin* 18:32-35.

- **Resettlement and Anthropology**
  United States, 1964

The Wagina Resettlement Scheme in the Western Pacific had anthropologists as administrators.

Cochrane, Glyn. 1970. The Administration of Wagina Resettlement Scheme. *Human Organization* 29(2):123-132.

- **Anthropologists Involved in African Resettlement**
  Zambia, 1966

The Kariba Dam Project led to major population displacement. To a limited extent, anthropologists were involved in basic documentation and policy-research on this attempt to increase agricultural output in the Zambezi basin.

Scudder, Thayer. 1965. The Kariba Case: Man-Made Lakes and Resource Development in Africa. *Bulletin of the Atomic Scientist* 21:6-II.
_____. 1968. Social Anthropology, Man-Made Lakes and Population Relocation in Africa. *Anthropological Quarterly* 41.
_____. 1969. Relocation, Agricultural Intensification, and Anthropological Research. In *The Anthropology of Development in Sub-Saharan Africa*. David Brokensha and Marion Pearsall, eds. Society for Applied Anthropology, Monograph No. 10.

- **Resettlement Scheme for Agriculture**
  Nigeria, 1966

The International Institute of Tropical Agriculture developed an agricultural resettlement project to increase agricultural production. Anthropologically trained personnel were included as researchers and planners.

Smock, David R. 1969. The Role of Anthropology in a Western Nigerian Resettlement Project. In *The Anthropology of Development in Sub-Saharan Africa*. David Brokensha and Marion Pearsall, eds. Society for Applied Anthropology, Monograph No. 10.

- **World Bank Resettlement Project Appraisal**
  Tanzania, 1972

Priscilla Reining was retained by the World Bank to do a "Project Appraisal" of a program to organize pastoral people into so-called ujamaa villages. The goal of the project was to increase the participation of pastoralists in the market economy. Reining was asked to make judgments about a number of different areas including the social suitability of the ujamaa approach and program participation recruitment criteria.

Husain, Tariq. 1976. Use of Anthropologists in Project Appraisal by the World Bank. In *Development from Below: Anthropologists and Development Situations*. David C. Pitt, ed. the Hague: Mouton Publishers.

- **Social Soundness of Integrated Development Project Assessed**
  Cameroon, 1976

At the request of the U.S. Agency for International Development's mission in Yaounde, Cameroon, Allen Hoben carried out a social soundness analysis of an integrated rural development proposal for West Benone. The project's purpose was to encourage resettlement from an adjacent, more heavily settled area. The report recommended against immediate further work on the project for a number of reasons. Among these were the anticipated deleterious effects on the adjacent area from which the relocatees would have originated and historic difficulty in relocating the people in question. Previous experiences with crops and marketing in this region suggested that agricultural development would result in increased income for the modern sector of the Cameroon economy rather than the rural poor.

Hoben, Alan. 1976. *Social Soundness Analysis of the West Benone Integrated Rural Development Proposal, and Suggestions for Alternative Interventions in Margui-Wandola.* Washington, DC: U.S. Agency for International Development.

- **Nutritional Impact of Relocation Assessed in Third World Settings**
  United States, 1980

Anthropologists William L. Partridge and Antoinette B. Brown reviewed literature on the nutritional impacts on populations displaced by rural development projects in order to better inform the U.S. Agency for International Development. The project resulted in a number of

200

recommendations concerning nutrition and resettlement, including advice on research needs in anticipation of population displacements.

Partridge, William L. and Antoinette B. Brown. 1980. *The Nutritional Impact of Resettlement, Settlement and Colonization.* Washington, DC: U.S. Agency for International Development.

- **Comparative Study of Resettlement Undertaken for Development Bank** Latin America, 1983

As a consultant to the Banco Interamericano de Desarrollo, William L. Partridge compared resettlement experiences in two hydroelectric dam projects in Costa Rica and Guatemala. Both projects had been financed by the Banco Interamericano de Desarrollo but were fundamentally different in their social planning and social effects. A number of themes are apparent in the analysis. These are 1) resettlement must be adequately planned, indifference will produce failure; 2) qualified professional staff must be hired; 3) "bottom up" approaches to planning that include mutual negotiation seem to be successful; 4) community livelihoods need to be replaced; 5) flexibility and choice for the relocated individuals is very important; 6) planning with the community has to occur well before the project is actually constructed; and 7) economic development needs to be appropriately facilitated.

Partridge, William L. 1983. *Comparative Analysis of BID Experience with Resettlement, Based on Evaluations of the Arenal and Chinoy Projects.* Atlanta, GA: Center for Applied Research, Georgia State University.

- **New-Lands Settlement Project Evaluated by IDA** Bolivia, 1984

The San Julian colonization project was an attempt to settle highland Quechua and Aymara peoples into subtropical lowlands of eastern Bolivia. The project which developed the reputation for being successful and innovative was the focus of evaluation research done by the Institute for Development Anthropology. This effort made use of their extensive work in the study of new-lands colonization done by Thayer Scudder and others. The San Julian colonization project developed out of the efforts of a religious agency and was ultimately supported by OXFAM, the Federal Republic of Germany, and the Bolivian AID mission. The numerous previous evaluations stressed a number of features of the project that were thought to be related to its success. These included a three-month settler orientation program; food and shelter assistance; a nucleated settlement pattern with associated 50 hectare farm plots; and a recruitment scheme that reduced the numbers of potentially less-successful colonists. The evaluation was done during eight weeks in 1984. The research team, consisting of two Bolivians and three Americans, made use of a variety of different data sources. These included archives and observations in the communities themselves. Based on this work, six communities were selected for more intensive study using an interview schedule based upon Scudder's earlier new-lands settlement studies. These interviews focused on land use, labor availability, farm commercialization, and family history.

Hamilton, Susan. 1985. *An Unsettling Experience: Women's Migration to the San Julian Colonization Project.* Binghamton, NY: Institute of Development Anthropology.

Painter, Michael, Carlos A. Perez-Crespo, Martha Llanos Alborno, Susan Hamilton and William L. Partridge. 1984. *New-Lands Settlement and Regional Development: The Case of San Julian, Bolivia.* Binghamton, NY: Institute of Development Anthropology.

Scudder, Thayer. 1981. *The Development Potential of New Lands Settlement in the Tropics and Sub-tropics: A Global State-of-the-Art Evaluation with Specific Emphasis on Policy Implications.* Binghamton, NY: Institute for Development Anthropology.

- **World Bank Involuntary Resettlement Guidelines Examined**
  International, 1988

Michael Cernea prepared basic guidelines and procedures for World Bank-financed development projects which result in involuntary resettlement as an assistance to those "involved in preparing, implementing or evaluating such projects" (1988:1). The foundation of the document were the internal policy statements issued by the Bank in 1980 and 1986. Cernea's analysis resulted in integration and contextualization of the earlier policy guidelines.

Cernea, Michael M. 1988. *Involuntary Resettlement in Development Projects, Policy Guidelines in World Bank-financed Projects.* World Bank Technical Paper Number 80. Washington, DC: The World Bank.

SOCIAL IMPACT ASSESSMENT

- **Early Social Impact Assessment Activities**
  United States, 1972

Three anthropologists enter the field of "Social Impact Assessment" required of all federal agencies under the National Environmental Policy Act of 1969. Magoroh Maruyama became Resident Social Scientist with the U. S. Corps of Engineers and began participating in the Corps' formulation of its social impact assessment guidelines. In 1973 Maruyama formed a consultant team that included anthropologists Sue-Ellen Jacobs and John H. Peterson.

Maruyama, Magorah. 1973. Cultural, Social and Psychological Considerations in the Planning of Public Works. *Technological Forecasting and Social Change* 5:135-143.

Vlachos, Evan, ed. 1975. *Social Impact Assessment: An Overview.* Corps of Engineers, IWR Paper 75-P7.

- **Social Impacts of McKenzie Valley Gas Pipeline Assessed**
  Canada, 1972

The Northwest Project Study Group of the Boreal Institute of Northern Studies contracted Larry R. Stucki to investigate cultural impacts of the proposed MacKenzie Valley Pipeline to be routed from new gas sources located at Prudhome Bay, through Canada's MacKenzie Valley to American consumers. The Group was funded by various pipeline companies. Stucki concluded that native employment opportunities which were discussed in the publicity given the project were unrealizable given the nature of the project.

Stucki, Larry R. 1972. Canada's "unemployable" Northerners: Square Pegs in Round Holes in the System to be Created for the International Transfer of Energy by Pipeline from Northern Canada to the United States, Unpublished Paper.

- **Impact of Power Production Assessed**
  United States, 1973

Anthropologists come to be involved in the analysis of the impact of power production on the Navajo Reservation population. Referred to as the Lake Powell Project, this effort involved anthropologists Jerrold E. Levy and Donald G. Callaway.

Callaway, Donald G., Jerrold E. Levy and Eric Henderson. 1976. *The Effects of Power Production and Strip Mining on Local Navajo Populations.* Lake Powell Research Bulletin No. 22, Los Angeles: University of California, Los Angeles.

- **New Handbook for Project Appraisal**
  United States, 1973

The Foreign Assistance Act of 1973 provided for "social soundness analysis" of overseas development projects. This dramatically increased the number of "contract" and "direct hire" opportunities for anthropologists in the Agency for International Development. Social soundness analysis focuses on cultural compatibility, diffusion of benefits, and extensiveness of impacts.

U.S. Agency for International Development. 1975. *Handbook 3, Project Assistance.* Washington, DC: U.S.A.I.D.

- **Coal Mining Impact Assessed**
  United States, 1973

The Institute for Social Science Research at the University of Montana began a research project to determine the social impact of the extraction of coal resources in the Northern Great Plains. The research made use of anthropological techniques. Data were gathered in and around Colstrip, Montana; Gillette, Wyoming and Stanton, North Dakota.

Institute for Social Science Research. 1974. *A Comparative Case Study of the Impact of Coal Development on the Way of Life of People in the Coal Areas of Eastern Montana and Northeastern Wyoming, Final Report.* Missoula, Montana: Institute for Social Science Research, University of Montana.

- **NEPA Progeny**
  United States, 1974

The passage of the National Environmental Policy Act of 1969 stimulated a substantial amount of related legislation requiring social impact assessment. One of the NEPA progeny having this effect was the Community Development Act of 1974 (PL 93-383). The Community Development Act requires that there be an assessment of the social impact of expenditures under the act. William Millsap carried out such an assessment in a small Texas community.

Millsap, William. 1978. New Tools for an Old Trade: Social Impact Assessment in Community and Regional Development. In *Social Science Education for Development*. William T. Vickers and Glenn R. Howze, eds. Tuskegee Institute, Center for Rural Development. Tuskegee Institute, Alabama.

- ## SIA in UK
United Kingdom, 1974

Although the legislative mandate is not as clear as in the United States environmental impact assessment is also practiced in Great Britain. Anthropologists are staff members of the Project Appraisal for Development Control group at the University of Aberdeen. This group has been working in environmental impact assessment since 1974.

Bisset, Ronald. 1978. Environmental Impact Analysis: A Review Article. *Royal Anthropological Institute News* (26):1-4.
Clark, B. D., K. Chapman, Ronald Bisset, and P. Wathern. 1978. Methods of Environmental Impact Analysis. *Built Environment* 4(1):111-121.

- ## Impact Assessment in an Army Corps of Engineers Project
United States, 1974

Sue-Ellen Jacobs was retained as part of a team that engaged in social impact assessment for the Springer-Sangamon Environmental Research Program of an Army Corps of Engineers reservoir project on the Sangamon River in central Illinois. Jacobs later participated in the development of guidelines for evaluating other Army Corps of Engineer projects.

Jacobs, Sue-Ellen, Barbara A. Schleicher and Raymond A. Ontiveros. 1974. *Preliminary Social and Cultural Profiles of the Human Communities in the Springer-Sangamon Impact Zones, Social Impact Assessment and Identification of Resource- Oriented Attributes of the Human Environment in the Springer-Sangamon Impact Zones - Phase I.* Springer-Sangamon Environmental Research Program, Department of Forestry and Illinois Agricultural Experiment Station University of Illinois, Urbana - Champaign, Ill.

- ## SIA Done in New Mexico
United States, 1975

Sue-Ellen Jacobs carried out a Social Impact Assessment for the Bureau of Reclamation. The zone of impact was to include portions of the Rio

Grande-Espanola Valley in New Mexico. Impact zone inhabitants included both Hispanics and Native Americans.

Jacobs, Sue-Ellen. 1977. *Social Impact Assessment: Experiences in Evaluation Research, Applied Anthropology and Human Ethics.* Mississippi State University Occasional Papers In Anthropology. John M. Peterson, Jr., ed. Mississippi State, MS:Department of Anthropology, Mississippi State University.

- **New York Highway SIA Finished**
  United States, 1976

A group of young anthropologists led by Karen L. Michaelson assessed the impact of the planned construction of Interstate 88 in up-state New York. The assessment was supported as a student-originated-study project of the National Science Foundation.

Van Tassell, Jon and Karen L. Michaelson. 1977. *Social Impact Assessment: Methods and Practice, (Interstate 88 in New York).* (Final Report: National Science Foundation, Student-Originated-Study Grant, Summer, 1976), Binghamton: NY: Department of Anthropology, SUNY, Binghamton.

- **SIA Technology Tested**
  United States, 1977

As part of a multi-disciplinary team, anthropologists Erve Chambers, Charles A. Clinton, and John H. Peterson, Jr. field tested the WRAM (Water Resources Assessment Methodology) procedure which had been developed at the U. S. Army Corps of Engineers Waterways Experiment Station, Vicksburg, Mississippi. The field test was carried out in the Tensas River Valley in Louisiana.

Clinton, Charles A. ed. 1978. *Social Impact Assessment in Context: The Tensas Documents.* Occasional Papers in Anthropology, Mississippi State University, Mississippi State, Mississippi.

Solomon, R. Charles, Billy K. Colfert, William J. Hansen, Sue E. Richardson, Larry W. Canter, and Evan G. Vlachos. 1977. *Water Resources Assessment Methodology (WRAM - Impact Assessment and Alternative Evaluation.* Report Y-77-l). Vicksburg, Mississippi: Environmental Effects Laboratory, U. S. Army Corps of Engineers Waterways Experiment.

206

- **Airport Construction Impact Assessed**
Truk, 1978

U.S.-administered Trust Territory of Pacific Islands' (TTPI) plan to enlarge the airport on Moen, Truk Island group, was opposed by many Trukese. Thomas King, an archaeologist working in the Historic Preservation Office, was assigned to mediate between the TTPI administration and the local community. Working with him was Patricia Parker who was doing ethnographic research on Moen and unofficially recognized as translator of villager's concerns into government language. Based on her observations of community meetings, she told of destruction by dredging of the reef, blocked access to the local disposal area, historic landmark destruction and the increase in dust and noise as well as other problems. King presented grievances to officials for resolution through mediation. As a result of their efforts many of the problems caused by the development were successfully mitigated.

Parker, Patricia L. and Thomas F. King. 1987. Intercultural Mediation at Truk International Airport. In *Anthropological Praxis: Translating Knowledge Into Action.* R. Wulff and S. Fiske, eds. Boulder: Westview.

- **Alternative Impact Analysis of Copper Mining Carried Out**
Panama, 1980

Cultural Survival, Inc., a non-profit research organization concerned with the continued existence of "ethnic minorities and indigenous people" throughout the world, provided support for an alternative "impact analysis" of a copper mining project occupied by the Guaymi Indians of Panama. Researchers associated with the project had concluded that the original social impact assessment was inadequate because it was not based on field work to a sufficient degree. Additional impact assessment was advised.

Gjording, Chris N. 1981. *The Cerro Colorado Copper Project and the Guaymi Indians of Panama.* Cultural Survival, Inc. Occasional Paper 3, Cambridge, MA.

- **AID Project Assistance Handbook Published**
United States, 1980

Because of the provisions of the Foreign Assistance Act of 1973 the U.S. Agency for International Development formulated procedures for doing social soundness analysis. This project planning tool was first implemented in 1975 and subsequently appeared in A.I.D. Project Assistance, Handbook

3. After about five years of experience with SAA's the accumulated documents were studied by a team of anthropologists led by Jasper Ingersoll. Forty-eight sets of project documents were reviewed. The review was directed at the identification of the qualities of social analyses that seemed most useful to the design of projects; the determination of how A.I.D. procedures influence the use of these planning documents; and the recommendation of new guidelines for doing SAA's.

Ingersoll, Jasper, Mark Sullivan and Barbara Lenkerd. 1981. *Social Analysis of A.I.D. Projects: A Review of the Experience.* Submitted in fulfillment of A.I.D. Contract # OTR-147- 80-79.

- **Social Impact Assessment of a Ski Resort Carried Out**
  United States, 1980

Foundation for Urban and Neighborhood Development (FUND), was commissioned to provide social impact assessment (SIA) for a proposed ski resort in Eagle County, Colorado. FUND was responsible to a Colorado joint Review Committee, that included the U.S. Forest Service, state and county governments, and the developer. FUND decided on a "issue-centered" SIA approach. The anthropologist, Kevin Preister and two field researchers worked to perform baseline social assessment, identify the range of issues, analyze social and economic effects of alternatives, promote information flow between pro- and anti-development interests, and promote resolution of issues. Baseline social assessment revealed rapid change already underway. Over 130 specific issues were identified which structured collection of social and economic data. Data was analyzed for the effects of project alternatives. The SIA effort reduced hostility between pro- and anti-development interests. Those with vested interests in maintaining status-quo decision-making were most threatened by the approach.

Preister, Kevin. 1987. Issue-Centered Social Impact Assessment. In *Anthropological Praxis: Translating Knowledge Into Action.* R. Wulff and S. Fiske, eds. Boulder: Westview.

(Steven E. Maas)

- **Forest Plan Development Aided by Anthropologist**
  United States, 1981

The National Forest Management Act of 1976 requires that each National Forest prepare a forest plan to direct management of the forest into the future. Anthropologist James Patterson did the "Socio-Economic

Overview" component of the Forest Plan for Malheur National Forest in Oregon. This "Overview" was focused on what Forest Service--USDA calls the Zone of Influence of the forest and made use of a variety of data sources to construct a socio-economic baseline of the region.

Patterson, G. James. 1981. *Socio-economic Overview of the Zone of Influence of the Malheur National Forest in Grant and Harney Countries, Oregon.* Eastern Oregon State College.

- **Impact of Real Estate Development on Papago Indian Life Assessed**
  United States, 1983

Developers proposed a project that would result in the construction of a planned residential community on 18,700 acres of the San Xavier District of the Papago Indian Reservation. A team from the Bureau of Applied Research in Anthropology at the University of Arizona, led by Thomas R. McGuire and Marshall A. Worden, carried out a social impact assessment under provisions of the National Environmental Policy Act of 1969 and the assessment criteria of the U. S. Bureau of Reclamation. These assessment criteria focus on probability of impact, duration of impact, reversibility of impact, numbers of persons impacted, and the spread of the impact effects across the community. The assessment process involved identification of baseline conditions in the community and assessment of potential impacts both with and without the project. Data from hearings were supplemented with informal interviews with community residents and a survey questionnaire administered to the San Xavier allottees. The literature on similar projects was supplemented by the general literature on reservation development. The data were used to frame the researcher's evaluation of the identified impacts into beneficial and adverse effects.

McGuire, Thomas R. and Marshall A. Worden. 1984. *Socio-cultural Impact Assessment of the San Xavier Planned Community, Papago Indian Reservation, Pima County, Arizona.* Prepared for the Bureau of Indian Affairs. (DRAFT) Tucson, AR: Bureau of Applied Research in Anthropology, University of Arizona.

- **Plans for Superconducting Super Collider Assessed**
  United States, 1986

The U.S. Department of Energy proposed the construction, somewhere in America, of a particle accelerator of a scale heretofore unknown. The device accelerates atomic particles through a 52 mile circumference oval, underground tunnel and then collides them, breaking them into their component parts providing research data on the physical properties of matter and energy. Thought to take at least seven years to construct, the project will bring thousands of workers and billions of dollars to the state that is the selected site. Further it will result in an influx of "world-class" scientists to the region and the development of many high technology spin-offs. A number of states proposed that the Super-colliding, Superconductor (SSC) be located in their states. The Michigan proposal included a social impact assessment of the SSC done by Anthropologist Richard W. Stoffle of the Institute of Social Research of the University of Michigan. The project was not constructed in Michigan.

Richard W. Stoffle, Michael W. Traugott, Florence V. Jensen, and Robert Copeland. 1987. *Social Assessment of High Technology: The Superconducting Super Collider in Southeast Michigan.* ISR Research Report Series. Ann Arbor, MI: Institute for Social Research, University of Michigan.

TRAINING PROGRAMS

- **French Colonial Administration Training Started**
  France, 1889

Ecole Nationale de la France D'Outre-Mer was founded to provide training for the colonial service. The school was an agency of the French government and offered training in the ethnology of Southeast Asia and Africa.

Leroi-Gourhan, A. 1953. France. In *International Directory of Anthropological Institutions.* William L. Thomas, Jr. and Anna Pikelis, eds. New York: Wenner-Gren.

- **Early Training Program Developed**
  Netherlands, 1864

Ethnology was included in a training program for civil servants to serve in the Netherlands East Indies. The Netherlands was one of the first countries to make use of anthropology as part of colonial administration training.

Held, G. Jan. 1953. Applied Anthropology in Government: The Netherlands. In *Anthropology Today.* A. L. Kroeber, ed. Chicago: University of Chicago.

Kennedy, Raymond. 1944. Applied Anthropology in the Dutch East Indies. *Transactions of the New York Academy of Sciences.* Ser. 2. VI:157-62.

- **Training Needs in Native Affairs Results in Faculty Slots**
  South Africa, 1905

A government inquiry into native affairs suggested that university positions be made available for teaching and ethnological research.

Forde, E. Daryll. 1953. Applied Anthropology in Government: British Africa. In *Anthropology Today.* A. L. Kroeber, ed. Chicago: University of Chicago Press.

- **Anthropology Training Provided Administrators**
  United Kingdom, 1908

Sir Reginald Wingate requested Oxford and Cambridge to offer anthropology as part of a training curriculum for civil servants being posted to the Sudan. Because of its status as a condominium of Great Britain and Egypt, the Sudan was administered by the Foreign Office rather than the Colonial Office. This seems to be related to earlier and more intensive use of anthropologists in government service there.

Myres, J. L. 1928. The Science of Man in the Service of the State. *Journal of the Royal Anthropological Institute of Great Britain and Ireland* LIX:19-52.

- **Radcliffe-Brown Establishes Training Program**
  South Africa, 1920

A. R. Radcliffe-Brown established a School of African Studies organized around a new anthropology department at the University of Cape Town. There he had some impact on government thinking both through special "applied anthropology" courses he established for government administrators and through lectures he delivered. The role of the anthropologist, as he saw it, was to provide scientific appraisals of the situations faced by administrators and not to advocate policy.

Kuper, Adam. 1973. *Anthropologists and Anthropology, the British School, 1922-1972.* London: Allen Lane.

- **Belgium Training Program Uses Anthropologists**
  Belgium, 1920

Institute of Universitaire des Territories d' Outre'Mer was created in Antwerp to train colonial administrators. This training included studies in ethnology.

Nicaise, Joseph. 1960. Applied Anthropology in the Congo and Rwanda-Urandi. *Human Organization* 19:112-117.

- **Colonial Officers Trained by Anthropologists**
  Netherlands, 1921

Colonial civil service training at the University of Leiden included training in the ethnology and customary law of Indonesia. The effect of this was that virtually all Dutch colonial administrators had ethnology training.

Josselin de Jong, P. E. 1960. Cultural Anthropology in the Netherlands. *Higher Education and Research in the Netherlands* 4:3-16.

- **Anthropological Training Center Advocated**
  Great Britain, 1921

The Anthropological Section of the British Association for the Advancement of Science advocated the establishment of a center to coordinate training in anthropology in service to the Empire. This proposition was approved and a center was established at the Royal Anthropological Institute.

Myres, J. L. 1928. The Science of Man in the Service of the State. *Journal of the Royal Anthropological Institute of Great Britain and Ireland* LIX:19-52.

- **Training Needs for Administrators Cited**
  New Guinea, 1923

Section II of the Pan-Pacific Science Congress, Melbourne, passed a resolution asking the Commonwealth Government to support a faculty position in anthropology at the University of Sydney and to appoint an official anthropologist for the mandated territory of New Guinea.

Chinnery, W. P. 1933. Applied Anthropology in New Guinea. *Report of the 21st Meeting of the Australian and New Zealand Association for the Advancement of Science* pp. 163-175.
Hogbin, H. Ian. 1949. Government Chiefs in New Guinea. In *Social Structure; Studies Presented to A. R. Radcliffe-Brown.* London: Oxford University Press.

- **Training Scheme Established**
New Guinea, 1925

A training scheme was organized for administrative personnel at the University of Sydney. It included special courses in anthropology.

Mair, Lucy P. 1948. *Australia in New Guinea.* London: Christophers.

- **Legislation Supports More Colonial Training**
United Kingdom, 1940

Parliament passed the Colonial Development and Welfare Act which included some support for policy-oriented anthropological research in Africa. In his *Africa Survey*, Lord Hailey called for additional research to improve the quality of colonial administration. Following the war these funds were allocated by the Colonial Social Science Research Council that included Raymond Firth and Audrey Richards.

Hailey, W. M. 1938. *An African Survey.* London.
Kuper, Adam. 1973. *Anthropologists and Anthropology, the British School 1922-1972.* London: Allen Lane.

- **Colonial Training Program includes Anthropology**
United Kingdom, 1943

The Devonshire Training Scheme developed for British Colonial Service Officers included anthropology.

British Colonial Service. 1946. *Post-War Training for the Colonial Service.* Report of the Committee appointed by the Secretary of State for the Colonies. London: H. M. Stationery Office.

- **Anthropology Included in Training for Administrators**
Australia, 1945

The inclusion of anthropological training for district and educational officers in Australian Papua and New Guinea. The training was necessary for promotion and included government, geography, land use, history, and tropical hygiene.

Mair, Lucy P. 1948. *Australia in New Guinea.* London: Christophers.

▪ Ethnology Training Provided in Pacific School
Australia, 1946

School of Pacific Administration was established to give training, including anthropology, to administrators of Papua and New Guinea. The school was supported by the Commonwealth Department of Territories.

Elkin, A. P. 1953. Australia and New Zealand. In *International Directory of Anthropological Institutions.* William L. Thomas, Jr. and Anna M. Pikelis, eds. New York: Wenner-Gren.

▪ Anthropologists Staff Lebanon Foreign Service Institute
United States, 1953

A branch of the Foreign Service Institute was established at the American Embassy in Lebanon for the training of younger foreign service officers being posted to the Middle East. The Institute staff included anthropologist Kepler Lewis and linguist Charles Ferguson.

McGregor, Gordon. 1955. Anthropology in Government: United States. In *Yearbook of Anthropology, 1955.* William L. Thomas, Jr., ed. New York: Wenner-Gren.

▪ Applied Anthropology Internship Project Funded
United States, 1976

Anthropology faculty at the University of South Florida initiated the Applied Anthropology Internship Project in conjunction with a MA program for training in applied anthropology. The project, which was supported by the National Institute of Mental Health, was intended to demonstrate an effective approach for the internship component of the MA program. The project has continued to the present based upon the model demonstrated under the grant.

Angrosino, Michael V. and Gilbert Kushner. 1978. Internship and Practicum Experience as Modalities for the Training of the Applied Anthropologist. In *Social Science Education for Development.* W.T. Vickers and G.R. Moore, ed. Tuskegee AL: Tuskegee Institute, Center for Rural Development.
Angrosino, Michael V. 1978. Applied Anthropology Training Programs. *Practicing Anthropology* 1(2):23.

214

Wienker, Curtis W. 1979. *Student Interns in Non-traditional Field Settings: Successful Adaptation is a New Eco-niche.* Washington, DC: Educational Resource Information Center.

Wolfe, Alvin W., Erve Chambers and J. Jerome Smith. 1981. *Internship Training in Applied Anthropology, A Five Year Review.* Human Resources Institute, University of South Florida.

▪ Mental Health Training Program for Latinos Developed
United States, 1980

Using grant support from the National Institute of Mental Health, the Anthropology Department of Catholic University of America implemented a M.A. level training program in applied anthropology for Latinos. The training consisted of a two year course sequence and a community field learning experience. The program, an integral part of the medical anthropology concentration of the department, was oriented toward training for careers in mental health.

Cohen, Lucy M. and Timothy P. Ready, eds. 1983. *Field Training in Applied Anthropology, Vol. II.* Washington, DC: Department of Anthropology, Catholic University of America.

_____. 1984. *Field Training in Applied Anthropology, Vol. III.* Washington, DC: Department of Anthropology, Catholic University of America.

Cohen, Lucy M., Timothy P. Ready, and Phyllis P. Chock. 1984. *An M.A. Applied Anthropology Mental Health Program for Latinos.* Final Report, NIMH Training Grant MH-16445-03. Washington, DC: Department of Anthropology, Catholic University of America.

Ready, Timothy P. and Lucy M. Cohen, eds. 1982. *Field Training in Applied Anthropology, Vol. I.* Washington, DC: Department of Anthropology, Catholic University of America.

TROUBLESHOOTING

▪ Mooney Does Problem-Solving Research on Ghost Dance
United States, 1891

Anthony Wallace suggests that an early occurrence of a policy study in anthropology is James Mooney's *The Ghost Dance Religion and the Sioux Outbreak of 1890.* Mooney considered the causes of the phenomenon. Hinsley questions whether Mooney was motivated by policy considerations.

Mooney, James. 1896. *The Ghost Dance Religion and the Sioux Outbreak of 1890.* Fourteenth Annual Report. Washington: Bureau of American Ethnology.

Hinsley, Curtis H., Jr. 1979. Anthropology as Science and Politics: the Dilemmas of the Bureau of American Ethnology, 1879 to 1904. In *The Uses of Anthropology.* Walter Goldschmidt, ed., Washington, DC: American Anthropological Association.

Wallace, Anthony F. C. 1976. Some Reflections on the Contributions of Anthropologists to Public Policy. In *Anthropology and the Public Interest, Fieldwork and Theory.* Peggy Reeves Sanday, ed. New York: Academic Press.

- **Williams Assists Australian Government with Cargo Cults**
  New Guinea, 1922

F. E. Williams began his tenure as the Australian Government Anthropologist by doing a trouble-shooting study of a cargo-cult which developed in response to European-native contact. The anthropologist recommended that the government not intervene in the movement. This recommendation was followed and minimized violence and bloodshed.

Williams, F. E. 1923. *The Vailala Madness and the Destruction of Native Ceremonies in the Gulf Division.* Port Moresby: Territory of Papua. Anthropology Report No. 4.

_____. 1934. The Vailala Madness in Retrospect. *Essays Presented to C. G. Seligman.* E.E. Evans-Pritchard, Raymond Firth, Bronislaw Malinowski and Issac Schapera, eds. London: Kegan Paul, French, Trubner.

- **Aba Riots Stimulate Hiring Anthropologists**
  Nigeria, 1929

An investigating commission, in response to what were called the Aba riots in Southeastern Nigeria, recommended that administrative officers be assigned the duty of doing ethnographic research. By 1934, over 200 ethnographic reports were prepared.

Perham, Margery. 1947. *Native Administration in Nigeria.* London: Oxford University Press.

- **Bureau of Indian Affairs Sponsors Peyote Research**
  United States, 1949

The Bureau of Indian Affairs hired anthropologist David F. Aberle to research the peyote religion and report the findings to the Bureau's Navajo Agency. Aberle made some policy recommendations in the course of his work. The BIA was especially interested in factors leading to increases in peyote use and the effects of peyote on individuals and family groups. Aberle examined the history of the development of Navajo peyotism, the content of ritual and the socio-economic correlates of peyote church membership. Aberle submitted reports to the Navajo Agency and also acted as an expert witness to the Navajo Tribal Council.

Aberle, David F. 1966. *The Peyote Religion Among the Navaho.* (VFPA No. 42) New York: Wenner-Gren Foundation.

- **Doukhobor Conflicts Examined**
  Canada, 1950

The inquiry into the causes of disturbances in Doukhobor communities in British Columbia was carried out by a research team that included an anthropologist. Project efforts included the formation of a committee that facilitated mediation between the Doukhobors and the provincial government.

Hawthorn, Harry B. ed. 1952. *The Doukhobors of British Columbia.* Report of the Doukhobors Research Committee. University of British Columbia.

- **Anthropologist Hired to Research Colonial Problems**
  Netherlands, 1954

Anthropologist J. W. Schoorl was assigned by the Governor of West Irian to carry out a research project in the Muyu region of that country. The research focused on various "administrative problems" such as the government's system of licensing "pig feasts," the practices associated with witchcraft, and the policy toward cowry money. Schoorl made policy recommendations as part of his study.

Schoorl, J. W. 1967. The Anthropologist in Government Service. In *Anthropologists in the Field.* D. G. Jongmans and P. C. W. Gutkind, eds. Assen: Van Gorcum.

- **Intra-Ethnic Conflict Examined**
  New Guinea, 1971

A dispute developed between two factions of the politically sophisticated Tolai language group. The two groups were divided in terms "nationalist" and "separatist" orientations.   Richard Salisbury was retained as a consultant to attempt to solve the problem.

Salisbury, Richard F. 1969. *Vunamam.* Berkeley: University of California Press.
_____. 1971. *Problems of the Gazelle Peninsula of New Britain, August 1971.* Port Moresby: Government Printer.
_____. 1976. The Anthropologist as Societal Ombudsman. In *Development from Below, Anthropologists and Development Situations.* David C. Pitt, ed. the Hague: Mouton Publishers.

URBAN DEVELOPMENT

- **Urban Studies Carried Out**
Northern Rhodesia, 1951

As part of an attempt to provide relevant information to "public authorities" concerning urbanization and urban life in Rhodesia the Rhodes-Livingstone Institute carried out surveys of urban dwellers to determine some basic demographic characteristics.   The director of the survey was J. Clyde Mitchell.

Mitchell, J. Clyde. 1954. *African Urbanization in Ndola and Luanshya.* Rhodes-Livingstone Communication Number Six, Lusaka: Rhodes-Livingstone Institute.

- **Action in Urban Areas**
United States, 1952

Application of action-anthropology techniques in urban redevelopment areas of South-side Chicago began when Sol Tax, participating in his own community, implemented the technique developed with the Fox. The goal of the project was neighborhood integration and continuity. Tax suggests that the experiences in Chicago as a citizen influenced his activities in Iowa as anthropologist.

Tax, Sol. 1959. Residential Integration: The Case of Hyde Park in Chicago. *Human Organization 18(1):22-27.*

- **Anthropologist Involved in Ciudad Guayana Planning**
Venezuela, 1962

Lisa Peattie served as staff anthropologist with a group from the Massachusetts Institute of Technology's Joint Center for Urban Studies that was contracted to provide technical assistance to the development of an urban plan for Ciudad Guyana. This city was part of a Venezuelan attempt to broaden the industrial base of the economy and was based on hydro electric power and iron ore and bauxite. The plan was to make the country less dependent on the petroleum that financed the development. Her role included serving as a liaison between the community and the design team consisting of urban designers, architects, economists, transportation planners, legal specialists, and a political scientist. She was encouraged to provide information on customs, values, and social problems which might be useful to the planners. Peattie took up residence in the newly developing city and made use of participant observation. This was a pioneering use of the services of an anthropologist in this kind of setting.

Peattie, Lisa. 1968. *The View from the Barrio*. Ann Arbor, MI: University of Michigan Press.

_____. 1969a Conflicting Views of the Project: Caracas Versus the Site. In *Regional Planning for Development: The Experience of the Guayani Program of Venezuela*. Lloyd Rodwin, ed. Cambridge, MA.: MIT Press.

_____. 1969b. Social Mobility and Economic Development. In *Regional Planning for Development: The Experience of the Guayani Program of Venezuela*. Lloyd Rodwin, ed. Cambridge, MA: MIT Press

_____. 1987. *Planning, Rethinking Ciudad Guyana*. Ann Arbor, MI: University of Michigan Press.

■ **Ethnoscience Informs Reforms**
United States, 1968

Using ethnosemantic research techniques, James Spradley investigated aspects of the life of the Seattle urban alcoholic. This project contributed to certain reforms in the Seattle legal system. These reforms included the decriminalization of public drunkenness and the establishment of a detoxification center for alcoholics.

Spradley, James P. 1970. *You Owe Yourself a Drunk, An Ethnography of Urban Nomads*. Boston: Little, Brown.

_____. 1970. Adaptive Strategies of Urban Nomads: The Ethnoscience of Tramp Culture. In *The Anthropology of Urban Environments*. Weaver and White, eds. Society for Applied Anthropology.

- **Minneapolis American Indian Movement Assisted**
  United States, 1969

Anthropologist Fay G. Cohen developed a thesis research project that focused on a component of the program of the Minneapolis-based American Indian Movement. Working with Dennis Banks and Clyde Bellecourt, Cohen was able to assist AIM in a number of areas. She did some basic writing and documentation for AIM and ultimately became a member. Her access to information became a reciprocal of the services she offered to AIM.

Cohen. Fay G. 1973. *The Indian Patrol in Minneapolis: Social Control and Social Change in an Urban Context.* Unpublished Ph.D. dissertation, University of Minnesota.

_____. 1973. The Indian Patrol in Minneapolis: Social Control and Social Change in an Urban Context. *Law and Society Review* 7:779-786.

_____. 1976. The American Indian Movement and the Anthropologist Issues and Implications of Consent. In *Dilemmas in Fieldwork, Ethics and Anthropology.* Michael A. Rynkiewich and James P. Spradley, eds. New York: John Wiley.

- **Grand Rapids Action Project**
  United States, 1973

Aquinas College, a small Catholic School in a deteriorating neighborhood of Grand Rapids, Michigan attempted to stimulate various kinds of development in the surrounding neighborhood. The area was undergoing rapid decay in the quality of community life and facilities. The project involved persons of various disciplinary backgrounds, including anthropologist Linda Elaine Easley.

Easley, Linda Elaine, Thomas Whitfield Edison and Michael Ronan Williams. 1978. *Eastown! A Report on How Aquinas College Helped its Local Community Reverse Neighborhood Transition and Deterioration.* Battlecreek, MI: W. K. Kellogg Foundation.

- **Quito Planned**
  United States, 1973

The U.S. Agency for International Development sponsored assistance for the planning of metropolitan Quito. Lisa R. Peattie was an anthropological consultant in this case.

Peattie, Lisa R. 1973. *Social Aspects of Planning for the Metropolitan Area of Quito.* Washington DC: U.S. Agency for International Development.

- **Project to Deal with Rapid Urban Growth Developed**
  Botswana, 1979

Botswana Ministry of Local Government and Lands invited AID to assist in the solution of rapid urban growth problems. AID guaranteed home loans to low-income, new urban dwellers and provided technical assistance and advisors. One aspect of the technical assistance was John Mason's sociocultural research to ensure that local preferences were reflected in program design. Mason constructed a survey to determine housing preferences. He also studied a major village, proposed as regional center to attract rural migrants. The survey and open-ended interviewing of leaders sought data on villagers' attitudes toward change.

Mason, John P. 1987. Promoting Socioculturally Feasible Housing and Community Upgrading Programs in Botswana. In *Anthropological Praxis: Translating Knowledge Into Action.* R. Wulff and S. Fiske, eds. Boulder: Westview.

- **Anthropologist Collaborates with Urban Natives in Calgary**
  Canada, 1979

Joan Ryan contributed to improving the services received by urban native Canadians when she became involved in the affairs of the Calgary Treaty Indian Alliance and its relations with the Canadian government (Price 1987:25).

Price, John A. 1987. *Applied Anthropology: Canadian Perspectives.* Downsview, Ontario: Society of Applied Anthropology in Canada.
Ryan, Joan. 1979. *Wall of Words: Betrayal of Urban Indians.* Toronto: Peter Martin Associates.

- **Squatter Settlement Development Policy Examined**
  Morocco, 1980

Acting in support of the Government of Morocco's squatter settlement development policy, FCH International, Inc. designed a plan for the development of a squatter settlement in Casablanca. This included improvement of 9,900 homes, construction of 1,200 core houses, installation of water, roads and electric systems and the construction of several educational and health centers. The FCH International Team, which included anthropologist John Mason, focused upon certain economic development aspects including job development, job training and small business upgrading. The plan proposed a number of specific developments these included, the development of an economic activity zone that was to create jobs and cash sources to subsidize other development projects and a program of loans and technical assistance for small businesses. The economic development goals of the project were also to be served by a proposed Building Materials Production Center. The research upon which this plan was based was funded by U.S. Agency for International Development.

FCH International, Inc. 1980. *An Operational Program for the Socio-Economic Development of Ben M'Sik Casablanca, Morocco.* Washington, DC: FCH International.

- **Night Shelter for Street People in Chattanooga Studied**
  United States, 1985

Like most other American cities the homeless population of Chattanooga, Tennessee is increasing. In response to the needs of these people two churches established St. Matthew's Night Shelter. Anthropologist Ralph A. Anderson of the Department of Human Services at the University of Tennessee at Chattanooga carried out an evaluation of the first year's operation for the shelter's board of directors. The evaluation focused on identifying some basic characteristics of shelter guests as well as identifying any significant program problems experienced by both the guests and volunteers. The evaluation also examined the effect of the experience of working at the shelter on the volunteers while it attempted to identify who would volunteer for work in the shelter during the next winter. The evaluation reported that the shelter was heavily used, often exceeding its capacity. This resulted in what was identified as the most difficult problem at the shelter, the difficulties in allocating sleeping space. Generally, however the guests were satisfied with the arrangements at the shelter. The research established that many of the volunteers valued their experience at the shelter.

Anderson, Ralph A. and Kyra J. Osmus. 1985. *St. Matthew's Night Shelter, The First Winter, 1984-1985.* Chattanooga, TN: Department of Human Services, University of Tennessee at Chattanooga.

- **Arab American Community Center Clientele Surveyed**
  United States, 1987

Anthropologist Barbara C. Aswad assisted in the survey of the clientele of
the Arab Community Center for Economic and Social Services [ACCESS]
of Dearborn, Michigan. She has been associated with the Center since its
founding in the early 1970s. The survey focused upon the users of one of
the Centers community mental health programs, to determine the basic
characteristics of the user population. Aswad and her associates determined
income, employment status, use of public assistance, country of origin, as
well as other attributes. They were also able to develop a clearer idea of
what aspects of the Center's services were used and what kinds of family
problems were presented.

Aswad, Barbara C. 1987. *Family Profile of Clients Entering the Family Counseling
Program.* Dearborn, MI: Arab Community Center for Economic and Social Services.

- **Hartford Neighborhoods Profiled**
  United States, 1988

The Institute for Community Research of Hartford, CT carried out a large-
scale survey of Hartford and nearby communities with the goal of
developing "a cooperative, systematic approach to gathering and regularly
updating information on the social and economic conditions of families,
households, neighborhoods, and communities." This activity, called the
Rapid Sociodemographic Assessment Project, involved a high level of
cooperation between various community organizations and funding from
various community sources. Data were collected through household
interviews. Anthropologist Jean J. Schensul was a key participant in the
project.

Institute for Community Research. 1990. *A Neighborhood Profile, Clay Arsenal.*
RSA Rapid Sociodemographic Assessment Project. Hartford, CT.

WAR

- **Committee on National Morale Established**
  United States, 1939

The Committee for National Morale was established to "consider the ways
in which anthropology and psychology could be applied to the

improvement of national morale during wartime" (Partridge and Eddy 1978:28). The committee consisted of Gregory Bateson, Eliott Chapple, Lawrence K. Frank, and Margaret Mead.

Bateson, Gregory and Margaret Mead. 1941. Principles of Morale Building. *Journal of Educational Sociology* 15:206-220.

- ## AAA Votes in Support of War Effort
United States, 1941

The American Anthropological Association passed a resolution which encouraged the participation of their members in the war effort. "Be it resolved: that the American Anthropological Association place itself and its resources and the specialized skills and knowledge of its members at the disposal of the country for the successful prosecution of the war."

American Anthropological Association. 1942. Resolution. *American Anthropologist* 44:289.
Beals, Ralph L. 1969. *Politics of Social Research, an Inquiry into the Ethics and Responsibilities of Social Scientists.* Chicago: Aldine Publishing.

- ## War Relocation Authority Established
United States, 1941

The War Relocation Authority was created to administer the camps established for the Japanese-Americans interned by military authorities during the Second World War. A social science research program was established at the one camp that was under the administrative control of the Bureau of Indian Affairs and Commissioner John Collier. After substantial administrative difficulty at various camps social science research programs were established at other locations. The researcher role termed "community analyst" was filled by anthropologists and sociologists.

Arensberg, Conrad M. 1942. Report on a Developing Community, Poston, Arizona. *Applied Anthropology* 2(1):2-21.
Brown, G. Gordon. 1945. War Relocation Authority, Gila River Project, Rivers, Arizona, Community Analysis Section, May 12 to July 7, 1945, Final Report. *Applied Anthropology* 4(4):1-49.
Embree, John F. 1943. Resistance to Freedom-An Administrative Problem. *Applied Anthropology* 2(4):10-14.

224

_____. 1943. The Relocation of Persons of Japanese Ancestry in the United States: Some Causes and Effects. *Journal of the Washington Academy of Sciences* 33(8).

_____. 1943. Dealing with Japanese-Americans. *Applied Anthropology* 2(2):37-43.

_____. 1944. Community Analysis--An Example of Anthropology in Government. *American Anthropologist* 46(3).

Hansen, Asael T. 1946. Community Analysis at Heart Mountain Relocation Center. *Applied Anthropology* 5(3):15-25.

Kimball, Solon T. 1946. *Community Government in the War Relocation Centers.* Washington, D.C.: Government Printing Office.

Leighton, Alexander N., et al. 1943. Assessing Public Opinion in a Dislocated Community. *Public Opinion Quarterly* 7(4).

_____. 1945. *The Governing of Men: General Principles and Recommendations Based on Experience at a Japanese Relocation Camp.* Princeton, NJ: Princeton University Press.

Loumala, Katharine. 1946. California Takes Back its Japanese Evacuees, The Readjustment of California to the Return of the Japanese Evacuees. *Applied Anthropology* 5(3):25-39.

_____. 1947. Community Analysis by the War Relocation Authority Outside the Relocation Centers. *Applied Anthropology* 6(1):25-31.

_____. 1948. Research and the Records of the War Relocation Authority. *Applied Anthropology* 7(1):23-32.

Provinse, John H. and Solon T. Kimball. 1946. Building New Communities During Wartime. *American Sociological Review* 11:396-410.

Spicer, Edward H. 1946a. The Use of Social Scientists by the War Relocation Authority. *Applied Anthropology* 5(2):16-36.

_____. 1946b. *Impounded People: Japanese-Americans in the Relocation Centers.* Department of the Interior, War Relocation Authority, Washington, DC.

_____. 1952a Reluctant Cotton-Pickers: Incentive to Work in a Japanese Relocation Center. In *Human Problems in Technological Change.* Edward H. Spicer, ed. New York: Russell Sage Foundation.

_____. 1952b. Resistance to Freedom: Resettlement from the Japanese Relocation Centers During World War II. In *Human Problems in Technological Change. Edward H. Spicer, ed.* New York: Russell Sage Foundation.

_____. 1979. Anthropologists and the War Relocation Authority. In *The Uses of Anthropology.* Walter Goldschmidt, ed. Washington, DC: American Anthropological Association.

War Relocation Authority. 1947. *WRA--A Story of Human Conservation.* Washington, DC:U.S. Department of the Interior.

- **Rosalie Wax Studies Relocation**
  United States, 1941

Rosalie H. Wax worked as a researcher in the University of California's Evacuation and Resettlement Study and worked as an anthropologist in both the Gila River and Tule Lake Relocation Centers of the War Relocation Authority.

Wax, Rosalie M. 1953. The Destruction of a Democratic Impulse. *Human Organization* 11(1):34-37.

- ### Early Anthropological Human Factors Research Done for Army Air Force
United States, 1941

Physical anthropologist E. A. Hooton was invited to investigate human aspects of aircraft design at the Aero Medical Laboratory, Wright-Patterson Air Force Base. This led to the establishment of the Anthropology Bureau of U.S. Air Force. This research organization contributed to improved design of aircraft cockpits, flight suits and gun turrets.

Clauser, Charles E. 1964. *The Role of Comparative Anthropometry in Aerospace Anthropology.* Anthropology, Psychology, Engineering, Occasional Paper No. 1 (April.)

- ### War Mobilization Studied in Rural California by Goldschmidt
United States, 1942

Walter R. Goldschmidt researched war mobilization of the California rural population while employed by the U.S. Department of Agriculture, Bureau of Agricultural Economics. The research focused upon "problems of protection in case of emergency," "problems of production with limited resources," and "problems of developing new awareness and activities." The data collection was carried out in one California county with the intent of demonstrating to other rural areas pitfalls that could be avoided. The data was collected through key informant interviews and survey techniques.

Goldschmidt, Walter R. and John S. Page. 1942. *A Study of the Methods of Mobilizing Rural People for War Emergencies, San Joaquin County.* Berkeley, CA: Bureau of Agricultural Economics, USDA.

- ### National Character Studies Implemented
United States, 1942

The World War II stimulated studies of national character of both enemies and allies. Geoffrey Gorer was requested a few months after Pearl Harbor to submit a report on "Japanese Character Structure and Propaganda" to the Committee on Intercultural Relations. Gorer suggested a relationship

226

between the Japanese patterns of toilet training and the way they fought their wars.

Gorer, Geoffrey. 1948. Themes in Japanese Culture. In *Personal Character and Cultural Milieu.* D. Haring, ed. Edwards Bros.: Ann Arbor, Mich.

- **Civil Affairs Training Program Started**
  United States, 1943

Far Eastern Civil Affairs Training School was established to provide personnel trained to deal with administering areas captured by the allies from the Japanese. The school, established at the University of Chicago, was directed by Fred Eggan. John Embree also participated.

Embree, John E. 1949. American Military Government. In *Social Structure, Studies Presented to A. R. Radcliffe-Brown.* M. Fortes, ed. London: Oxford University Press.

- **Foreign Morale Analysis Follows National Character Line**
  United States, 1944

The Foreign Morale Analysis Division was created as part of the Office of War Information. This organization provided social science analysis of various data sources concerning the Japanese and their morale. The organization provided service to the Departments of State, War, and Navy for various outposts in Asia and the Pacific. The project developed out of an early attempt to make studies of the Japanese as represented by the internees of the relocation camps. The anthropologists on the project team included Clyde Kluckhohn, Morris Opler, Ruth Benedict, John Embree, Frederick Hulse, Dorothea Leighton, Katherine Spencer, David Aberle, Alexander Leighton, and Iwao Ishino.

Benedict, Ruth. 1946. *The Chrysanthemum and the Sword.* Boston: Houghton Mifflin.
Leighton, Alexander. 1949. *Human Relations in a Changing World, Observations on the Use of the Social Sciences.* New York: Dutton.

- **Ethnological Content in Civil Affairs Handbooks**
  Oceania, 1944

"Civil Affairs Handbooks" were published by the Office of the Chief of Naval Operations. These handbooks included ethnological data for administrative staff in anticipation of the occupation of Japanese held

Pacific Territories. This work was largely the responsibility of George P. Murdock. This resulted in monographs on the Marshalls, Marianas, the Carolines, and others.

Office of the Chief of Naval Operations. 1944. *Civil Affairs Handbook, West Caroline Islands, DPNAV 50E-7.* Washington, DC: Office of the Chief of Naval Operations, Navy Department.

- **Naval Administration School Established**
  United States, 1945

The School of Naval Administration at Stanford was established to prepare Naval personnel for work in Guam, American Samoa, as well as former Japanese Mandate territories. The associate director in charge of training was an anthropologist.

Kessing, Felix N. 1949. Experiments in Training Overseas Administrators. *Human Organization* 8(4):20-22.
United States Navy Department. 1948. *Handbook on the Trust Territory of the Pacific Islands.* Washington, DC: Office of the Chief of Naval Operations, Department of the Navy.

- **Anthropologists Serve with American Military Governments**
  United States, 1945

Various anthropologists served the American Occupation forces in the post-war period. Anthropologists came to be associated with the American Military Governments in Japan, the Pacific, and Germany. In these situations they served as researchers and consultants. This involvement resulted in a number of studies. Two of the most complex were Rodnick's study (1948) of civilian attitudes toward occupation and reconstruction in the Hesse region of Germany, and Leighton's study (1949) of aspects of the Japanese response to the war.

Bennett, John W. 1951. Community Research in the Japan Occupation. *Clearing House Bulletin of Research, Human Organization* 1(3):1-2.
Gladwin, Thomas. 1950. Civil Administration on Truk: A Rejoinder. *Human Organization* 9(4) 15-23.
Embree, John F. 1946. Military Government in Saipan and Tinian, a Report on the Organization of Susupe and Chuco, Together with Notes on the Attitudes of the People Involved. *Applied Anthropology* 5(1):1-39.
Hall, Edward T. 1949. Military Government on Truk. *Human Organization* 9(2):25-30.

Leighton, Alexander H. 1949. *Human Relations in a Changing World: Observations on the Use of the Social Sciences.* New York: E. P. Dutton.

Rodnick, David. 1948. *Postwar Germans: An Anthropologist's Account.* New Haven: Yale University Press.

- **Anthropologists Serve in Administrative Roles**
  Libya, 1945

S. F. Nadel served the British Military Administration as Secretary for Native Affairs. E. E. Evans-Pritchard was appointed tribal affairs officer in Cyrenaica with the British military administration. Evans-Pritchard worked as a consultant and made policy recommendations.

Evans-Pritchard, E. E. 1949. *The Sanusi of Cyrenaica.* London: Oxford University Press.

Fortes, Meyer. 1957. Siegfried Frederick Nadel 1903-1956, a Memoir. In *The Theory of Social Structure.* S. F. Nadel, ed. London: Cohen and West.

James, Wendy. 1973. The Anthropologist as Reluctant Imperialist. In *Anthropology and the Colonial Encounter.* Talal Asad, ed. New York: Humanities Press.

- **Navy Hires Anthropologists**
  Micronesia, 1948

The Navy Department hired staff anthropologists for work in Micronesia. Anthropologists were later hired by the civilian administration. They tended to be placed in staff as opposed to line positions.

Barnett, H. G. 1956. *Anthropology in Administration.* Evanston, Illinois: Row, Peterson.

Criswell, John H. 1958. Anthropology and the Navy. In *Anthropology in the Armed Services: Research in Environment, Physique and Social Organization.* L. Dupree, ed. University Park, PA: Pennsylvania State University, Social Science Research Center.

Drucker, Philip. 1951. Anthropology in the Trust Territory. *The Scientific Monthly* 72(5).

Useem, John. 1945. Governing the Occupied Areas of the South Pacific: Wartime Lessons and Peace Time Proposals. *Applied Anthropology* 4(3):1-10.

- **Anthropologists Support Occupation**
  Japan, 1949

American anthropologists participated in the occupation of Japan following the treaty. These included John W. Bennett who was employed as Chief of the Public Opinion of Civil Information and Education Section of the

Supreme Commander Allied Powers and Robert B. Textor who was Assistant Civil Information and Education Officer for I Corps at Kyoto. Bennett engaged in a number of research efforts including attempts to assess the effects of the land reform program.

Bennett, John W. 1951. Community Research in the Japan Occupation. *Clearinghouse Bulletin of Research in Human Organization* 1(3):1-5.
_____. 1952. Social and Attitudinal Research in Japan: The Work of SCAP's Public Opinion and Sociological Research (PO and SR) Division. *Journal of East Asiatic Studies (Manila)* 2(1):21-33.
Bennett, John W. and Ishino Iwao. 1955. Futomi: A Case Study of the Socio-Economic Adjustments of a Marginal Community in Japan. *Rural Sociology* 20:41-50.
_____. 1963. *Paternalism in the Japanese Economy: Anthropological Studies of Oyabun-Kobun Patterns.* Minneapolis: University of Minnesota Press.
Textor, Robert B. 1951. *Failure in Japan.* New York: John Day Company.

- **Evaluation of Conditions in Micronesia**
  Micronesia, 1950

A survey of conditions in Micronesia was made in anticipation of the administrative transfer from U.S. Navy administration to the U.S. Department of Interior.

Department of the Interior. 1951. *Management Survey of the Government of the Trust Territory of the Pacific Islands.* Washington, DC: Office of Territories, Department of the Interior.

- **Japanese Labor Practices Researched for Occupation Forces**
  Japan, 1950

Staff members of the Public Opinion and Sociological Research Division, General Headquarters, Supreme Commander of Occupation Forces carried out research on the Japanese "labor-boss" system. The research may have been motivated by problems associated with attempts to do away with the system. Research personnel included Iwao Ishino and John W. Bennett.

Society for Applied Anthropology. 1954. Research in Progress. *Clearinghouse Bulletin of Research in Human Organization* 2(4).

WATER RESOURCES DEVELOPMENT

- **River Basin Policy Studies Started**
  United States, 1949

The Missouri River Basin Investigations Staff was created. The group was to research the impact of water resources development.

Cushman, Frances and Gordon MacGregor. 1949. *Harnessing the Big Muddy.* Lawrence, Kansas: Indian Service.

MacGregor, Gordon. 1949. Attitudes of the Fort Berthold Indians Regarding Removal from the Garrison Reservoir Site and Future Administration of their Reservation. *North Dakota History* 16(1).

- **Another Dam Impact Assessment**
  Mexico, 1952

Anthropologist Aguirre Beltran researched the Tepalcatepec basin region to determine the social impacts of a large dam construction project. This project was similar to the Papaloapan project.

Beltran, Aguirre. 1952. *Problemas de la Poblacion Indigena de la Cuenca del Tepalcatepec.* Memorias de I.N.I.

- **Mekong River Projects**
  Southeast Asia, 1957

The Mekong River Project was initiated by the United Nations Economic Commission for the Far East and Asia (ECAFE). The plan involved the construction of a series of multiple purpose projects on the Mekong River which flows through Cambodia, Laos, Vietnam, and Thailand. Anthropologists were actively involved in planning and evaluation of the planned projects.

Bardach, John E. 1972. Some Ecological Implications of Mekong River Development Plans. In *Careless Technology: Ecology and International Development.* M. Taghi Farvar and John T. Milton, eds. Garden City, NY: The Natural History Press.

Ingersoll, Jasper. 1968. Mekong River Basin Development: Anthropology in a New Setting. *Anthropological Quarterly* 41:147-167.

231

_____. 1969. *The Social Feasibility of PaMong Irrigation, A report to the U.S. Bureau of Reclamation and the U.S. Agency International Development.* Washington, DC.

Solheim, Wilhelm. 1961. The Importance of Anthropological Research to the Mekong Valley Project. *France-Asia* (Sept.-Oct.).

Halpern, Joel. 1972 Mekong River Development Schemes for Laos and Thailand. *Internationales Asian Forum (Munich)* Heft 1. Jahrgang 3, (Jan).

- ## Volta River Project Planned
Ghana, 1962

The Volta River Project resulted in the construction of a major hydro-electric dam and the displacement of 67,000 people. The project made use of anthropological data in the planning stages.

Brokensha, David. 1963. Volta Resettlement and Anthropological Research. *Human Organization* 22(4) 286-290.

- ## Arizona's Salt River Project Studied by Anthropologists
United States, 1966

This project was part of the larger research effort entitled, "Economic Implications of Public Water Policy in Arizona." The research integrated efforts of agricultural economists, political scientists and anthropologists in studying Arizona's water problem. The Salt River Project was the State's leading water management agency. It controlled water use in most of Maricopa County. The critical issue was the impact of urbanization on water use. The anthropological component was directed by Harland Padfield with the assistance of E.B. Eiselein, Nicholas Houser and Courtland L. Smith.

Eiselein, E.B. 1969. *Water for Weststate, U.S.A.: the Association in the Politics of Water Resources Development.* Unpublished Ph.D. dissertation, University of Arizona.

Padfield, Harland and Courtland L. Smith. 1968. Water and Culture. *Rocky Mountain Social Science Journal* 5(2): 23-32.

Smith, Courtland L. 1968. *The Salt River Project of Arizona: Its Organization and Integration with the Community.* Unpublished Ph.D. Dissertation, University of Arizona.

- ## Impacts of Corps of Engineers Dam Projects Assessed
United States, 1968

The Corps of Engineers built two flood control dams in the vicinity of Sweet Home, Oregon between 1963-66. Thomas C. Hogg received funding for a two-year project to assess the impacts of this construction on a community of less than 12,000. During the second year Hogg was joined by Courtland L. Smith. Research findings showed Sweet Home went through a boom and bust cycle which paralleled construction expenditures. Expectations were that the dam construction would start Sweet Home on sustained economic growth. When asked about the growth and decline cycle, many Sweet Home residents said they liked it and hoped for another growth cycle with new construction projects. The expectation of growth led community leaders to overexpand facilities and residents were left with the higher tax burdens. The results of this study were widely used by environmentalists to argue the detrimental impacts of large scale construction projects. The study was reported nationally and used by activist groups to testify against construction programs by water development agencies. This study was a precursor to the field of social impact assessment.

Hogg, Thomas C. 1968. *Socio-cultural Impacts of Water Development.* Proceedings of the People and Water Seminar, Water Resources Research Institute, Oregon State University, pp. 11-24.

_____. 1966. *Toward Including Ethnological Parameters in River Basin Models.* Proceedings of the Committee on Economics of Water Resources Development, Western Agricultural Economics Research Council, Las Vegas.

Hogg, Thomas C. and Marlin R. McComb. 1969. Cultural Pluralism and its Implications for Education. *Educational Leadership* 27(3):235-238.

Hogg, Thomas C. and Courtland L. Smith. 1970. *Socio-cultural Impacts of Water Resource Development in the Santiam River Basin.* Corvallis, Water Resources Research Institute, Oregon State University, WRRI-5.

Smith, Courtland L., Thomas C. Hogg and Michael J. Reagon. 1971. Economic Development: Panacea or Perplexity for Rural Areas? *Rural Sociology* 26(2):173-186.

Smith, Courtland L. 1974. Contrasts in Community Action and Opinion. *Water Resources Bulletin* 10(5).

- **Influence of Domestic Water on Diarrhoea Rates Investigated on Behalf of UNICEF**
  Bangladesh, 1975

A research team from the International Centre for Diarrhoeal Disease Research, Bangladesh (ICDDR,B) carried out an assessment of the control of cholera by increasing the availability of clean drinking water from tubewells. The project, located in Matlab Thana, Bangladesh, was directed in the field by anthropologist K.M.A. Aziz. Overall, the project was directed by George T. Curlin, a medical epidemiologist. The amount of data collected was immense. About 20,000 residents of 12 randomly selected villages were followed during the calendar year 1975. Field workers visited each family weekly to enquire about diarrhoea over the past week, and basic data regarding the source of water for domestic purposes was recorded one day in each month. Funded by UNICEF, the Matlab project served as a reference study for subsequent field studies of the relationship between water quality and cholera. Project results shaped basic health education recommendations in that the study demonstrated that it was necessary to provide clean water for all domestic purposes; cooking, washing, as well as drinking in order to have an impact on diarrhoeal disease incidence.

Curlin, G.T., K.M.A. Aziz and M.R. Khan. 1976. The Influence of Drinking Tubewell Water on Diarrhoea Rates in Matlab Thana, Bangladesh. Paper presented at a meeting of the U.S.-Japan Cholera Panel, Sapporo.

- **Water Supply and Waste Disposal Comparison**
  United States, 1977

The World Bank sponsored a research project entitled, Appropriate Technology for Water Supply and Waste Disposal in Developing Countries, within the Energy, Water and Telecommunications Department. Directed by Mary Elmendorf and Patricia K. Buckles, the project used the case study method to analyze "the choice, adoption, and diffusion of technological innovations for water supply and excreta disposal." The project collected case materials in Guatemala, Mexico, El Salvador, Colombia, Nicaragua, and Haiti.

Elmendorf, Mary and Patricia K. Buckles. 1978. *Socio-cultural Aspects of Water Supply and Excreta Disposal.* The World Bank, Energy, Water and Telecommunications Department, Public Utilities Notes (P.U. Report No. RES 15) Washington, DC: The World Bank.

- **PAHO Team Studies Dam Impact in Mexico**
  Mexico, 1977

A research team from the University of Southern California was contracted by the Pan American Health Organization, Center for Human Ecology to study some of the ecological and health consequences of the construction of the Aleman Dam constructed in 1954 as a major component of the Papaloapan River Basin Development Project. The research attempted the evaluation of impacts more than thirty years after the start of construction,

234

thus making the study a rare post-project assessment. The research design called for the identification of distinctive socio-economic settlement types, termed socioeconomic spheres. Topics for analysis included diet, health history, use of health care facilities, income and wealth, work group organization, work history, credit use, household structure and social, occupational and geographic mobility. Anthropologists William L. Partridge and Antoinette B. Brown were associated with the project as co-principal investigator and nutritional anthropologist.

Aguirre Beltran, Gonzalo. 1975. *Pobladores del Papaloapan: Biografia de Una Hoya*. Mexico: Direccion General de Arte Popular.

_____. 1976. *Obra Polemica*. Mexico: Instituto Nacional Indigenista

Attolini, Jose. 1949. *Economia de la Cuenca del Papaloapan: Agricultura*. Mexico Gobierno del Estado de Vera Cruz.

McMahon, David F. 1973. *Antropologiz de una Presa: Los Mazatecos y el Projecto del Papaloapan*. Mexico: Instituto Nacional Indigenista.

Nugent, Jeffery B., William L. Partridge, Antoinette B. Brown and John D. Rees. 1978. *An Interdisciplinary Evaluation of the Human Ecology and Health Impact of the Aleman Dam*. Mexico City, Center for Human Ecology and Health, Pan American Health Organization.

- **Dinkey Creek Hydroelectric Project Area
  Surveyed Ethnographically**
  United States, 1981

Based on testimony before the California State Water Resources Control Board about the proposed Dinkey Creek Project, the Kings River Conservation District decided to reevaluate the content of a draft environmental impact statement issued in 1978. Deficiencies revealed by this reevaluation resulted in an ethnographic evaluation of the region carried out by Theodoratus Cultural Research. The survey addressed the history and cultural life of the Mono population of the region which had been very poorly documented through prior ethnographic research or the EIS. An interesting component of the research was the identification and review of notes from ethnographic work done by C. Hart Merriam located at the Bancroft Library. These data were supplemented with interviews with Mono consultants both inside and outside the project area. Some of these interviews were recorded with video equipment. Botanical collections were carried out in the project area.

Johnson, Ann Hagerman and Helen McCarthy. 1982. *A Review of the Historic Resources of the Dinkey Creek Hydroelectric Project*. Prepared for Kings River Conservation District. Fair Oaks, CA: Theodoratus Cultural Research.

Theodoratus, Dorothea J., Clinton M. Blount and Clark L. Taylor, Jr. 1982. *An Ethnographic Survey of the Proposed Dinkey Creek Hydroelectric Project.* Prepared for the Kings River Conservation District. Fair Oaks, CA: Theodoratus Cultural Research.

▪ **Assessing Cultural Attributes in Water Resources Development Projects**
United States, 1982

The U.S. Army Corps of Engineers requested that the National Research Council evaluate the procedures recommended by the U.S. Water Resources Council for assessing the impact of proposed water resources projects on "cultural attributes" of the environment. The committee was chaired by anthropologist John H. Peterson and included anthropologist Ruthann Knudson. The committee concluded that both historical properties and traditional lifeways should be considered cultural resources.

Panel on Cultural Attributes in Water Resources Projects. 1982. *Assessing Cultural Attributes in Planning Water Resources Projects.* Washington, DC: Environmental Studies Board, Commission on Physical Sciences, Mathematics, and Resources, National Research Council.

▪ **Tennessee-Tombigee Corridor Development Examined**
United States, 1985

Anthropologist Claudia M. Rogers of the Mobile District of the Army Corps of Engineers undertook the compilation of a guide to public development efforts in the Tenn-Tom Corridor. Based on a variety of data, the guide included an inventory of developments and general recommendations for design of projects. Substantial portions of the analysis were focused on barge terminal and port facilities.

U.S. Army Corps of Engineers, Mobile and Nashville Districts. 1985. *A Guide to Waterfront Development Activities within the Tennessee-Tombigbee Corridor.* Mobile, AL: U.S. Army Corps of Engineers, Mobile District.

▪ **Rengali Multipurpose Dam Project Study Initiated**
India, 1986

P. K. Nayak of Utkal University's Post-Graduate Anthropology Department was engaged by OXFAM to assess the problems faced by village people who were resettled as a result of the construction of the Rengali Multipurpose Dam in Orissa. The dam across the Brahmani River that was built for flood control, irrigation, and power generation purposes resulted in a large reservoir. This caused 2972 households to be displaced. The research revealed that the displaced population underwent tremendous hardship. Agricultural production decreased, making it difficult for farmers to pay the service providing castes in kind. The evaluation documented the inadequacy of all government planning for mitigation of the problems caused by the construction of the Rengali Dam.

Nayak, P. K. 1987. Anthropology of the Displaced: Problems of Resettlement and Development Alternatives. In *Anthropology, Development and Nation Building*. A.K. Kalla and K.S. Singh, eds. New Delhi: Concept Publishing Company.

■ IDA Researchs the Effects of Manantali Dam
Mali, 1986

When the construction of the Manantali Dam started in 1986, the project donor, the U. S. Agency for International Development also supported social research into its effects. Carried out by the Institute for Development Anthropology, the research involved a number of anthropologists, including Michael Horowitz, Delores Koenig, Thayer Scudder, Yacouba Kanate, Curt Grimm, and Muneera Salem-Murdock. IDA was connected to the project through the Social and Monitoring Section of the project itself. Though defined as having a monitoring role, IDA also came to be involved in project administration. Monitoring included discovering any acute problems such as disease or nutritional stress in the short run. In a longer time frame, the project was monitored to determine whether the relocatees were able to "reestablish their preproject production systems and quality of life" (Koenig and Horowitz 1990:72).

Koenig, Dolores and Michael M. Horowitz. 1990. Involuntary Resettlement at Manantali, Mali. In *Social Change and Applied Anthropology, Essays in Honor of David W. Brokensha.* Miriam S. Chaiken and Anne K. Fleuret, eds. Boulder: Westview Press.

WILDLIFE MANAGEMENT

- **Wildlife Conservation Area Management Plan Assessed**
  Tanzania, 1980

Anthropologist Kaj Arhem, employed by the Bureau of Resource Assessment and Land Use Planning at the University of Dar es Salaam, Tanzania, contributed to the development of a development and management plan for the Ngorongoro Conservation Area in northern Tanzania. This area, home to 15,000 Maasai pastoralists, was established as a response to conflict between the needs of the Maasai residents and the conservation goals of the park. The government authority responsible for the newly established area required a reassessment and management plan. A major focus of the research was to be the relationship of the Maasai with the management plan. It became apparent that the agency required the Maasai to live outside the Conservation Area. Arhem was given the responsibility to provide data during the planning process. Data on human and livestock populations, land use, living standards, and subsistence strategies were included. Data were collected using a village survey implemented through group interviews with leaders. The research team concluded that the Maasai and their stock did not pose a threat to the wildlife population, but had experienced a decline in living standards because of conservation policies. The team recommended a plan that allowed the Maasai to stay in place. The plan was not implemented for a number of reasons.

Arhem, Kaj. 1985. Anthropology in Action: A Tanzanian Experience. In *Anthropological Contributions to Planned Change and Development.* H.O. Skar, ed. Gothenburg Studies in Social Anthropology.

- **Sitka, Alaska, Wild, Renewable Resource Use Analyzed**
  United States, 1983

The Alaska Department of Fish and Game supported a series of research projects directed at improving understanding of the use of wild, renewable resources by residents of urban communities. Anthropologists George Gmelch and Sharon Bohn Gmelch carried out a baseline study of resource use in Sitka as part of this effort. They established the Sitka baseline with data collected through an interview survey of a random sample of Sitka households, in-depth interviewing and participant observation. The research found that large numbers of Sitka residents of all ethnic backgrounds used wild resources.

Gmelch, George and Sharon Bohn Gmelch. 1985. *Resource Use in a Small Alaskan City - Sitka.* Technical Paper Series No. 90. Juneau: Alaska Department of Fish and Game.

- **Anthropologist Studies Cincinnati's Pigeon Population Problem**
  United States, 1983

Sharlotte N. Donnelly evaluated an array of measures for control of Cincinnati's pigeon population. The research was carried out for the Cincinnati Environmental Advisory Council made recommendations concerning city ordinances and the activities of various city departments. The proposed program included public education, roost stoppage, and dropping cleanup. Donnelly treated the pigeon problem as basically a problem in human ecology. The project was praised by the National Association for the Prevention of Cruelty to Animals.

Donnelly, Sharlotte Neely. 1983. *Environmental Evaluation of the Urban Pigeon Situation in Cincinnati, Ohio.* A Report for the City of Cincinnati Environmental Advisory Council. Cincinnati, OH.

WOMEN IN DEVELOPMENT

- **Women's Development Programs Evaluated for UNICEF**
  Malawi, 1980

The Centre for Social Research at the University of Malawi was requested to evaluate the UNICEF - assisted women's programs in Malawi. The research focused on the performance of the female Community Development Assistants in the Community Development Assistants Programs, the Homecraft Workers' program, and the Home Management Program. The evaluation considered recruitment, financing, basic and in-service training, teaching effectiveness, field conditions, supervision, staff support, and overall program effectiveness. The data collection and design was largely the responsibility of anthropologist Bruce T. Williams.

Williams, Bruce T. 1981. *UNICEF-assisted Women's Programs in Malawi, An Evaluation and Summary of Findings on the Homecraft Workers' Programs and the*

Female Community Development Assistant's Program. Centre for Social Research, University of Malawi.

- **Women in Dayak Development Researched**
  Indonesia, 1980

Carol J. Pierce Colfer provided consultant services to a German development team's project in transmigration area development. She had been engaged in policy relevant, basic research in a Dayak resettlement village in the East Kalimcentan region of Java. Her consultancy focused upon the potential role of women in the development project.

Colfer, Carol J. Pierce. 1980. *Report Women of Long Segar (For Women's Promotion Study).* submitted to Transmigration Area Development.
_____. 1980. *Changes in an Indigenous Agroforestry System.* Report, Indonesian-U.S., Man and Biosphere Project Report.

- **Women's Role in Water and Sanitation Programs Assessed**
  United States, 1981

Working under a U.S. Agency for International Development contract, Mary L. Elmendorf and others reviewed and reported on the existing literature which dealt with the role of women as, "acceptors, users, managers, and diffusers (change agents) for the introduction of innovative water supply and sanitation technologies." The project made recommendations concerning how to address women's roles in programs in project evaluation.

Elmendorf, Mary L. and Raymond B. Isely. 1981. *The Role of Women as Participants and Beneficiaries in Water Supply and Sanitation Programs.* Water and Sanitation for Health Project (WASH) Technical Report No. 11, Office of Health, Bureau for Science and Technology, U.S.A.I.D.

- **Women in Colonization Studied by IDA**
  Bolivia, 1984

Susan Hamilton investigated the experiences of women in the San Julian Colonization Project in conjunction with a general evaluation of the project. The San Julian project is an attempt to settle highland people into subtropical lowlands of eastern Bolivia. The Institute for Development Anthropology carried out an evaluation as part of an understanding with

AID and Clark University. The research demonstrated a number of patterns of women's circumstances in San Julian. Women were infrequently land owners. Handicraft production had ceased to be a significant source of income. Food preparation was influenced by the relative lack of knowledge of local foods by these migrant women. Women of the project held few political offices.

Hamilton, Susan. 1986. *An Unsettling Experience: Women's Migration to the San Julian Colonization Project.* Binghamton, NY: Cooperative Agreement on Human Settlements and Natural Resource Systems Analysis, Clark University/IDA.

- **Economic Position of Women Assessed**
  Somalia, 1987

This assessment was part of the Privatization and Policy Initiatives Project carried out with sponsorship from USAID. The assessment focused upon the economic role of Somali women with special reference to 1983-1987, a period of economic reform that emphasised the growth of the private sector and development of the market economy. Topics considered included female circumcision and polygamy, women's access to economic opportunity, and participation in agriculture and the modern economy. Many data were provided by secondary sources.

McFerson, Hazel M. 1989. *Women in the Economy of Somalia.* Mogadishu, Somalia: Privatization and Policy Initiatives Project, USAID/Somalia

INDEX